THE ORDINANCE MAKING POWERS OF THE PRESIDENT OF THE UNITED STATES

THE ORDINANCE MAKING POWERS OF THE PRESIDENT OF THE UNITED STATES

By James Hart

DA CAPO PRESS • NEW YORK • 1970

A Da Capo Press Reprint Edition

This Da Capo Press edition of *The Ordinance Making Powers of the President of the United States* is an unabridged republication of the first edition published in Baltimore in 1925 as Series XLIII, No. 3, of the Johns Hopkins University Studies in Historical and Political Science.

Library of Congress Catalog Card Number 78-87482
SBN 306-71487-6

Published by Da Capo Press
A Division of Plenum Publishing Corporation
227 West 17th Street, New York, N.Y. 10011

Manufactured in the United States of America

THE ORDINANCE MAKING POWERS OF
THE PRESIDENT OF THE UNITED STATES

THE ORDINANCE MAKING POWERS
OF THE
PRESIDENT OF THE UNITED STATES

BY

JAMES HART, Ph. D.

Instructor in Political Science, University of Michigan

BALTIMORE

THE JOHNS HOPKINS PRESS

1925

J. H. FURST CO., PRINTERS, BALTIMORE

TO
MY MOTHER AND FATHER
TO WHOM I OWE EVERYTHING
WORTH WHILE

PREFACE

This treatise is an expansion of a dissertation submitted in 1923 to the Johns Hopkins University in partial fulfillment of the requirements for the Ph. D. degree. It was originally undertaken at the suggestion of Professor Lindsay Rogers, now of Columbia University, and pursued first at the University of Virginia, under his guidance, and later in Baltimore under the supervision of Professor W. W. Willoughby. To them and to President Goodnow, his three teachers who have most influenced his conception of law and politics, and most contributed to his stock of knowledge, the present writer is indebted in ways that are not indicated in the footnotes. Acknowledgments are also due to Professor Frankfurter, of the Harvard Law School, some meetings of whose graduate seminar in administrative law the writer attended, in 1921-1922, with great profit. Professor Frankfurter discussed at considerable length the problem dealt with in chapter VI. The author desires to take this opportunity to thank Professor Jesse S. Reeves for several very fruitful ideas. It is only fair to state, however, that for errors of fact and of judgment entire responsibility rests with the author.

J. H.

ANN ARBOR, MICHIGAN,
 May 25, 1924.

vii

CONTENTS

TABLE OF CASES

(It will be noted that some of the cases in the following Table have no page references. These cases are not referred to in the text, but are included here as they bear on the subject).

PAGE

Nos efforts tendront à déterminer la nature juridique des règlements, les conditions de leur légalité, les sanctions qui les accom-
pagnent, les guaranties et voies de recours qui prémunissent les
citoyens contre les abus qui peuvent survenir, enfin les règles
d'abrogation.

—RAIGA, *Le pouvoir réglementaire du Président de la République.*

THE ORDINANCE MAKING POWERS OF THE PRESIDENT OF THE UNITED STATES

PART I

JURISTIC ANALYSIS

CHAPTER I

INTRODUCTION

Few people are aware of the great extent to which public administration in the United States national government is controlled by means of administrative regulations or orders, in the nature of subordinate legislation.

Important as such executive regulations have been, even in time of peace, they are of much greater importance in time of war; and during the recent emergency, regulations of this kind have been brought to the attention of many outside the circle of government officials.

There are indeed, besides presidential proclamations and executive orders, many elaborate systems of executive regulations governing the transaction of business in each of the executive departments, and in the various services both within and without these departments. These include organized codes of regulations for the army, the navy, the postal service, the consular service, the customs service, the internal revenue service, the coast guard, the patent office, the pension office, the land office, the Indian service, the steamboat inspection service, the immigration and the naturalization bureaus, and the civil service rules. In addition to long established types of regulations, there have been many new series of regulations issued in recent years both before the war, and more recently by the new war agencies, such as the Food and Fuel Administration, the War Industries Board, and the War Trade Board.

In addition to the systematized and codified regulations, there is perhaps an even more extensive body of more specialized rules, orders, and instructions issued by the various departments, bureaus, commissions, and local agents, knowledge of which is often limited to the persons who have to apply them and to those whom they affect.
—FAIRLIE.[1]

The lawyer as well as the layman is often puzzled by the phrase ' ordinance making '[2] as applied to powers of the President. He understands by the term, and rightly enough, powers of a legislative nature exercised by executive officials. Yet does not the Constitution expressly vest " all legislative

---

[1] " Administrative Legislation," in Michigan Law Review, January, 1920, passim.

Powers herein granted " in Congress? Is it not a fundamental principle that *delegata potestas non potest delegari?*
Has it not been taught in the books that the Chief Executive
of the nation has no legislative powers? Where in contemporaneous evidence is the claim or admission by any of the
fathers that the President is given such powers by the supreme
law or may be given them by Congress? Do not the pages of
the Supreme Court Reports contain denials of any such proposition?

This is all true. Yet, despite the orthodox theory, we find
a constitutional practice which is comparable in character
if not in degree with that known on the continent of Europe
as executive ordinance making. What the Supreme Court
has denied, moreover, is not the authority of the Chief Magistrate in respect to this practice, but merely the fact that
the powers so exercised are legislative. It has preferred to
call them administrative. In thus refusing to call a spade
a spade the Court has sought to allow needed flexibility in
governmental arrangements without admitting that Congress
can devolve its constitutional powers upon the Executive.

The extent of Presidential legislation should not be exag-

---

² The term 'ordinance-making power' is used by Professor Willoughby, while President Goodnow speaks of the 'ordinance power'
or the 'power of ordinance.' There are several reasons which
render the term 'ordinance' preferable to any other term. In the
first place, it is the word which is most often used by those American writers, like President Goodnow and Professor Willoughby,
who through their study of the administrative law of continental
Europe have come to recognize this power as a distinct category
of our jurisprudence. Then, too, the corresponding power in the
hands of public corporations is styled the power of ordinance,
so that the proposed use of the term is but an extension of this
existing use. Finally, it is historically fitting that such functions
of a legislative character as are now exercised by the executive
should be called by the same name as was the legislative power of
the English king in the fourteenth century. In the sixteenth century it was called the power of proclamation. But a proclamation
is essentially a form of promulgation, the contents of which may be
legislative, as in Lincoln's emancipation proclamation, or merely
declaratory or hortatory or the like. The President's annual Thanksgiving proclamation creates no legal rights and duties. The term
ordinance connotes, on the other hand, both distinctive features of
the thing to be defined, namely, that it is legislative in nature
while it proceeds from some authority other than the regular legislative body. On this and other points in this chapter see the
present writer's article on "The Ordinance Making Powers of the
President," in North American Review, July, 1923.

gerated. In fact, as one runs through the volumes of the statutes-at-large,[3] one finds that only in connection with three great crises has Congress made delegations of legislative powers a prominent feature. These crises were the periods of the Napoleonic Wars, the War of Secession, and the War with Germany. In general, our laws have been based upon a conception of the relation between legislation and administration entirely different from that in vogue in Europe. There, general legislation passed with the knowledge that the Executive has the independent power to supplement statutory generalizations, is the normal method.[4] With us it is conceived to be the function of the legislative department to define with completeness and in concrete terms the right and duties which are to be created, and not simply to set forth a general policy to guide the Executive. The enactments of Congress have accordingly been characterized by concreteness, specificness, explicitness, detail, the limitation of generalities by provisos, and the anticipation (so far as possible) of all future contingencies. Sometimes, to be sure, abstractions appear in the laws; but until recently the interpretation of these was left in the last analysis to the courts in the decision of controversies, rather than to the Executive by the issuance of ordinances to meet concrete conditions.[5]

Nevertheless, from the Presidency of Washington to that of Coolidge the Chief Magistrate has issued ordinances under both Congressionally delegated and constitutional authority, and affecting the interests of private persons as well as the duties of officials. The Proclamations of the President and his Executive Orders embody various sorts of executive action, but among them are many ordinances in the technical sense as hereinafter defined. Certainly since Congress in 1917-1918 endowed President Wilson with multi-

---

[3] The present writer has made a fairly careful study of the volumes of the statutes-at-large covering the period from 1813 to 1887 with a view to checking up on the frequency of delegations of ordinance making powers to the President.

[4] Lowell, The Governments of France, Italy, and Germany, pp. 44-45, 139-140, 200.

[5] Freund, " The Substitution of Rule for Discretion in Public Law," in American Political Science Review, November, 1915.

tudinous extraordinary powers involving the exercise of exceptionally broad discretion,[6] the general public as well as
the closeted scholar has begun to realize that it is an unreal
fiction that the President cannot legislate.

Then, too, although the Constitution vests the legislative
power in the Congress, it delegates to the President powers
which are, or involve, ordinance making as that function will
be defined.   The most striking example of this is found in
his power by and with the advice and consent of the Senate
to make treaties; for in our system treaties are the law of
the land, and in them we have executive legislation without
the consent of the House of Representatives.   Again, while
individual pardons are executive acts of clemency, amnesties
or general pardons are law in substance though not in form.
As commander-in-chief, also, the Chief Magistrate issues
administrative Regulations to the army and navy, and gov-
erns enemy territory conquered in time of war.   As the
possessor of the executive power and of the duty to take
care that the laws be faithfully executed, he may issue administrative directions to his subordinates to guide them in
the exercise of the powers given them by law.   Finally, the
President derives from his power and duty to see to the
execution of the laws, occasional powers of legislation in
American dependencies in carrying out treaty obligations
of the United States, or in regions like the Canal Zone, where
in order to carry out the statutory mandate to build the
canal, President Roosevelt had to govern the Zone when Congress failed to give him specific power to do so.

The following study of the ordinance making powers of
the President will embrace an examination of the subject
from the viewpoints successively of analytical jurisprudence,
the historical method, constitutional law, political science,
and administrative technique.   First we shall consider the
word ordinance as a technical term and establish its meaning as a distinct category of general jurisprudence.   In this
connection an effort is made to analyze the ordinance making

---

[6] 40 Stat. L., passim.   Cf. Rogers, "Presidential Dictatorship in
the United States," in Quarterly Review, January, 1919.

power in its relation to the other chief aspects of the governmental process. Then follows a section in which ordinances are distinguished from other products of governmental activity with which they might be confused, and a section in which ordinances are classified from four distinct points of view. These portions of the treatise comprise Part I.

After this Part on Analytical Jurisprudence comes, in Part II, an outline of the main periods into which the constitutional history of the practice of executive legislation falls.

Part III deals with problems in constitutional law which are raised first by the delegation to the President by Congress of ordinance making powers, and secondly by the exercise by the President of such powers under the functions which are by the Constitution directly vested in him. Especial consideration is given to such questions as: By what construction of the supreme law can delegations be reconciled with the separation of powers? What is the scope and what the limitations of this power of Congress to delegate to the Chief Magistrate subordinate powers of legislation? Can Congress make the violation of Presidential ordinances a penal offense? Can it vest in the Executive final discretionary determination of the contents of a rule having the force of law? What is the relation of the ordinances of heads of departments and commissions to the power of the President as the administrative head? What independent or constitutional powers of the President are or involve ordinance making?

Part IV is concerned with the political aspects of the power under review: What is the importance of the emergency ordinance making power, of the power to issue administrative ordinances, of the power of co-legislation? Why should the determination of rules of law which at one and the same time affect classes of private citizens and " give manifestation to some original idea " be left almost exclusively to the popular assembly? What are the potentialities of administrative co-legislation? What are its political implications for democracy and for the theory of the relation of the executive and legislative departments to each other? How can this function be regularized and systematized in such a fashion as to place it upon an effective footing and substitute something like government by science for government by opinion or political manipulation? What are the proper methods of popular control of the organs which elaborate complementary ordinances? What are the means by which the individual may be protected from illegal exercise or actual usurpation of ordinance making powers? Such are some of the questions to be considered.

The Appendix treats of matters of technique. The forms of ordinances, and the methods of preparation and of publication, are among the points discussed.

Some of the results which will follow from the examination of the Presidential ordinance making power may be summarized as follows:

1. It will reveal a unity in powers which have heretofore been studied separately. In this unity they will all be seen in a new light and from a novel angle.

2. It will for the first time show that there is no irreconcilable contradiction between the delegation of ordinance making powers to the President and the constitutional doctrine of the separation of powers.

3. It will dispel the myth that under the Constitution the Chief Executive has no independent legislative powers.

4. It will establish at least one precisely defined category of American jurisprudence, and emphasize the value, for the clearness of legal thinking, of working out, by scientific analysis of the material furnished by American public and private law in action, a complete system of accurate juristic terminology.

5. It will throw light upon the vital problem of the relation in a governmental system of the executive department to legislation.

6. It will emphasize the need for the regularization and

systematization of the preparation and publication of ordinances.[7]

7. It will indicate that, while in modern constitutional governments it is a basic principle that legislation affecting private rights be enacted by or with the consent of the representative assembly, nevertheless more or less numerous exceptions have in all governments to be made by constitutional or statutory provisions or both.

8. It will suggest a method by which modern regulation of industrial and social problems can be mapped out by the legislature and then worked out in detail by executive agencies acting under the influences both of popular control and of scientific knowledge.

---

[7] The best discussion of this problem is that in the article of Professor Fairlie, " Administrative Legislation," in Michigan Law Review, January, 1920.

CHAPTER II

ANALYSIS OF THE GOVERNMENTAL PROCESS

Almost all of the problems of jurisprudence come down to a fundamental one of rule and discretion, of administration of justice by law and administration of justice by the more or less trained intuition of experienced magistrates.

—POUND.[1]

Normally the progress of law should be away from discretion toward definite rule.

—FREUND.[2]

Den materiellen Gegensatz zwischen Rechtsvorschrift und Verwaltungsvorschrift kann man also darin fassen, dasz, während erstere ein rechtliches Verhalten fordert, letztere die Technik in der Ausführung einer rechtlich geforderten Handlung bestimmt. Der Gegensatz liegt also in den Begriffen des Rechtlichen und des Technischen.

—AFFOLTER.[3]

L'acte législatif ou réglementaire se connaît à ce qu'il organise; il crée une situation juridique générale, impersonelle, objective; il contient essentiellement une règle de droit, une norme juridique. . . . Dans tous ces cas, quelles que soient la qualité de l'auteur de l'acte, les formes suivée, le nom donné à l'acte juridique, nous trouvons comme effet juridique voulu la création d'une situation juridique générale, impersonelle, objective. Cela est nécessaire pour qu'il y ait acte législatif au sens matériel, mais cela est suffisant.

—JÈZE.[4]

One reason why the ordinance making powers of the President were not earlier recognized as such was the lack in the English speaking world of a scientific jurisprudence such as exists in countries like Germany and France. Terminology in our law was historical rather than scientific; hence it was easy to call the legislative powers of the Chief Magistrate by another name. Even those scholars who through their familiarity with continental juristic distinctions recognized the connection between Presidential rule making and the *pouvoir réglementaire* of the French and the *Verordnungsrecht* of the Germans failed to arrive at any commonly

---

[1] An Introduction to the Philosophy of Law, p. 111.
[2] " The Substitution of Rule for Discretion in Public Law," in American Political Science Review, November, 1915.
[3] Archiv für Öffentliches Recht, Bd. 27, S. 370.
[4] Principes généraux du droit administratif, p. 9ff.

accepted term. They referred to the legislative powers of the Executive, and to ordinances without explicitly defining their meaning. President Goodnow wrote of the ordinance power or the power of ordinance;[5] Professor Willoughby of the ordinance making power;[6] Professor Fairlie of administrative legislation.[7] There was lacking, therefore, both fixity in nomenclature and exactness of definition.

In a strictly formal sense there can be no ordinance making powers in American constitutional law. Only executive powers are vested in the President,[8] except at the most where the Constitution itself grants to him participation in legislation.[9] For the present, however, we are not concerned primarily with the nomenclature of the Constitution but with an analysis of the facts of the governmental process. To make clear the precise place of the ordinance making power in that process it is necessary to adopt a number of precisely defined terms after the fashion of analytical jurisprudence. To undertake this task will be to repeat classical distinctions of German jurisprudence; but that will be well worth while if these distinctions can be applied to the phenomena of American government in a manner never before attempted in any complete way. Incidentally, also, emphasis will be laid upon the absolute necessity of building up an acceptable system of technical terminology. Such a system is the indispensable handmaiden to the profitable study of analytical jurisprudence.

Let it be repeated that we shall define ' ordinance ' in terms not of historical connotation but of analytical jurisprudence. Of late this science has come into disfavor with certain self-styled realists. These men are interested in trying to photograph concrete phenomena, and have little patience with abstract ideas. They fail to realize that the perception of an

---

[5] Comparative Administrative Law, passim.
[6] The Constitutional Law of the United States, sec. 781.
[7] " Administrative Legislation," in Michigan Law Review, January, 1920.
[8] This is because the opening sentence of Art. 2 of the Constitution describes his powers as ' executive ' powers.
[9] It is significant that the so-called veto power of the President is contained in the article on the legislative department.

apple is a form of abstraction, and that the logic of law and politics is as legitimate a study as the analysis of law and politics in action.

Analytical jurisprudence is the formal science which furnishes logical coherence, consistency, and unity to the provisions of the law. This it does by arranging them under precisely defined categories and developing basic jural concepts out of the elements they have in common.[10] The chief of such concepts are: right, or any interest which the law protects; duty, or the correlative obligation to respect a legal right; person, or the subject of right and duty; and thing (including services owed), or the object of right and duty.[11] The method is the simultaneous use of analysis and correlation to discover relative similarities and differences in legal ideas. The results are classifications, generalizations, and definitions. It is the supreme triumph of formal jurisprudence that, carrying to their logical conclusion principles implicit in the law, it has given unity to the whole legal system by evolving the concept of the state as a corporate personality possessed of sovereignty. For sovereignty is the unlimited subjective right of the supreme legal person to set the rights and duties both of itself and of all other legal persons and with reference to all things whatsoever.[12] The formula is completed by defining government as the concrete organs, machinery, or agency through which the state formulates and executes its will, and law as the expressed formulations of that will in the creation of rights and duties.[13] The state is not only an ordinary legal person with objective rights and duties,[14] but it is unique in its possession of abso-

---

[10] W. W. Willoughby, "The Study of the Law," in Virginia Law Review, April, 1920, p. 461 ff.

[11] Holland, Elements of Jurisprudence, 12th ed. 1916, chap. viii; Gray, The Nature and Sources of the Law, chap. i. See Hohfeld, Fundamental Legal Conceptions.

[12] W. W. Willoughby, "The Juristic Conception of the State," in American Political Science Review, May, 1918; Vinogradoff, Introduction to Historical Jurisprudence, p. 88 ff.

[13] W. W. Willoughby, The Nature of the State, chaps. vii, viii, ix, and xi.

[14] But its objective rights and duties are self-set. "Rechte und Pflichten der Einzelnen empfangen ihre Kraft und Verbindlichkeit aus dem von dem objectiven Rechte festgesetzten Grunde. Der

lute subjective right.   As thus conceived the state is an
abstract medium of legal thinking rather than a concrete
thing.   Yet in this respect it is analogous to atom and ether
in the physical sciences; [15] and like those concepts its validity
must be adjudged by its usefulness.

Starting with these premises analytical jurisprudence un-
dertakes to make generalizations, classifications, and definitions with reference to the functioning of the state through
government.   In juristic study, as elsewhere, classification
is merely the discovery of relative similarities and dissimilar-
ities, by the method of analysis and correlation, and with
reference to a defined point of view.[16]   The classification that
follows is not offered as the ' correct ' one, therefore, but as
one that is not frivolous and is prolific of fairly satisfactory
results in the interpretation of the given phenomena.   The
basis of distinction or point of view is the relation of the
process, act, or product in question to the régime of law.
By this term is meant the system of modern constitutional
government whereby social regulation takes the form of formally set and uniform rules of conduct which are impartially applied to all particular cases which come within the
rules.[17]

This system is typical of the government of modern

Staat findet den Grund seiner Rechte und Pflichten in sich selbst "
(Jellinek, Gesetz und Verordnung, p. 196).

[15] Pearson, Grammar of Science.   See especially the Preface to
the edition of 1911.

[16] Mill, A System of Logic, book 4, chap. vii.   Bastable, Public
Finance, pp. 157-158, 163-164, 167, shows how economists dispute
over the ' correct ' classification of taxes.   Political philosophers
might profit by his reminder that " the principle of classification is
relative to the matter in hand. . . . An arrangement suitable for
one purpose may be unsuitable for another. . . . This is a com-
monplace to logicians."

[17] M. Hauriou states that the reign of law (état de droit) involves two principles: (1) the subordination of particular acts to
general rules previously established; and (2) the subordination of
the political point of view to that of juridical relationship (Précis
de droit administratif et de droit public, huitième édition, 1914,
p. 38).   Locke speaks of " settled standing rules, indifferent and
the same to all parties " (Second Treatise of Civil Government,
chap. vii).   Typically these ' rules ' are embodied in formal ' enactments.'

states.[18] Unwritten legal principles developed under a case system may cover a large field, but are nevertheless historical survivals, exceptions to the modern scheme. Under that scheme governmental activity is said to be divisible into two and only two distinct phases. These are variously distinguished as the expression and the carrying out of the will of the state; as the formation and the enforcement of the commands of the state; as the creation and the execution by the state of legal rights and duties; and as the enactment and the administration by the state of general rules of conduct. The matter is not so simple as this might indicate, yet we may accept it as the primary distinction from the standpoint of the reign of law.

Legislation is the discretionary determination of the legal rights and duties of private persons generally, or private persons of a reasonably defined class, and the provision of means of enforcing these rights and duties. By discretion is meant the exercise of choice involving not the scientific application to the facts of objective standards but a subjective evaluation of the advisability of alternatives. The régime of law does not eliminate discretion, but substitutes discretion as to a uniform rule for discretion in individual cases. The classical distinction of the Massachusetts constitution is really one between a government of man-made laws and a government of men. Legal means of enforcement is a necessary element in legislation. A rule of conduct which lacks a means of enforcement is not an expression of the will so much as of the mere wish of the state; and such a rule, if not enforceable by legal processes, should not even be graced with the title of a law of imperfect obligation.[19] It should be understood, however, that laws may enact privileges as well as commands,[20] and that means of enforcement is to be taken

---

[18] Cf. Laband, Deutsches Reichsstaatsrecht (Das Öffentliche Recht der Gegenwart, Band 1), sec. 15.

[19] The international lawyers usually insist upon stretching the meaning of the term law so as to include the 'law' of nations; but, clearly, to do so makes the term cover two quite different sorts of rules.

[20] The idea of 'command' was distinctively Austin's; see Brown, The Austinian Theory of Law, chap. i.

as broader than the penal sanction.[21]   The injunction of
equity, for example, is a more direct method of compelling
obedience than is either a damage suit or punishment by the
state.   Finally, we note that the provisions of a law may
be in concrete or in abstract terms.   Perhaps some specific
act will be required to be performed once [22] or periodically;
or maybe an abstract obligation such as the exercise of ' due
care ' will be imposed.

We have used the term uniformity [23] rather than generality, for the reason that the latter is ambiguous.   Many
writers have put forward generality as a criterion of
law.   Among the prominent ones are Rousseau,[24] Jèze,[25]
Esmein,[26] Duguit,[27] Austin,[28] Jethro Brown,[29] and the Meyer-
Anschütz Lehrbuch des deutschen Staatsrechtes.[30]   Unfortunately they do not mean the same thing in all cases.   Some
mean uniformity of application; [31] while Austin deliberately
rejects that meaning and terms law any command whether
to a person or to persons generally which obliges to a course
of action as distinguished from a particular act.[32]   Brown
cites these two meanings and accepts them both; while Amos
rejects both.[33]   Jellinek rejects generality as an essential
criterion in the following language: " Wenn daher auch in
der Mehrzahl der Fälle der Rechtsatz eine allgemeine Regel

---

[21] We may say of Austin's ' threat of evil ' what we said of his
' command,' that it is too narrow a term (Brown, Austinian Theory
of Law, p. 6 ff.; cf. Vinogradoff, Common Sense in Law, chap. ii).

[22] Austin denied the character of law to a command, even one of
uniform application, which obliged a person or persons to do or
refrain from doing a particular act (Brown, The Austinian Theory
of Law, pp. 11 ff., 16-17).   This limitation we reject.

[23] Wigmore, Problems of Law, Lecture I.

[24] Le contrat social, book 2, chap. iv.

[25] Les principes généraux du droit administratif (deuxième édition, 1914), pp. 147, 217.

[26] " De la délégation du pouvoir législatif," Revue politique et
parlementaire, 1-2 (1884), p. 212.

[27] Manuel de droit constitutionnel (1907), sec. 40.

[28] Brown, Austinian Theory of Law, pp. 11 ff, 16-17.

[29] Ibid., pp. 18-19 n.

[30] Page 570.

[31] This meaning Austin attributes to Blackstone (Brown, Austinian Theory of Law, p. 14).

[32] Ibid., p. 11 ff.

[33] Science of Jurisprudence, p. 74.

enthalt, so ist das Moment der Allgemeinheit doch höchstens ein Naturale, kein Essentiale des Gesetzes im materiellen Sinne." [34]   He protests that Rousseau's dictum that the object of the general will must be a general object is a play upon the logically ambiguous meaning of the term general.[35] He points out that in a society where there were no " constant types " there could be no uniform rules.[36] The best discussion of this whole problem which has appeared in English is that by Dr. Tomio Nakano in his recent work on The Ordinance Power of the Japanese Emperor.[37] With Nakano's conclusion, however, to the effect that uniformity is not an essential criterion of law [38] the present writer cannot agree. At one time, he was inclined to hold that a particular act might be a law as well as a uniform act, provided it created legal rights and duties by the exercise of full discretion in the premises.   Thus one has to distinguish between an order of an administrative officer addressed to an individual directing him to pay fifty dollars into the treasury when such officer was merely applying, by a simple mathematical calculation, the uniform statutory tax rate to the assessed value of said individual's property, and another order to the same effect issued by the arbitrary decision of the legally omnipotent British Parliament.   But this distinction taken by itself is not sufficient.   We could agree with Dr. Nakano if he merely held that one criterion of legislative acts is that they " are original, primary and spontaneous commands defining the free sphere of conduct of individuals in their relations with the state or between themselves." [39] But when he ends here, without adding that such acts are creative of law only when uniform, he fails to include a second criterion which the present writer considers essential. That criterion is uniformity in the sense of providing rights

---

[34] Gesetz und Verordnung, p. 239.
[35] Ibid., p. 237.
[36] Ibid., p. 238.
[37] Nakano, op. cit., chap. ii.
[38] Ibid., pp. 56-58.
[39] Ibid., p. 58.

or duties for persons of a class as distinguished from individuals.

It is the broad function of the administrative branch to run the machinery of government in the application and enforcement of the law. Administration in the narrower sense includes a multitude of non-discretionary proceedings by which public officers put into operation legislative rules of conduct. Some of these proceedings are merely mechanical acts, which do not even involve judgment. To such physical acts we give the name ' ministerial '.[40]   There are, nevertheless, acts of administration which involve not discretion to be sure, but a greater or less degree of judgment. Such are ' administrative determinations ' whether of fact or of law. Between the two, however, there is an important distinction. Under our system an administrative officer may be vested by statute with the final determination of a fact, but with only preliminary determination of a point of law. Final determination of a question of law is really a question of jurisdiction, which as we shall presently see is judicial in nature and must, under Article III of the Constitution, be left to the courts.[41]   It should be added that the determination of a fact, preliminarily as well as finally, as well as the determination of a matter of law preliminarily is administrative in character whether it be performed by an administrative officer or by a lower court of law.

If we stop with this dual division we relegate adjudication to a subordinate place as a mere phase of execution. This theory of judicial power is indeed quite logical for the government of France, where it originated.[42]   The distinctive function of the judiciary is the authoritative but non-discretionary determination of jurisdiction, or, in other words, the final decision whether a given act or course of action of a

[40] Marbury v. Madison (1 Cr. 137).

[41] Albertsworth, " Judicial Review of Administrative Action by the Federal Supreme Court," in Harvard Law Review, December, 1921.

[42] Ducrocq, Cours de droit administratif (sixième édition, 1881), vol. i, p. 27. Goodnow, Politics and Administration, p. 9, accepts this idea. But cf. also Paine, The Rights of Man, Everyman's ed., part 2, p. 198.

private person was (or, under a system of declaratory judgments, will be)[43] within the sphere of the legal competence of the performer or pursuer.   In France [44] the administrative courts, in English-speaking countries [45] the ordinary courts, perform the same function with reference to acts of the administration.   In the United States, however, the jurisdiction of the legislature is a judicial question.[46]   Here the courts may in a proper case determine whether the popular assembly has stepped outside its circle of power as well as whether the sheriff or the town clerk has exceeded his authority.   Thus the courts bring unity into the legal system by keeping all private and governmental persons within the range of their allotted powers.   For this very reason it seems illogical for American jurisprudence to treat the judicial process as an aspect of the administrative instead of as a function coordinate with the other two.

The rule of law involves the impartial application of uniform prescriptions to particular cases.   This stage of the governmental process requires a more or less elaborate administrative machinery.[47]   There is necessary, therefore, a body of rules which have to do with the organization and regulation of the administrative services.   Where those services are organized into a hierarchy, there may be commands issued by administrative superiors to their subordinates.   In German jurisprudence, as in the practice of German states, it has been considered a proper function of administrative heads to organize and regulate the services.[48]   In the States

---

[43] Borchard, " The Declaratory Judgment—A Needed Procedural Reform," in Yale Law Journal, vol. xxviii.

[44] Duguit, " The French Administrative Courts," in Political Science Quarterly, September, 1914; Garner, "Judicial Control of Administrative and Legislative Acts in France," in American Political Science Review, vol. ix, pp. 637-665.

[45] Cf. Goodnow, Principles of the Administrative Law of the United States, pp. 394-395.

[46] Marbury v. Madison (1 Cr. 137).

[47] In this connection note the development of administrative machinery that has accompanied the growth of governmental activity in recent decades.

[48] Laband, Deutsches Reichsstaatsrecht, pp. 135 ff.; Meyer-Anschütz, Lehrbuch des deutschen Staatsrechtes, pp. 571-573. Cf. Lowell, Governments and Parties in Continental Europe, vol. i, pp. 345-346.

of the American Union, on the other hand, not only did the popular election of many administrative officers make impossible a hierarchical system, but the creation of all administrative offices and the definition of the powers and duties appertaining thereto have been considered matters for either constitutional or legislative determination. Likewise, the federal Constitution, though making the President the real head of the administration,[49] placed in the hands of the Congress the power to make all laws necessary and proper for carrying into execution not only its own powers but also all other powers vested by the Constitution in the federal government or any department or officer thereof.[50] With reference to this power it will be noted that while of great importance it is ancillary to the enforcement of the uniform rules of conduct with respect to private interests which the reign of law entails.   For this reason we include in the power not only uniform rules governing administrative conduct [51] but also regulations respecting a single officer, provided these set forth general powers and duties,—powers and duties in connection with the administration of uniform laws or the performance of regular administrative duties.[52]

If we are to analyze government as it actually works, we must take note of the fact that two agencies may cooperate in the formulation and the bringing into operation of a given scheme of rights and duties.   Sometimes, indeed, especially in the United States, the legislative body elaborates in concrete detail every phase of a given regulation.   In this event the rôle of the administrative department is confined to administration proper or at the most to administration combined with a degree of subordinate discretion.   At other

---

[49] Through his power of removal, which is not expressed in the document, but is implied from his executive power.

[50] Art. 1, sec. 8.

[51] Such as the executive order of the President forbidding federal officers from holding simultaneously state, territorial, or municipal offices (Richardson, Messages and Papers of the Presidents, vol. ix, pp. 4172-4173; pp. 4173-4174).

[52] Such as the regulations issued by the Director of the Budget under the provision of law which enacts that " The Assistant Director shall perform such duties as the Director may designate " (42 Stat. L. 20-27).

times it falls out for one reason or another that the legislature expresses its rules in terms of abstractions which the Executive is to complete, or perhaps leaves it to the discretion of the Executive to determine the circumstances under which the rules are to become operative.   In the one case the administration may be given the function of rendering concrete the legislative abstractions by concrete ' rules '; in the other case its part may be not to prescribe a completing rule but to proclaim formally that a legislative rule is to come into operation.   To make the matter clear we may set forth the main elements involved in full discretion in the premises.   These are: (1) the decision as to whether any regulation of the given phenomena is expedient; (2) the determination of what substantive legal rights and duties shall be created; (3) the setting forth of the time when or the circumstances under which the rights and duties are to become operative; (4) the designation of the class or classes of persons to whom the rights and duties shall be applied; (5) the definition of what penalty (if any) shall be inflicted for the violation of the rights and duties; and (6) the prescription of the administrative and judicial means which shall be employed in enforcing the rights and duties.   Discretion as to any phase of an enactment save the first may be left to the Executive; and in such case we have co-legislation, provided the product of such discretionary determination applies to persons generally or to persons of a class or to a single official in connection with general duties.

Formerly the American legislatures left their legislative abstractions to be interpreted by Mr. Dicey's twelve shopkeepers.[53]   Nowadays they are more apt to authorize the appropriate administrative officer or commission to render such abstractions concrete by the issuance of uniform and concrete rules and regulations.   The body of rights and duties does not come from the legislature complete, but is supplemented by complementary ordinances translating the legislative abstractions into concrete terms.[54]   As yet

[53] The Law of the Constitution, 8th edition, p. 242.
[54] An example of concretizing ordinances was involved in the case

the potentialities of this practice have scarcely begun to be realized, and the discretionary functions of administrative tribunals often have more of an executive than a legislative complexion.[55] Yet the principle of administrative cooperation in the process of legislation has latent possibilities which are bound to be developed; and for this reason emphasis should be given to its existence even now. It must be added that in the field of administrative organization and regulation the same principle applies. In fact it is probably both constitutional and wise to carry the principle much further here than in the sphere of legislation in the material sense of the word. This raises the whole question 'Who should organize the administration?'[56]

It must not be thought, however, that all creations of rights and duties can, or at any rate do, take the form of the enactment of uniform rules. Because, as Jellinek points out,[57] uniformity is possible only where there are uniformities in the phenomena to be regulated, therefore there are in all governments cases where it is manifestly out of the question to attempt to realize justice by the application of uniform rules to situations no two of which are even approximately alike. Then, too, the principle of uniformity is not always applied where it might be. Where the discretionary creation of rights and duties of particular persons crystallizes into recognized types of action that are independent of legislation, we may term the acts involved 'executive.' An example is a pardon or a private act of a legislative assembly. Where such particularized discretion is rather incidental to

---

of Buttfield v. Stranahan (192 U. S. 470). An example of an ordinance issued under an abstract statement of the third element of full discretion in the premises was involved in Field v. Clark (143 U. S. 649).

[55] See for example, the power given the Interstate Commerce Commission in 24 Stat. L. 384, as amended by 34 Stat. L. 589, 36 Stat. L. 551, and 40 Stat. L. 272. See Compiled Statutes, sec. 8583.

[56] Cf. Blachly, "Who Should Organize State Administration?" in Southwestern Political Science Quarterly, September, 1923; Mathews, "State Administrative Reorganization," in American Political Science Review, August, 1922.

[57] Gesetz und Verordnung, p. 238.

the administration of a given statutory rule, we may denominate it 'sub-legislative.' Likewise, we may have particular discretion with reference to a governmental official instead of a private person. This we may call, for the want of a better name, an 'official order.' Such is the provision that a named official give bond, as also are appointments and removals where the appointing and removing officer is not rigidly bound by the merit system.[58] The ideal is everywhere uniformity,[59] but only rarely can the pardon be discarded for the amnesty, and only gradually in the United States is a uniform merit method being substituted for the arbitrary, particular action of the spoils system. There will always be need for what Dean Pound has aptly called individualization in the law.[60]

Here, then, are the main phases of the functioning of government in the modern constitutional state. We distinguish certain 'processes,' which culminate in types of 'governmental acts.' Most of such acts result in corresponding 'governmental products.' Thus we find that the legislative process includes such preliminary matters as committee hearings, the adoption of rules of procedure, and parliamentary debates thereunder. The legislative act is the final authoritative act of government which makes law what is not-law.

---

[58] As an example of an 'official order' we may cite the following letter:

"Executive Mansion,
"Washington, D. C., May 3, 1899.
"Sir: You are hereby removed from the office of general appraiser of merchandise, to take effect upon the appointment and qualification of your successor.

WILLIAM McKINLEY."

[59] Of course, no two cases are ever exactly alike. The 'event' never repeats itself. But the law can and does select certain important characteristics which are, roughly speaking, recurrent, the uniform rules to be applied whenever those characteristics are found to be present.

[60] An Introduction to the Philosophy of Law, chap. iii. Mr. Pound is referring primarily to individualization through the judiciary, but he refers to 'administrative tribunals' as one agency "for individualizing the application of law" (pp. 129-130). It would seem, moreover, that the judgments of courts are 'executive' or 'sub-legislative' rather than 'judicial' acts in those cases on which stress is laid in Cardozo, The Nature of the Judicial Process, Lecture III.

The result or product of such an act is, of course, a law.[61]
In like manner we have administrative acts, which may be
ministerial acts (physical) or administrative determinations.
A judicial act is the rendering of a judgment in a question
of jurisdiction. Similarly we have the ordinance,[62] prescribing rules of governmental as distinguished from social conduct, and co-laws and co-ordinances to supplement and concretize legislative and ordinance making abstractions. Outside the reign of law and standing as exceptions thereto are
executive orders and official orders; while sub-legislative
orders and sub-ordinance making orders issue in the one
phase of administration proper which is discretionary.

These are not distinctions of American constitutional law,
to be sure. Law as defined above is defined in the material
sense of the term. The same is true of ordinance and the
rest. Now definition in the material sense looks to the
nature of the process and of the result and not to the character of the performer of the act. That is said to be a formal
definition which is based upon the latter criterion.[63] Thus
we are taught in the text books that the separation of powers
is a fundamental principle of American government and con-

---

[61] "La loi est une règle impérative ou prohibitive qui statue
non dans un intérêt particulier, mais dans l'intérêt commun, non à
l'égard d'un individu isolé mais à l'égard de tous, pour l'avenir et
à toujours" (Esmein, Eléments de droit constitutionnel, 2e édition,
p. 10).
[62] The difference between law and ordinance in the material sense
is the difference between Rechtsvorschrift and Verwaltungsvorschrift (Laband, Deutsches Reichsstaatsrecht, sec. 16).
[63] According to Jellinek, it was Laband who first raised to a
sharp juristic formulation the contrast between law in the material and in the formal sense (Gesetz und Verordnung, p. 252). See
Laband, Staatsrecht des deutschen Reiches, vol. ii, p. 59 ff., and his
Deutsches Reichsstaatsrecht, secs. 15-16, for his distinctions between
formal and material law, and between formal and material ordinance. The writer has found helpful summaries of the German
theories on these matters in Boelling, Das Recht der Prüfung von
Verordnungen nach dem Staatsrechte des Reiches und Preussens,
1912, sec. 2, and Schmidt, Das Verordnungsrecht des Bundesrates
des deutschen Reiches, 1913, sec. 11. Cf. with the theory of the
text the brilliant analyses of the problem of classification of governmental functions in Green, "The Separation of Governmental
Powers," in Yale Law Journal, February, 1920; and Brown, "The
Separation of Powers in British Jurisdictions" in Yale Law Journal,
November, 1921. The writer is in debt to both these authors.

stitutional law. We are further taught that, according to that principle, the three phases of the governmental process (namely, the making, executing, and construing of the law) should be and in our system are placed in separate and coordinate departments (namely, the legislature, the executive, and the judiciary). Hence, in the formal sense of the Constitution, the three kinds of governmental acts are legislative, executive, and judicial. Any act of Congress is formally a law, whether such act embody law in the material sense,[64] ordinances in the material sense,[65] or private acts which are executive decrees in the material sense.[66] By the same token we describe as executive in the formal sense Presidential legislation levying under constitutional authority tariff duties in conquered enemy territory in time of war,[67] wartime Presidential Proclamations prohibiting under authority from Congress the exportation of certain articles to certain countries,[68] and Executive Orders prescribing under Congressional delegation the duties of United States consuls.[69] The term ordinance is unknown to our constitutional law in its formal as well as in its material meaning.

Yet what are the facts? Government in action and constitutional law in the concrete are more varied than the opening sentences of the first three Articles of the Constitution would indicate. The traditional dogma of the separation of powers is an over-simplification of the governmental process as it actually takes place and as it is recognized by the courts. The variety and complexity of that process is hidden by the confusing use of a term like law without reference to content. The word as used in the United States covers at once too much and too little.[70] This is so even if

---

[64] Such as the Sherman Anti-Trust Act.

[65] Such as the act creating and organizing any of the Executive Departments and prescribing its functions.

[66] Such as the grant of a pension to a named individual.

[67] See Dooley v. United States, 182 U. S. 222.

[68] 40 Stat. L., part 2, 1746-1747.

[69] Embodied in the 'Consular Regulations' issued under Rev. Stat., sec. 1752.

[70] It covers too much because it includes statutes which organize the administrative services and grant money to individuals; too

we except from it certain acts of Congress (like impeachments) which the Constitution authorizes as clear exceptions to the strict principle of the separation of powers. Then, too, by judicial interpretation practices like the delegation of discretionary and even rule-making powers by Congress to the President are upheld.[71] Fortunately the courts have construed the supreme law not without an eye to history and governmental efficiency; and the lines of demarcation between the three departments have been somewhat blurred.

In view of these facts it appears entirely legitimate for analytical jurisprudence to define the processes, acts, and products of governmental activity with reference to the nature of the mental process involved and of the legal results produced instead of with reference to the character of the department concerned. On the other hand, it is of both political and juristic significance whether material laws or material ordinances be passed by Congress or issued by the Chief Magistrate. Hence it is expedient for the analytical jurist to elaborate his own formal classification to supplement his material classification of the phenomena. The former may differ from the formal classification of the Constitution; and, in point of fact, a much more serviceable one can be found. For formal acts of legislation are properly not all acts of the legislature, but only those which produce material laws or ordinances;[72] while formal ordinances are those acts emanating from the executive department which embody either material laws or material ordinances.[73] If terms are

---

little, because it does not include Rechtssätze if they happen to be embodied in executive proclamations and orders.

[71] Field v. Clark, 143 U. S. 649; United States v. Grimaud, 220 U. S. 506; and many other cases.

[72] "Im formellen Sinne ist nur dasjenige *ius scriptum* Gesetzrecht, welches unter Zustimmung der Volksvertretung entstanden ist" (Laband, Das Staatsrecht des deutschen Reiches, vol. ii, p. 62). Formal law should properly include not only such material law as is created by or with the consent of the representative assembly, but also such material ordinances as emanate from the same source.

[73] "Le règlement diffère de la loi proprement dite, non par son contenu juridique, mais par sa forme, par l'autorité de qu'il émane. Une règle générale posée par les Chambres législatives est une loi proprement dite; la même règle générale, si elle est formulée par une autre autorité publique, est un règlement" (Jèze, "Les prin-

needed to cover all products of action by the popular assembly and by the Executive, respectively, the words ' statute ' and ' decree ' might serve. For present purposes there is no need to go further than to distinguish ' formal law ' as an act passed by the legislative department containing either ' material law ' or ' material ordinance ', and ' formal ordinance ' as an act issuing from the Executive containing either ' material ordinance ' or ' material law.'

French authorities disagree as to whether ordinances are law.[74] It is clear that they are not law in the formal sense; but certain writers deny them a place in the category of material law. For this three reasons are given. In the first place, it is pointed out that the sanction for ordinances is provided by the legislature and not the executive.[75] This

---

cipes généraux du droit administratif," deuxiéme édition, 1914, p. 217). M. Duguit defines "règlement" as "toute disposition par voie générale émanant d'un organe autre que le parlement, ou si l'on veut toute disposition par voie générale en une forme autre que la forme législative (c'est-à-dire, vote par le parlement et promulgation par le président de la république)" (Manuel de droit constitutionnel, Paris, 1907, p. 191, sec. 40). Formal ordinances should properly include all Verwaltungsvorschriften as well as all Rechtsvorschriften which emanate from the Executive.

[74] Duguit holds that ordinances are law in the material but not in the formal sense (Droit constitutionnel, pp. 107-108). Dufour says: "L'acte réglementaire a la même autorité et produit les mêmes effets que l'acte législatif; il est vrai de dire en ce sens que tout acte réglementaire n'est qu'une loi secondaire " (Cours de droit administratif, vol. i, p. 58). Esmein, on the contrary, claims that they are not laws. He says: " A vrai dire, le pouvour réglementaire ne rentre pas nécessairement dans le pouvoir législatif, et le règlement n'est point la loi. Le règlement est, en effet, simplement une préscription qui a pour but d'assurer l'exécution de la loi en la complétant dans les détails, mais sans pouvoir en changer ou modifier ni le texte ni l'esprit. Aussi le droit de faire des règlements ne revient-il pas nécessairement, ni même naturellement, au pouvoir législatif. Il droit être confié naturellement au pouvoir exécutif; car étant chargé d'exécuter les lois, c'est lui qui peut le plus utilement les compléter de cette manière." He admits, however, that they are like laws in being generally obligatory (Droit constitutionnel, sixième édition, 1914, p. 535, sec. 6).

[75] A middle view is that held by Laferrière, who says (vol. i, p. 11, deuxième édition): "Entre le pouvoir législatif et le pouvoir exécutif il y a une attribution intermédiaire, celle qui consiste à faire les règlements, à édicter les préscriptions secondaires nécessaires à l'application des lois; cette difficulté sera attribuée au législateur ou au gouvernement, ou bien elle sera diversement

is certainly true of at least most of the ordinances of France,[76] England,[77] and the United States.[78] Secondly, an ordinance is said not to be law because it is on a subordinate plane. An ordinance may not abrogate a statute, but a statute may abrogate an ordinance. An ordinance is bound by the existing statute law and may not contradict its letter or spirit, or (in the case of delegated ordinances) go beyond the scope of the statutory delegation.[79] Thirdly, it is pointed out that the French administrative courts may annual ordinances, while there is no judicial body which can annul statutes.[80] But to all of these points it may be said that they prove not that ordinances are not law, but that they are a form of law which in France is subordinate to statutes.

For the exact relation of statute and ordinance we must look to the particular constitutional system in question. Where ordinance making power is specifically given to the Executive in a written constitution, it is usually provided what relation such constitutional ordinances shall bear to the statutes. Thus the Japanese constitution provides for emergency ordinances " in the place of laws "; [81] while it says of other ordinances that " No ordinance shall in any way alter any of the existing laws." [82] Many constitutions grant to the Executive the power to issue ordinances to complete the laws; and the usual provision is something to the effect that

---

partagée entre eux, selon que la Constitution générale de l'Etat tendra à faire plus ou moins prévaloir l'influence du Parlement ou celle du pouvoir exécutif."

[76] A general penal sanction for ' ordinances legally made ' is provided in art. 471, sec. 15, of the French Penal Code (as revised in 1832). Special statutory sanction may be provided in individual cases, of course (See Garner, " Judicial Control of Administrative and Legislative Acts in France," in American Political Science Review, November, 1915).

[77] See Carr, Delegated Legislation, p. 54, n. 2.

[78] See chap. vi. Cf. United States v. Grimaud, 220 U. S. 506.

[79] See Hauriou, Précis de droit administratif et de droit public, pp. 35, 36-37, 53, 54, 59, 60. But see p. 62. Cf. also Merritt v. Welsh, 104 U. S. 694, and Morrill v. Jones, 106 U. S. 466.

[80] See Jèze, Les principes généraux du droit administratif, deuxième édition, 1914.

[81] Art. 8.

[82] Art. 9.

such ordinances may not alter the laws (statutes).[83]   That such ordinances are limited strictly by the text of the statutes which they supplement might be implied from the very nature of this phase of the ordinance making power. In the exercise of such power the jurisdiction of the authority possessing it involves completion, without violation, of the enactment to be supplemented. And of course that authority, as all other, must be kept within its jurisdiction. Whether the authority find its source in statutory or constitutional delegation, it is conditioned by the terms of the grant. It may, indeed, be the case that the power is derived from prerogatives recognized by an unwritten law, or even from the theory of autocracy that the ruler, being the source of all political power, has himself all authority which he has not delegated to others.[84] In such cases, the power of ordinance is not based upon a definite text, and is therefore vaguer and more capable of expansion.[85] Even in such cases, however, the general rule in modern constitutional governments is that, as between statute and ordinance, the former prevails. The chief exception is where the constitution specifically provides that in certain cases ordinances may override statutes.

Otherwise statutes are superior to ordinances. And this superiority is emphasized by the fact that (under at least the systems of England, France, and the United States) the penal sanction of ordinances is attached by the legislature. The Executive has no inherent power to make the violation of its rules (even when it has authority to issue them) a crime or misdemeanor. And in the United States the legislature itself can not delegate to the Executive the power to decide what punishment is ' reasonable.' The creation of the punishment is so clearly the very teeth of legis-

---

[83] See, for example, the Constitution of Italy, art. 6.
[84] See W. W. Willoughby, Prussian Political Philosophy, chap. v, especially p. 94 ff.   Contrast the *dictum* of the Supreme Court in the Floyd Acceptances, 7 Wall. 666.
[85] Lowell, Government of England, vol. i, p. 19.

lation, that the most that, under our rigid constitutional system, can be allowed is the delegation to the Executive of the power which is sometimes left to the courts [86] of determining within defined limits the amount of the punishment.

---

[86] As where the law provides that the violator of an enactment shall be liable to a fine of not less than ten nor more than thirty thousand dollars, or to imprisonment for not less than one nor more than two years, or both.

CHAPTER III

The Ordinance: Distinctions and Classifications

On est d'accord pour définir le règlement toute disposition par voie générale émanant d'un organe autre que le parlement, ou si l'on veut toute disposition par voie générale edictée en une forme autre que la forme législative (c'est-à-dire, vote par le parlement et promulgation par le président de la république).

—Duguit.[1]

Die Verordnungen unterscheiden sich von den Gesetzen durch die fehlende Mitwirkung der Volksvertretung.

—Meyer-Anschütz, Lehrbuch des Deutschen Staatsrechtes.[2]

It is important to distinguish between rules issued by the head of a department for the guidance of his subordinates and the regulations of which we are speaking. The former are merely directions given to the officials for the purpose of instructing them in their duties, and are binding on no one else. The right to issue them must belong, to some extent, to every one who has persons under his orders, although they are used much more systematically in France than in the United States. The regulations with which we are concerned here are of quite a different kind, for they are binding on all citizens who may be affected by them, and have, in fact, the character of laws.

—A. Lawrence Lowell.[3]

The American conception of the term law makes no distinction between material laws and material ordinances, but includes them both. It is furthermore in accord with American ideas on government for the enactment of both sorts of rules to be left to the legislative department. Thus the Constitution of the United States in effect gives to the Congress the power to pass the ' necessary and proper ' material ordinances as well as material laws. Congress has the power to pass acts organizing the executive departments as well as acts affecting private interests with respect to the subjects committed to its control. Both sorts of acts are technically ' laws,' and under the Constitution the law-making powers

---

[1] Droit constitutionnel, sec. 40.
[2] Page 570.
[3] The Governments of France, Italy, and Germany, pp. 44-45.

of the popular assembly cannot be delegated by it to the President or to any other authority.[4]

Yet, as has been indicated above, Congress may delegate through its 'laws' discretion as to the creation of subordinate rules. This is true whether Congress is enacting 'laws' affecting personal and property interests of individuals, or 'laws' respecting administrative operations. Thus, in the war with Germany, the national legislative body passed the Overman Act[5] as well as the Selective Draft Act,[6] the Trading with the Enemy Act,[7] and Food and Fuel Control Acts.[8] Each of these authorized the Chief Magistrate or subordinates acting under his general control to issue ordinances, the first with respect to departmental organization, the others with reference both to administrative practice and procedure and to private conduct.

Herein we find a practice which raises interesting and significant problems in the realms both of jurisprudence and of political theory. As long as Congress itself prescribes the appropriate material laws and ordinances in detail, the situation is in harmony with orthodox American conceptions and methods. The moment, however, that that body grants to the President power to enact material laws or material ordinances even of a subordinate character, we are faced with juristic and political issues which demand a solution. In Germany this is partly true of the delegation of power to enact material laws, but not of the delegation or constitutional possession of the power to enact material ordinances.[9] But our ideas regarding the proper location of this latter power have differed from those of the Germans; the broad

---

[4] "That Congress cannot delegate legislative power to the President is a principle universally recognized as vital to the integrity and maintenance of the system of government ordained by the Constitution" (Field v. Clark, 143 U. S. 649).

[5] 40 Stat. L., part 1, 556-557.

[6] Ibid., 76 ff.

[7] Ibid., 411 ff.

[8] Ibid., 273 ff, 276 ff, 1348 ff.

[9] For the reason, already mentioned, that material ordinances are by the Germans considered as properly emanating from the head of the administrative system.

delegation of power in the Overman Act excited opposition and discussion just as in the case of the other acts named. In fact, it excited more opposition for the reason that it was broader than the others and authorized changes in, and not mere applications of, the statutes.   There would thus seem to be ample justification for the consideration in this treatise of the power of the President to issue both material ordinances and material laws, or, in other words, for the discussion of the formal ordinances of the Executive and the problems connected with his issuance thereof.   This will, of course, include the ordinances issued under his constitutional as well as his delegated powers, and the ordinances issued by his subordinates under his supervision or responsibility in accordance with statutory authorization.

I

It will serve to clarify our ideas concerning the formal ordinances of the President if we distinguish ordinances from several other kinds of products, some governmental and some non-governmental, with which they might be confused. Take first uniform rules of conduct laid down by a club or some similar organization for its members.   Their enforcement rests upon the pressure of opinion, social comity, and maybe even upon expulsion of members who disobey them.   But can it be said of them that what the state permits it commands?   The expelled member could appeal to the courts of the state and secure relief where the rules or the manner of enforcing them infringed upon any material interest of his which the state sees fit to protect.   If, however, he were without redress in court we could say that the state 'commands' or, more aptly, grants that the club may enforce certain rules in a certain way.   The rules themselves, however, are not commands of the state but of the club.   The state wills to permit them, but the club wills to enforce them. They are not governmental products.[10]

The next class of acts is entirely different.   The Execu-

---

[10] See Gray, The Nature and Sources of the Law, secs. 329-334.

tive may be permitted to issue proclamations of warning to persons who are violating or about to violate the law. President Washington issued proclamations of this sort during the Whiskey Rebellion in western Pennsylvania.[11] They were clearly governmental products, but of what type? Their nature was clearly set forth by Coke in 1610 in the famous Case of Proclamations.[12] The king may issue his proclamation, said Coke, to warn the subjects of what the law is, but he may not by his proclamation make that an offense which was not one before. In other words, he showed that such proclamations are not creative of law, but merely declaratory thereof. Coke and later writers after him said that such warnings " aggravated " the offense, and Professor Maitland has remarked that in England this is probably still true.[13] In the United States, such proclamations of warning might or might not influence the trial court to impose the maximum legal penalty. It might be more apt to do so when (as sometimes happens) Congress specifically provides that the enforcement of the law be preceded by a proclaimed warning. It is important to add that such a warning does become an ordinance if the law has set forth rights and duties which are to come into operation only when the Executive in his sound discretion shall have so decided and have given warning to that effect by proclamation.

Presidential ordinances are issued chiefly if not solely in the form of Proclamations or Executive Orders. But these two forms are also used for Presidential acts which are not in any sense ordinances. In order to emphasize this fact, we may note that many proclamations are hortatory or declaratory and not legislative in character. A classic example is the annual Thanksgiving Proclamation. Then again we find among the ordinance making proclamations of President Wilson an exhortation to his countrymen to support the Boy Scout movement.[14]

---

[11] Richardson, Messages and Papers of the Presidents, vol. i, pp. 117, 149.
[12] 12 Co. Rep. 74.
[13] The Constitutional History of England, p. 302.
[14] 41 Stat. L., part 2, 1747-1748.

Another type of official act, which may or may not be embodied in the form of a proclamation, is the formal statement of the official determination of a fact in the administration of a law. Sometimes a statute states that its provisions shall become operative only when the President has by proclamation set forth the existence of certain facts. In such a case it is not easy to draw the line between non-discretionary fact-findings and determinations which involve discretion; and thus we find administrative and ordinance making functions shading into each other. The American courts are especially prone to regard as 'fact-finding' processes which come dangerously near discretionary determinations. It is in this somewhat disingenuous manner that they justify delegation of discretionary authority to the Executive without having to modify in terms the separation of powers. An Act of Congress of May 1, 1810, provided in section 4 "that in case either Great Britain or France shall before the third day of March next, so revoke or modify her edicts, as that they shall cease to violate the neutral commerce of the United States, which fact the President of the United States shall declare by proclamation." [15] To what extent did this involve mere judgment, to what extent if any did it involve discretion? In the case of the Brig *Aurora* v. United States [16] the Supreme Court declared that it did not involve the delegation of legislative power to the President. Again, section 3 of the tariff act of October 1, 1890, read: " whenever and so often as the President shall be satisfied that the government of any country producing and exporting " designated articles " imposes duties or other exactions upon the agricultural or other products of the United States, which in view of the free introduction of such " articles " into the United States he may deem to be reciprocally unequal and unreasonable, he shall have the power and it shall be his duty to suspend, by proclamation to that effect, the provisions of this act relating to the free introduction of such " articles, " the production of such

---

[15] 2 Stat. L., 605, 606.   [16] 7 Cr. 382.

country, for such time as he shall deem just, and in such case and during such suspension duties shall be levied, collected and paid upon " such articles coming from such country " as follows." [17]   Does it involve subjective evaluation to determine whether commercial exactions of another country are " reciprocally unequal and unreasonable," and to decide how long the suspension of certain provisions of a tariff act shall continue? Yet here again, in the leading case of Field v. Clark,[18] the Court called the part of the President fact-finding, except with reference to the length of time of the suspension.

Then there is the case of ' rulings ' of administrative officers, which are technically merely their interpretations of the meaning of the law, but which are in fact of more practical importance than many ordinances having the force of law.[19] For where such rulings can be brought before the judiciary, the courts will give every presumption in their favor, and in case of doubt will accept them as the true meaning of the law.[20]   The rule, however, is that they do not bind the courts when they are clearly in conflict with the law.[21]   A second reason for the practical importance of such rulings is that where no private rights are involved, or where such rights are not asserted, the administrative rulings do not come before the courts at all.[22]   In case they cannot be reviewed

---

[17] 26 Stat. L., 567, chap. 1244.

[18] 143 U. S. 649.

[19] " Statutory construction is practically one of the greatest of executive powers " (Taft, Our Chief Magistrate and His Powers, pp. 78-79).

[20] Powell, " The Separation of Powers, II," in Political Science Quarterly, vol. xxviii, pp. 39-40 n.; Albertsworth, " Judicial Review of Administrative Action by the Federal Supreme Court," in Harvard Law Review, December, 1921.

[21] Compare the following cases: Houghton v. Payne, 194 U. S. 88, 1904, and United States v. Hill, 120 U. S. 169, 1887.

[22] " Of course ultimately where a statute affects private right, it is likely to come before the courts in actual litigation and to put upon the courts the duty of its construction. But there are many statutes that do not affect private right in such a way that they come under the court's interpretation; and in such cases Executive interpretation is final. Even where it is not, it is very persuasive with courts who subsequently are obliged to adjudge the meaning of the statutes " (Taft, Our Chief Magistrate and His Powers, pp. 78-79).

by the courts, should we call them ordinances? Strictly speaking, no. For while in such an event they practically have the force of law, they are, after all, interpretative rather than discretionary. The mental process is different from that where the law itself gives the Executive the right to elaborate its contents or concretize its abstractions. Yet where the law is general, and perhaps somewhat inconsistent and vague, the distinction between administrative rulings as to its meaning and ordinances is almost without a difference. However, the same situation arises with reference to interpretations by the courts in the frequent cases where final determination of jurisdiction shades into discretion.[23]

Another sort of action to be distinguished is emergency action by the English Crown under its prerogative right of defending the realm.[24] Because of such action the responsible ministers could be sued for damages at common law; and in such suits the courts would determine in each case for themselves whether the action taken was justified by the necessities of the case. If the Crown had proceeded by the method of issuing general rules, such rules would thus not be law but mere statements of policy by the Executive. The Crown would not be bound by them itself; and if it did follow them the courts could go behind the rules and determine as a matter of fact whether, aside from the rules, the act in each case was justifiable.[25] Clearly such rules are different from ordinances having the force of law.

II

Having set forth the meaning of ordinance and distinguished it from several other products of the governmental

---

[23] This is especially true where a court of appeal is testing some new departure in social or industrial legislation by the standard of a Constitutional generalization like the ' due process ' clause (Cardozo, The Nature of the Judicial Process, p. 76 ff.). The principle of stare decisis makes such a decision practically a rule for the future.

[24] James Hart, " The Emergency Ordinance: A Note on Executive Power," in Columbia Law Review, June, 1923, pp. 528, 532-533.

[25] Baty and Morgan, War: Its Conduct and Legal Results, 1915, chap. i.

process, we may now classify ordinances from selected points of view. Our method will be to start with significant points of view, and, with reference to each of them, to divide all ordinances into two classes. In addition it will be expedient to make sub-classifications of one of the main classes in accordance with the same procedure.

The primary basis of distinction for the purposes of this treatise is the source of the authority by which the ordinance making official acts. In American law there are only two such sources,—constitutional and statutory.[26] In the federal government at least the President is the only officer who is granted ordinance making authority directly by the Constitution; the source of the ordinance making power of his subordinates is constitutional only when and in the sense that they act as agents of the Chief Executive in carrying out his constitutional functions. For the rest they must find their authorization in the statutes of Congress alone.[27] The Chief Magistrate, however, exercises powers which come distinctly within the definition of ordinance making powers both by virtue of constitutional grants and by virtue of statutory delegations.

These two types of ordinances are distinguished by the French with reference to the ordinance making powers of the President of the French Republic as *les décrets réglementaires spontanés* and *les règlements d'administration publique*.[28] By German authorities they are referred to as *verfassungs= und gesetzmässige Verordnungen,* respectively.[29]

Illustrations of each kind of Presidential ordinance are not far to seek. It was under his authority as commander-

---

[26] Taft, Our Chief Magistrate and His Powers, pp. 139-140; The Floyd Acceptances, 7 Wall. 666, 676.

[27] The Executive Departments are created, not by the Constitution, but by statutes of Congress, the Constitution merely referring to them and their heads incidentally and in general terms (Art. ii, sec. ii).

[28] Duguit, Droit constitutionnel, sec. 141; Jèze, Les principes généraux du droit administratif, deuxième édition, 1914, pp. 218-219.

[29] Jellinek, Gesetz und Verordnung, Zweite Abteilung, Zweiter Abschnitt, Kap. vi.

in-chief of the army that President Lincoln issued his emancipation proclamation,[30] the aim of which seems to have been to produce a paralysis of production in the South if not a slave uprising behind the Confederate lines. His earlier blockade of Southern ports was also a proper exercise of the same constitutional power.[31] When, however, we turn to Lincoln's proclamations suspending the writ of habeas corpus, we find that the authority for the earlier proclamations [32] was formally declared by Chief Justice Taney in Ex parte Merryman [33] to be non-existent; but that the proclamation of September 15, 1863,[34] was issued under authority of an act of Congress of March 3, 1863,[35] which also by a retroactive delegation ratified the previous action of the President in suspending the writ. We have here a clear case of statutory delegation. The question is no longer whether the President is given by the supreme law the power to suspend the writ, but whether Congress, in the exercise of its power in this regard, may delegate such broad discretion to the President.

Now we find that in some monarchical countries the Executive may claim ordinance making powers on grounds of inherent authority,[36] while in England he claims them as customary or in other words under the common law.[37] In both cases we may reduce the claims to a constitutional basis if we use the term constitutional in the sense not of a written document but of the body of maxims and principles by which the government is organized. But that is not the sense in which we have spoken of the ordinance making powers of the President as being sometimes under constitutional authoriza-

---

[30] 12 Stat. L., 1267-1268.
[31] 12 Stat. L., 1259.
[32] 12 Stat. L., 1260; 13 Stat. L., 730. See McPherson, History of the Rebellion, pp. 177 ff; Dunning, Essays on the Civil War and Reconstruction, chap i.
[33] Campbell's Rep., 246.
[34] 13 Stat. L., 734-735.
[35] 12 Stat. L., 755.
[36] Cf. W. W. Willoughby, Prussian Political Philosophy, chap. v, p. 94 ff.
[37] Cf. Dicey, Law of the Constitution, pp. 50-51.

tion. By that we have meant that they were sometimes delegated to the President in the text of the instrument itself.

The second important criterion for the classification of ordinances is the relations which they regulate. In this respect they are by German authors divided into *Rechtsverordnungen* and *Verwaltungsverordnungen*.[38] Of these classes the former comprises those ordinances which may be described as uniform rules of social conduct which the state will enforce; the latter administrative regulations, or general rules prescribing the manner in which government officials shall conduct their offices. In other words, the former includes material laws as we have defined them above, while the latter consists of material ordinances as they are hereinbefore defined. As we have seen, formal ordinances are divisible into these two classes of material laws and material ordinances. To put the matter somewhat differently, *Rechtsverordnungen* undertake to regulate relations between private persons and their fellows, or between private persons and the state. As such they include uniform rules of private law as well as uniform rules of criminal law, and uniform grants of privileges or franchises by the state to private individuals. On the other hand, *Verwaltungsverordnungen* control relations between the state and its agents in the administration of *Rechtsverordnungen,* or, in other terms, between the sovereign person and its governmental organs. It may be added that relations between officials and private persons and those between superior officials and their subordinates are in reality included in the above series. For in such cases the ' political superior ' either is the mere agent or representative of state action, or else is exceeding his official capacity and acts as a mere private usurper.[39]

---

[38] Laband, Deutsches Reichsstaatsrecht, sec. 16; Meyer-Anschütz, Lehrbuch des deutschen Staatsrechtes, 570-574. Cf. Lowell, Government of England, vol. ii, p. 363 ff.; and Governments and Parties in Continental Europe, vol. i, pp. 43-46, 345.

[39] That is to say, a relation between a private individual and an official is really a relation between such individual and the state; and, similarly, a relation between a subordinate official and his superior official is really a relation between the subordinate and

In actuality these two kinds of ordinances are inextricably inter-related. The creation of private rights and duties inevitably gives specific content to the general duties which are assigned to administrative officials; while the regulation of official conduct necessarily affects at least indirectly the private interests which are made subject to that conduct. In fact, one finds the same statute prescribing rules of social conduct, and the duties of one or more officials in connection with the administration thereof, or else laying down powers of officers and making it the duty of all private persons concerned to obey the orders of such officers issued in pursuance of such powers. The two things are but opposite sides of the same shield.[40]

Here again we may pause to give at random illustrations from the ordinances of the President. In 1794 Congress delegated to President Washington both the power to lay an embargo during the impending recess of that body and the authority to issue the orders necessary for the administrative enforcement, presumably by the navy, of such embargo.[41] The President did not find it necessary to exercise the power thus delegated; but if he had, the proclamation ordering the embargo and setting forth the classes of vessels to which it applied would have been material law, while the executive orders for the prevention of violation would have been material ordinances. The amnesty proclamation of President Lincoln, which was authorized by Congress, but which he might have issued under his pardoning power alone, was material law;[42] while the following Executive Order of President Roosevelt was a material ordinance:

EXECUTIVE ORDER.

No officer or employee of the Government shall, directly or indirectly, instruct or be concerned in any manner in the instruction of any person or classes of persons with a view to their special

---

the state. The official in the first case, and the superior official in the second, act merely as the agents through whom the will of the state arrives at concrete formulation.

[40] A like mutuality subsists between the rules prescribing the powers of superior officers and those setting forth the correlative duties of their subordinates.

[41] 1 State. L. 372.   [42] See 13 Stat. L. 737.

preparation for the examinations of the United States Civil Service Commission.

The fact that any officer or employee is found so engaged shall be considered sufficient cause for his removal from the service.

THEODORE ROOSEVELT.

The White House,
   October 13, 1905.

This order, which is the third in the first volume of the United States Executive Orders,[43] is an illustration of a material ordinance which concerns the general conduct of officials rather than their functions in immediate connection with the enforcement of law. It applies to all officers and employees of the Government, and is thus a uniform rule of governmental conduct; while the sanction lies in the President's power of removal.

Our third point of departure is the question: does the ordinance under consideration consist of an independent regulation or does it merely complete or supplement the terms of some statute? If the former, the process by which it is evolved is an exercise of full or almost full discretion in the premises; if the latter, the process involves discretion as to subordinate premises only. By almost full discretion in the premises is meant discretion which is limited only by general constitutional provisions, such as the prohibition of the taking of life, liberty or property without due process of law,[44] or the clause of the Constitution which states that " all duties, imposts, and excises shall be uniform throughout the United States." [45]   In England, to be sure, there is no written constitution, and a legally omnipotent parliament has with reference to all matters a theoretically full discretion in the premises.[46]   In the United States, on the other hand, there is no body or person with unlimited discretion with reference to any matter whatsoever. Perhaps the broadest discretion under our system is seen when Congress is legislating for unincorporated territories and when

---

[43] See Appendix.
[44] Constitution of the United States, Amendments v and xiv.
[45] Ibid., art. i, sec. viii.
[46] Dicey, Law of the Constitution, chap. i.

the President is legislating for enemy territory conquered in time of war. In the former case only the ' fundamental ' guarantees of private rights apply,[47] while in the latter case the constitutional limitations mainly embody those established by the law of nations.[48]

We have already described the two classes of ordinances which are under discussion as legislative and ordinance making (in the material sense) on the one side, and co-legislative and co-ordinance making on the other. Laws and ordinances, in the acute words of Count Ito,[49] give manifestation to some original idea; while co-laws and co-ordinances are best described in the apt phrase of the French as *une législation sécondaire et dérivée*.[50] The distinction is important both legally and politically; legally because Congress may delegate to the Executive co-legislative power but not legislative power without violating the principle *delegatus non potest delegare;* [51] politically because one may justify the constitutional or statutory delegation of a power of issuing completing ordinances while condemning at the same time the practice of giving to the Executive the authority to issue self-contained legislative measures. The latter power may wisely be allowed to the President only in emergencies, in connection with the organization and regulation of the administration, and in special cases. Yet it is ordinarily better to have the Executive supplement legislative abstractions by complementary regulations or by individual discretionary determinations than to have the legislature either attempt the detailed regulation of complex social and industrial problems or leave it to juries to give varying interpretations to statutory abstractions.

An example of an ordinance which embodies a law in the material sense is the President's order establishing a

---

[47] Downes v. Bidwell, 182 U. S. 244.
[48] N. Orleans v. N. Y. Mail S. S. Co., 20 Wall. 387. But see also Dooley v. United States, 182 U. S. 222.
[49] Commentaries on the Constitution of the Empire of Japan, pp. 18-20. This work gives an exceptionally acute and concise analysis of the ordinance making power.
[50] Cf. Duguit, Droit constitutionnel, deuxième édition, sec. 115.
[51] See the cases cited in chapter vi below.

schedule of tariff duties in Porto Rico during the occupation of that island in the Spanish War;[52] while in the Army Regulations of the President we have perhaps the nearest approach in ordinary times to ordinances embodying material ordinances.[53] For it should be clear that the distinction between laws and co-laws is not a rigid one, especially in the United States, where there can be no laws in the absolute sense. On the other hand, co-laws and co-ordinances are the normal products of Presidential ordinance making; and examples are not difficult to find. Thus, many of the proclamations of President Wilson in conformity with the wartime legislation of the sixty-fifth Congress embodied just such products.[54] His proclamation fixing the minimum price of wheat was a co-law,[55] while his executive orders under the Overman Act were ordinances.[56]

Of completing ordinances there are several kinds, corresponding to the several elements involved in full discretion in the premises.[57] In other words, supplementary ordinances vary in accordance with the nature of the element the abstract expression of which they concretize. In one class the Executive issues an order setting forth in concrete terms the circumstances under which the rule of law in question is to go into effect, or more frequently issues an order stating officially that the circumstances anticipated in the legislative phraseology do now exist.[58] Still another class consists of

---

[52] See Dooley v. United States, 182 U. S. 222.

[53] These are issued now by virtue of statutory as well as constitutional authority. See 18 Stat. L., 337.

[54] See 40 Stat. L., part 2, passim.

[55] 40 Stat. L., part 2, 1749-1751. For the delegation authorizing this co-law, see 40 Stat. L., part 1, 281.

[56] For the act itself see 40 Stat. L., part 1, 556.

[57] For these elements see chapter ii above.

[58] Of course, such legislative phraseology must be sufficiently abstract, so that the Executive decision involves subjective evaluation, not a mere determination of 'fact' by the application of objective standards; else there would be no discretion involved (See the definition of 'discretion' in chap. ii). Furthermore, the discretionary declaration of the Executive must have the effect, under the statute, of bringing the rule into effect with reference to a whole class of persons, not just one individual at a time; else it would be a 'sub-legislative' rather than a 'co-legislative' act.

those ordinances which complete the statutory definitions of the rights and duties to be created,[59] the class or classes of persons to whom they are to attach, or the penalties which are to be inflicted for their violation.[60]   Finally, a third class comprises the ordinances which prescribe the administrative [61] and judicial processes for carrying out the ordinances and enforcing them in case of disobedience.   German jurists distinguish the last two classes by the terms *Ergänzungsverordnungen* and *Ausführungsverordnungen*,[62] respectively.   The former are complementary to the contents of a statutory rule which prescribes in general terms rights and duties; the latter either originally or in a supplementary fashion deal with the means of executing the said rule.   It may be added that the question whether there shall be any action taken at all, by way of creating either immediately effective or anticipatory rights or duties, is a matter which must, in the

---

An admirable example of the difference may be had by comparing the nature of the 'Proclamation' to be issued by the President under sec. 3 of the tariff act of October 1, 1890, 26 Stat. L., 567, and the 'notice' to be issued by the Secretary of War under sec. 18 of the river and harbor act of March 3, 1899, 30 Stat. L., 1121, 1153. The two sections were discussed in Field v. Clark, 143 U. S. 649, and in Union Bridge Co. v. United States, 204 U. S. 364, and Monongahela Bridge Co. v. United States, 216 U. S. 177, respectively.

[59] Buttfield v. Stranahan, 192 U. S. 470.

[60] Under our system, it would be unconstitutional for Congress to prescribe that there should be a 'reasonable' penalty for the violation of a statute or ordinance, leaving it to the President to concretize that legislative abstraction.   It might, perhaps, prescribe specific limits, and leave to him the decision whether violation should be punishable at all, and if so what the penalty (within those limits) should be.   I refer to a decision for all future cases, not in particular instances.   But such delegations are practically never made in practice.   As for particular or individual acts, the President through his power of pardon can release a person from penalties; while the courts are often left to decide (within limits) the quantum of the punishment in individual cases (Pound, An Introduction to the Philosophy of Law, pp. 134-135).   Such individual decisions involve, however, 'sub-legislative' discretion only.

[61] See 1 Stat. L. 372.   For a classification of different types of 'delegated legislation' in England, see Carr, Delegated Legislation, chap. ii.

[62] James, Principles of Prussian Administration, pp. 156-158. They are termed completing ordinances, and executing ordinances, respectively.   The former are supplementary to the contents of the substantive part of the statute; the latter are supplementary to the adjective part or else originally supply the adjective part.

nature of the case, be determined by the authority having full or almost full discretion in the premises.

The fourth and final basis of classification has to do with the question whether an ordinance is issued in connection with ordinary social and industrial problems or whether it is issued in connection with a special emergency.[63] Ordinances of the latter type are called by German writers *Notverordnungen*. These are considered as a distinct category by reason of their political significance in relation to the preservation of security from external aggression and the safeguarding of internal order, as well as by reason of the special constitutional problems that are raised by governmental action in wartime or other times of crisis. With respect to ordinary ordinances the power is granted to the Executive because it is considered the proper sphere of the administration, or because the multiplicity and complexity of the problems of modern social and industrial life make it expedient or even necessary that at least the details be decided by a branch of government that is more efficient, more experienced, and better informed than a popular assembly can be. There the question is whether the Executive cannot deal with some matters more adequately or with readier adjustment than the legislature. But in the case of the *Notverordnungsrecht* the prime consideration is that the Executive can act more quickly than the legislature. The crisis may arise when the legislature is not in session, as happened at the outbreak of the War of Secession; or, if it be in session, its necessary slowness may cause a delay that will endanger the safety or vital interest of the state. In foreign relations, in war, and in internal crises of various sorts, the unpredictable character of the events and the necessity for quick action make it essential for the Executive to be given broad discretion and strong power to meet the many critical situations. Emer-

---

[63] See the author's article: " The Emergency Ordinance: A Note on Executive Power," in Columbia Law Review, June, 1923. This section of this treatise is a summary of that article. The term Notverordnungen as herein used includes emergency ordinances of all sorts.

gency power of this kind may be opposed to the ideal of democracy,[64] but it is none the less inevitable.[65]

Emergencies are of various sorts, as are also the methods of meeting them. A belligerent may unlawfully attack neutral commerce and travel; a foreign state may invade or otherwise commit acts of aggression against the nation; alien enemies may become a menace in time of war; and so on. In internal affairs, life and property may be placed in jeopardy through famine or flood; there may be armed riots of citizens against citizens, or of citizens against resident aliens; insurrections against law enforcement may take place; even rebellions against the established government itself may be set afoot. Hence we have the executive declaration of war [66] and of the state of siege; [67] executive suspension, in emergencies, of bills of rights; [68] executive discretion as to the use of military and naval forces in maintaining order and repelling invasions; [69] the power of the Executive to issue rules, within the limits of statutes, to provide for named contingencies; [70] and a general power granted to the Executive of issuing emergency ordinances.[71] Most of these forms of action seem to embody ordinances.

We may now summarize the five chief methods of providing in a governmental system for the issuance of emergency ordinances. In the first place the power to issue them may be delegated to the Executive in the constitution itself. This was done in the Austrian,[72] Prussian,[73] and Russian [74]

---

[64] See Burns, Political Ideals, pp. 294-295.
[65] Cf. Stubbs, Constitutional History of England, vol. ii, p. 619.
[66] Constitution of Japan, art. xiii.
[67] Ibid., art. xiv.
[68] Ibid., art. xxxi.
[69] Martin v. Mott, 12 Wheat. 19.
[70] See 40 Stat. L., passim. Also worthy of scrutiny in this connection are: 1 and 2 Stat. L., passim, and 12 and 13 Stat. L., passim. See examples cited in a later chapter.
[71] Constitution of Japan, art. viii; See Ito, Commentaries, pp. 13-17.
[72] Sec. 14, Staatsgrundgesetz über die Reichsvertretung, 12 Dec. 1867, R. G. B. 141.
[73] Art. 63 of the Constitution of 1850.
[74] Art. 45.

constitutions of the old régime, as it is done in the constitution of Japan and other countries.[75]   There is, of course,
no such provision in the Constitution of the United States.
The second method is a modification of the first.   It is the
constitutional provision for ordinances not by the Executive
but by a legislative committee at the instance of the Executive.   The best illustration is in Article 54 of the constitution of Czechoslovakia.[76]   In the third place we have permanent statutes delegating to the Executive the power to meet
crises, and in the fourth special and temporary laws for the
same purpose.   Usually Congress has waited for the emergency to arise instead of providing beforehand for possible
occurrences.   There are probably fewer constitutional difficulties in this method, because anticipatory delegation must
often be broader than delegations relating to an existing situation.   The method proved sufficiently efficient, also, in
the War with Germany, because the enemy was remote and
there was time for Congress to meet and debate and pass the
necessary measures.   Its inadequacy in a really critical situation was demonstrated at the outbreak of the War of Secession, when President Lincoln could preserve the Union
only by taking action of doubtful legality without waiting
for legislative authorization.[77]   However, a way out was
found; and this brings us to the fifth and final method.   That
is, the bill of indemnity, which amounts to a sort of retroactive delegation.   This procedure was developed in England,[78]
and was found convenient in the American Civil War.   Congress passed an act " approving, legalizing, and making valid
all acts, proclamations, and orders of the President, . . . as

---

[75] For example, the constitution of Denmark of 1866; the new
Constitution of the German Reich, art. 48, translated in McBain and
Rogers, The New Constitutions of Europe (1922), pp. 185-186.   See
also Lowell, Governments and Parties in Continental Europe, vol. i,
p. 341.
[76] See McBain and Rogers, The New Constitutions of Europe,
pp. 310, 321-323; cf. art. 55 of the new Prussian Constitution, in
ibid., p. 226.
[77] Dunning, Essays on the Civil War and Reconstruction, chap. 1.
[78] Anson, Law and Custom of the Constitution, part i, pp. 263-
264; Dicey, Law of the Constitution, pp. 47-48, 228 ff.

if they had been issued and done under the previous express authority and direction of the Congress of the United States." This was sanctioned by the Supreme Court in the Prize Cases [79] as a sound application to public law of the principle of agency that *omnis ratihabitio retrotrahitur et mandato equiparatur*. But of course Congress could not by such an act excuse subordinates of the President from the legal responsibility for enforcing unauthorized or illegal Presidential ordinances which Congress under the Constitution could not in the first place have authorized him to issue. This limitation does not, however, hold with reference to the British Parliament.[80]

Of these five methods the first, third, and fourth are also used with respect to ordinary ordinances, where there is no emergency. The first is authorized by a number of constitutions,[81] and is implied in the French constitution.[82] The President of the United States, on the other hand, has no constitutional ordinance making powers except such as may be involved in the so-called ' executive ' powers which he is granted by the supreme law of the land. In other words, he is given by that instrument ordinance making powers as such neither with reference to emergencies nor with reference to ordinary problems.

Let us now mention examples of both emergency and ordinary ordinances of the President. In a sense at least the proclamation of President Wilson directing the taking over of Dutch vessels may be termed an emergency proclamation. That proclamation read in part: [83]

Whereas, the law and practice of nations accords to a belligerent power the right in times of military exigency and for purposes essential to the prosecution of war, to take over and utilize neutral vessels lying within its jurisdiction:

And whereas the act of Congress of June 15, 1917, entitled "An

---

[80] Dicey, Law of the Constitution, pp. 47-48, 228 ff.
[79] 2 Black 635.
[81] See the Constitution of Italy, art. 6.
[82] Constitutional Law on the Organization of the Public Powers, February 25, 1875, art. iii; see Duguit, Droit constitutionnel, sec. 141.
[83] 40 Stat. L., part 2, 1761.

act to, etc.," confers upon the President power to take over the possession of any vessel within the jurisdiction of the United States for use or operation by the United States:

Now, therefore, I, Woodrow Wilson, President of the United States of America, in accordance with international law and practice and by virtue of the act of Congress aforesaid, and as Commander in Chief of the Army and Navy of the United States, do hereby find and proclaim that the imperative military needs of the United States require the immediate utilization of vessels of Netherlands registry, now lying within the territorial waters of the United States; and I do therefore authorize and empower the Secretary of the Navy to take over on behalf of the United States the possession of and to employ all such vessels of Netherlands registry as may be necessary for essential purposes connected with the prosecution of the war against the Imperial German Government.   The vessels shall be manned, equipped, and operated by the Navy Department and the United States Shipping Board, as may be deemed expedient; and the United States Shipping Board shall make to the owners thereof full compensation, in accordance with the principles of international law. . . .

Another example may be found in the proclamation of February 14, 1918, concerning exports from the United States, from which we quote: [84]

Whereas, Congress has enacted, and the President has on the 15th day of June, 1917, approved a law which contains the following provisions:

" Whenever during the present war the President shall find that the public safety shall so require, and shall make proclamation thereof, it shall be unlawful to export from or ship from or take out of the United States to any country named in such proclamation any article or articles mentioned in such proclamation, except at such time or times, and under such regulations and orders, and subject to such limitations and exceptions as the President shall prescribe, until otherwise ordered by the President or by Congress; provided, however, that no preference shall be given to the ports of one State over those of another."

And, whereas, the President has heretofore by proclamations dated July 9, 1917, September 7, 1917, and November 28, 1917, declared certain exports in time of war unlawful, and the President now finds that the public safety requires that such proclamations be amended and supplemented in respect to the articles and countries hereinafter mentioned;

Now, therefore, I, Woodrow Wilson, President of the United States of America, do hereby proclaim to all whom it may concern that the public safety requires that the following articles, namely:

. . and all other articles of any kind whatsoever shall not, on and after the 16th day of February, in the year 1918, be exported from, or shipped from, or taken out of the United States or its Territorial possessions to . . . except under license granted in

[84] Ibid., 1746-1747.

accordance with regulations or orders and subject to such limitations and exceptions as have heretofore been, or shall hereafter be prescribed in pursuance of the powers conferred by said act of June 15, 1917. The said proclamations of July 9, 1917, August 27, 1917, September 7, and November 28, 1917, and paragraph 11 of the Executive Order of October 12, 1917, are hereby confirmed and continued and made applicable to this proclamation. . . .

A proclamation in almost the same terms was on the same date issued with respect to imports.[85] It may be noted in passing that the section of the act of June 15, 1917, which is quoted in the proclamation resembles a check signed by Congress which leaves it to the President, to whose order it is written, to fill out the amount.

Other examples of emergency proclamations of 1917-1918 issued in meeting the problems of the war might easily be cited: the proclamation of alien enemy regulations in pursuance of Section 4067 of the Revised Statutes;[86] the promulgation of Rules and Regulations for the management and protection of the Panama Canal and the maintenance of its neutrality;[87] the proclamations under the Food and Fuel Control Act of August 10, 1917, concerning the licensing of the importation, manufacture, storage and distribution of necessaries;[88] the proclamation taking over the railroad lines, December 26, 1917;[89] etc. It may be added that the last named proclamation was issued in pursuance of a provision of law enacted in 1916 as part of the army appropriations act for the next year;[90] and that, while the terms of the act were broad enough to include the action of the Chief Executive in the ordinance referred to, in the opinion of Mr. W. F. Willoughby it is doubtful whether in enacting the provision Congress actually had in mind the entire control and operation by the government of all railroad lines.[91] The clause under which President Wilson acted was as follows:

---

[85] Ibid., 1747-1749.
[86] Ibid., 1650-1652.
[87] Ibid., 1667-1669.
[88] Ibid., 1700-1702.
[89] Ibid., 1733-1735.
[90] 39 Stat. L., part 1, 645.
[91] Government Organization in War Time and After, p. 173.

The President, in time of war, is empowered, through the Secretary of War, to take possession and assume control of any system or systems of transportation, or any part thereof, and to utilize the same to the exclusion, as far as may be necessary, of all other traffic thereon for the transfer or transportation of troops, war material, and equipment, or for such other purposes connected with the emergency as may be needful or desirable.

Here is a case where Congress, spurred on by the Preparedness Movement that reached its climax in 1916, enacted a permanent emergency delegation which proved extremely serviceable when a crisis arose.

Finally, it is proper to mention that these examples of emergency ordinances might be supplemented by others from the War with Germany and other crises, and especially by several from the War of Secession,[92] where, in cases like the call for volunteers in May of 1861,[93] the suspension of the writ of habeas corpus in 1862,[94] and the like, the element of a very critical crisis was more acute and more apparent than at any other times of our constitutional history. In the critical stages of American neutrality during the Napoleonic Wars, we have examples of what amounted to emergency ordinances in a time when technically the nation was at peace.[95]

By way of contrast we may take note of one or two ordinances of the Chief Magistrate which were issued in time of peace and in connection with the ordinary course of governmental regulation of official conduct or social or industrial relations. Thus in Richardson's Messages and Papers of the Presidents [96] we find an executive order of February 2, 1888, which President Cleveland entitled " Revised Civil-Service Rules." The order set forth that these rules were issued

---

[92] See Dunning, Essays on the Civil War and Reconstruction, chap. i; McPherson, History of the Rebellion, passim.

[93] 12 Stat. L. 1260. This is to be distinguished from a proclamation of the month before calling for 75,000 of the state militia (12 Stat. L. 1258), which gave as its statutory authority an act of 1795 (1 Stat. L. 424). The May proclamation was under assumed authority, and it promised its measures would be "submitted to Congress as soon as assembled."

[94] 12 Stat. L. 1261; 13 Stat. L. 720; 13 Stat. L. 734-735 (the latter under authority of 12 Stat. L., 755).

[95] See 1 and 2 Stat. L., passim, and examples cited in a later chapter.

[96] Richardson, vol. xii, pp. 5329-5347.

under the President's power under the Constitution and by authority of Rev. Stat. 1753 and an act of January 16, 1883, which was the original civil service reform act. Of the same character were the " Railroad Mail Rules " contained in the same volume; [97] as also an executive order of President Arthur from which we quote: [98]

Rule I

No person in said service shall use his official authority or influence either to coerce the political action of any person or body or to interfere with any election.

Rule XXI

The Civil Service Commission will make appropriate regulations for carrying these rules into effect.

Rule XXII

Every violation by any officer in the executive civil service of these rules or of the eleventh, twelfth, thirteenth, or fourteenth sections of the civil service act, relating to political assessments, shall be good cause for removal.

CHESTER A. ARTHUR.

To take a quite different example, we may cite the proclamation of President Taft fixing Panama tolls. It is true that Congress had confirmed the action of President Roosevelt in governing the Panama Zone and had authorized its continuance in a very liberal delegation; [99] but while Congress thus recognized its inability to cope with the problem as efficiently as the President could, it can hardly be said that Presidential proclamations relative to ordinary tolls are emergency ordinances. The proclamation of President Taft may be cited in full: [100]

By the President of the United States of America

A PROCLAMATION

To the People of the United States:

I, William Howard Taft, President of the United States of America, by virtue of the power and authority vested in me by the Act of Congress, approved August twenty-fourth, nineteen hundred

---

[97] Ibid., pp. 5432-5436.
[98] Ibid., vol. xi, pp. 4748-4753.
[99] 37 Stat. L., 560 ff.
[100] 37 Stat. L., part 2, 1769.

and twelve, to provide for the opening, maintenance, protection, and operation of the Panama Canal and the sanitation and government of the Canal Zone, do hereby prescribe and proclaim the following rates of toll to be paid by vessels using the Panama Canal:

1.   On merchant vessels carrying passengers or cargo one dollar and twenty cents ($1.20) per net vessel ton—each one hundred (100) cubic feet—of actual earning capacity.

2.   On vessels in ballast without passengers or cargo forty (40) per cent less than the rate of tolls for vessels with passengers or cargo.

3.   Upon naval vessels, other than transports, colliers, hospital ships and supply ships, fifty (50) cents per displacement ton.

4.   Upon army and navy transports, colliers, hospital ships and supply ships one dollar and twenty cents ($1.20) per net ton, the vessels to be measured by the same rules as are employed in determining the net tonnage of merchant vessels.

The Secretary of War will prepare and prescribe such rules for the measurement of vessels and such regulations as may be necessary and proper to carry this proclamation into full force and effect.

In witness whereof I have hereunto set my hand and caused the seal of the United States to be affixed.

Done at the city of Washington this thirteenth day of November, in the year of our Lord one thousand nine hundred and twelve and of the independence of the United States the one hundred and thirty-seventh.

WILLIAM H. TAFT.

By the President:
P. C. Knox,
Secretary of State.

We have now set forth four basic points of view for the classification of ordinances. Each point of view covers the whole range of the ordinance making powers of the President; and with reference to each all such powers may be grouped into one of two categories. If we combine the four methods we arrive at sixteen combinations for the cataloguing of executive ordinances. Thus, for example, one combination in the series comprises ordinances which are (1) constitutional with reference to the source of the President's authority to issue them; (2) self-contained and independent of statutes in respect to scope; (3) creative of material law with reference to subject matter; and (4) emergency in regard to purpose.[101]   Another combination includes all ordi-

---

[101] An example is the Emancipation Proclamation (12 Stat. L., 1267-1268).

nances which at one and the same time are (1) based upon statutory authority; (2) issued to supplement or complete the terms of a statute; (3) creative of material co-laws; and (4) aimed to meet a normal rather than an emergency situation.[102] And so on through the sixteen possibilities. It may be added that rarely if ever will examples of some theoretical combinations be found, while examples of others lie upon the surface of things. It is not necessary at this point to cite illustrations; it is enough to furnish a method by the employment of which one can subject ordinances to classification in accordance with the scheme which the exact definitions of analytical jurisprudence have enabled us to work out.

---

[102] An example is involved in Buttfield v. Stranahan, 192 U. S. 470.

PART II

CONSTITUTIONAL PRACTICE

CHAPTER IV

Delegated Ordinance Making in Constitutional Practice

There are a number of such bills, and may be many more, tending to direct the most minute particle of the President's conduct. If he is to be directed, how he shall do everything, it follows he must do nothing without discretion. To what purpose, then, is the executive power lodged with the President, if he can do nothing without a law directing the mode, manner, and, of course, the thing to be done? May not the two Houses of Congress, on this principle, pass a law depriving him of all powers? You may say it will not get his approbation. But two thirds of both Houses will make it a law without him, and the Constitution is undone at once.

—Journal of William Maclay.[1]

That the General Assembly doth particularly protest against the palpable and alarming infractions of the Constitution in the two late cases of the "Alien and Sedition Acts," passed at the last session of Congress; the first of which exercises a power nowhere delegated to the Federal Government, and which by uniting legislative and judicial powers to those of (the) executive, subvert the general principles of free government, as well as the particular organization and positive provisions of the Federal Constitution. . . . .

—Virginia Resolutions (1798).[2]

No one can be more deeply impressed than I am with the soundness of the doctrine which restrains and limits, by specific provisions, executive discretion as far as it can be done consistently with the preservation of its constitutional character. . . . The duty of the Legislature to define, by clear and positive enactments, the nature and extent of the action which it belongs to the executive

---

[1] Page 109; cf. p. 103.

[2] MacDonald, Select Documents Illustrative of the History of the United States, 1776-1861, pp. 156-157; cf. the Kentucky Resolutions (1798), ibid., pp. 151-162:

VI. Resolved, that the imprisonment of a person under the protection of the laws of this Commonwealth on his failure to obey the simple order of the President to depart out of the United States, as is undertaken by the said act entitled "An act concerning aliens," is contrary to the Constitution, one amendment to which has provided, that "no person shall be deprived of liberty without due process of law." . . .

to superintend springs out of a policy analogous to that which enjoins upon all the branches of the Federal Government an abstinence from the exercise of powers not clearly granted.

—ANDREW JACKSON.[3]

The perennial struggle of American administrative law with nineteenth-century constitutional formulations of Aristotle's [sic] threefold classification of governmental power, the stone wall of natural rights against which attempts to put an end to private war in industrial disputes thus far have dashed in vain, and the notion of a logically derivable super-constitution of which actual written constitutions are faint and imperfect reflections, which has been a clog upon social legislation for a generation, bear daily witness how thoroughly the philosophical legal thinking of the past is a force in the administration of justice of the present.

—POUND.[4]

The Interstate Commerce Commission was authorized to exercise powers the conferring of which by Congress would have been, perhaps, thought in the earlier years of the Republic to violate the rule that no legislative power can be delegated. But the inevitable progress and exigencies of government and the utter inability of Congress to give the time and attention indispensable to the exercise of these powers in detail forced the modification of the rule. Similar necessity caused Congress to create other bodies with analogous relations to the existing legislative, executive, and judicial machinery of the Federal government, and these in due course came under the examination of this court. Here was a new field of administrative law which needed a knowledge of government and an experienced understanding of our institutions safely to define and declare. The pioneer work of Chief Justice White in this field entitles him to the gratitude of his countrymen.

—MR. CHIEF JUSTICE TAFT.[5]

We turn now to a sketch of delegation in practice. We shall not present a complete history of Presidential ordinance making, but shall merely cite typical illustrations of delegated ordinance making powers at different periods. There are discernible six broad periods in the history of the delegation of legislative powers to the President. (1) The first extended from 1789 to 1815. In it Congress granted to the Chief Executive little discretionary power except in connection with one great problem, namely, the protection of the neutral commerce of the United States from French decrees and English orders in council. In that connection, however,

---

[3] Seventh Annual Message, December 7, 1835 (Richardson, Messages and Papers of the Presidents, vol. ii, pp. 1386-1837).
[4] Introduction to the Philosophy of Law, pp. 15-16.
[5] 259 U. S., Appendix.

there were numerous delegations which were important, especially as setting precedents for the practice in later times. (2) The second period stretched from the close of the second war with England in 1815 to the outbreak of the War of Secession in 1861. During that era there were scattered delegations, but they were not frequent, nor were they connected with any one problem like those of the preceding period. (3) Then came the period of the War and Reconstruction, from 1861 to about 1875, when in connection with the political issues of the day Congress delegated rule-making powers of great importance to the Chief Magistrate. (4) Again there was a long stretch of time, from 1875, or earlier, to 1917, when delegations did not center as in the times of emergency around any central problem. However, in the second half of this period, beginnings of federal government by commission took place; while it is probable that the ordinary delegations to the President and heads of departments increased, both in numbers and scope. (5) In the brief war period of 1917-1918 Congress delegated to President Wilson powers more extensive and in greater numbers than in any similar length of time, or in fact at any other time in our history. (6) Finally, with 1919 began the period upon which we are now entering, when government by commission and Presidential legislation will in all likelihood both be greatly expanded. This is partly because of the example of the practice in the recent war, partly because of the fact that the causes that have produced co-legislation in the past may be expected to appear in intensified form in the future.

It is significant that two of the three periods when the delegated ordinance making powers of the President really loomed large were periods of actual warfare and that the other was an era of commercial war. The international aspects of the problems were dominant in the first and third of these periods, while in the second the unity of the nation was at stake. In the world war, however, internal problems were important for the reason that a whole nation had to be organized for industrial as well as military warfare. Examples of delegations of these three periods will be in point;

while for the rest we shall give typical delegations of various sorts, and shall in particular enumerate some of the delegations of the early years of our constitutional history, because of their bearing upon constitutional construction. Exhaustive catalogues will not be undertaken, although these might prove much.

I

1. Because of their significance for constitutional construction the delegations of discretionary power to President Washington may be set forth in full. In this list we shall include delegations of power involving the issuance of sub-legislative and sub-ordinance making orders as well as ordinances. Perhaps a few instances are omitted.

The President was authorized to decide upon a site for a lighthouse near the entrance of Chesapeake Bay.[6] Various appropriation acts authorized him to borrow money not to exceed specified sums. Examples are cited in the footnotes.[7] The acts relating to the army and the militia granted discretionary power to the President.[8] The Chief Executive was empowered to draw not over forty thousand dollars for foreign intercourse, with specifications of maximum salaries for negotiations. To this a two year limit was set.[9] The Chief Magistrate was authorized to direct the surveying and

---

[6] 1 Stat. L. 54.

[7] Nearly every appropriation act authorized the President to borrow; various other acts also (such as those relating to the public debt or foreign relations) authorized him to borrow money not to exceed specified sums (see Sess. 2, ch. 4, sec. 7, 1790; Sess. 2, ch. 34, sec. 2, 1790; Sess. 2, ch. 47, sec. 4, 1790; Sess. 3, ch. 16, 1791; Sess. 1, ch. 27, sec. 16, 1792; Sess. 1, ch. 42, sec. 3, 1792; Sess. 2, ch. 18, sec. 3, 1793; Sess. 1, chs. 7 and 8, 1794; Sess. 1, ch. 63, sec. 2, 1794; Sess. 2, ch. 4, 1794; Sess. 2, ch. 33, 1795; Sess. 2, ch. 46, sec. 6, 1795; Sess. 1, ch. 21, sec. 1, 1796; Sess. 1, ch. 41, 1796; Sess. 1, ch. 51, sec. 3, 1796; Sess. 2, ch. 12, 1797; Sess. 2, ch. 23, 1797).

[8] All of the acts relating to the army and the militia granted discretionary power to the President (see 1st Cong., sess. 1, cn. 26, 1789; 1st Cong., sess. 2, ch. 10, 1790; 1st Cong., sess. 3, ch. 28, 1791; 2nd Cong., sess. 1, ch. 9, 1792; 2nd Cong., ch. 28, 1792; 3rd Cong., sess. 1, ch. 9, 1794, also ch. 14; 3rd Cong., sess. 1, chs. 25 and 27, 1794; 3rd Cong., sess. 2, ch. 1, 1794; 3rd Cong., sess. 2, ch. 36, 1795; 3rd Cong., sess. 2, ch. 44, 1795; 4th Cong., sess. 1, ch. 39, 1796).

[9] 1 Stat. L. 128.

building plans in connection with the establishment of the seat of government.[10] He was given discretion in regulating the issuance of licenses to trade with the Indians or in allowing trade without license respecting tribes surrounded by citizens of the United States.[11] In another act we find the clause: "And the President is moreover further authorized to cause to be made such other contracts respecting the said debt as shall be found for the interest of the said States." [12] Again, he was given authority to have built revenue cutters not to exceed ten, the expense not to exceed ten thousand dollars.[13] Such were the delegations of the first two years of our constitutional history.

Congress declared that the President's loan in Holland netting only one-half of one per cent interest, the legality of which under Congressional authorization of the debt had been questioned, came within the true intent of the law, as should future loans.[14] In a joint resolution the President was granted power to engage " artists " to establish a mint, to stipulate the terms and conditions of their services, and to cause the necessary apparatus to be procured.[15] He was authorized to have provided and put in proper condition for the mint such buildings as he deemed requisite in such manner as he saw fit.[16] He was empowered to select a site suitable for a lighthouse on Montauk Point, New York, and to approve of the plans of the secretary of the treasury for the building and furnishing of the same.[17]

The President was empowered to allow annual salaries to consuls sent to states on the Barbary coast, the salary of each consul not to exceed two thousand dollars, and that for only one consul to each state on that coast.[18] He was authorized to appoint such place as he might deem expedient

---

[10] Ibid., 130.
[11] Ibid., 137.
[12] Ibid., 139.
[13] Ibid., 175.
[14] Ibid., 218.
[15] Ibid., 225.
[16] Ibid., 248; see also ibid., 241-243.
[17] Ibid., 251.
[18] Ibid., 256.

to be the port of entry and delivery in Vermont.[19] He was authorized and empowered to grant certain quantities of land to John Cleves Symmes and decide upon the limits and lines of boundary agreeably to a former statute.[20] He was also granted power within limits to make such allowances to supervisors and collectors of revenue as he should deem reasonable and proper.[21] Such were the authorizations of 1791 and 1792.

In an act to regulate intercourse with the Indians, Congress authorized the President to have citizens removed from Indian lands; and to furnish friendly Indian tribes with domestic animals, etc., and temporary agents, not in excess of twenty thousand dollars per annum; and to have violators of the act arrested and tried.[22] Because of the Algerian controversy, Congress authorized the Chief Executive to provide a specified number of ships, or to provide a naval force —in lieu of the said ships—not exceeding that directed by the act.[23] Again, the Chief Magistrate was empowered to alter the place for holding a session of Congress if in his opinion an epidemic of a contagious disease warranted it.[24] To him was also given supervision over the building of lighthouses, under contracts made by the secretary of the treasury with the President's approval, on Cape Hatteras and the Island of Seguin.[25] He was also given a power to lay embargoes, a power which was so important that it will be set forth in full at the end of this section. He was authorized, in the recess of Congress, if the same should appear to him necessary for the protection of the United States, to build or buy, fit out, man, arm and equip, as many as ten vessels; and for that purpose to borrow as much as eighty thousand dollars.[26] Also, Congress gave him power to erect new (revenue) districts and alter old ones as appeared, " in his judgment, expedient and necessary "; to allow further compensation to inspectors, etc., up to one-third more than

---

[19] Ibid., 263.
[20] Ibid., 266.
[21] Ibid., 270.
[22] Ibid., 329.
[23] Ibid., 350.

[24] Ibid., 353.
[25] Ibid., 368-369.
[26] Ibid., 376.

was before allowed; and to provide officers of inspection in special cases, the expense not to exceed ten thousand dollars.[27] Further, Congress enacted that he might allow to officers of inspection not more than two and one-half per cent of duties collected.[28] It is interesting to note that President Washington was authorized to use land and naval forces in order to keep cruisers, etc., fitted out here from carrying on hostile action against a state with whom the United States was at peace, and to make foreign vessels depart when by the law of nations or treaties of the United States they ought not to remain.[29] He was authorized to increase up to a certain amount the rations of soldiers on the frontier.[30] He was again authorized, as above, to allow to officers of inspection not more than two and one-half per cent of the duties collected.[31] Then comes the authorization to use such revenue cutters as dispatch boats " as the public exigencies may require." [32] After declaring an embargo for thirty days Congress authorized the Executive " to give such instructions to the revenue officers of the United States, as shall appear best adapted for carrying the said resolution into full effect." No clearances were permitted to vessels " except ships or vessels, under the immediate direction of the President of the United States."[33] The President was authorized, despite the embargo, to grant clearances to vessels then loaded, owned by citizens and bound for a port beyond the Cape of Good Hope.[34] Thus ended the delegations of the years 1793 and 1794.

The first delegation of 1795 authorized the President to compensate inspectors, etc., and provide for incidental expenses, not exceeding five per cent of the total amount collected.[35] He was empowered to reduce the weight of copper coins to a certain extent.[36] He was granted authority to have twenty-four thousand acres surveyed on the Ohio River, to cause the French inhabitants of Gallipolis to be enumer-

[27] Ibid., 378.
[28] Ibid., 378.
[29] Ibid., 384.
[30] Ibid., 390.
[31] Ibid., 399.
[32] Ibid., 400.
[33] Ibid., 400.
[34] Ibid., 401.
[35] Ibid., 429; see also ibid., 430-432.
[36] Ibid., 440.

ated, and to issue a patent for four thousand acres to John G. Gervais, and to distribute the remainder to the actual settlers of Gallipolis.[37] "In cases connected with the security of the commercial interest of the United States, and for public purposes only," the President was authorized to permit the exportation of arms, cannon and military stores, "the law prohibiting the exportation of the same to the contrary notwithstanding."[38]

The year 1796, which is the last year to be considered during the Presidency of Washington, witnessed the following enactments: Men were to be put on the invalid service list of the army "at such rate of pay, and under such regulations as shall be directed by the President of the United States for the time being."[39] Power was granted him to establish trading houses in Indian country, to appoint to each one agent, whose duties were to be regulated by the President, and to pay agents and clerks, not to exceed eight thousand dollars.[40] Power also was given to have sold perishable material not wanted for completing certain frigates, and to have the rest of the surplus safely kept for future use.[41] The Chief Magistrate might cause new revenue cutters to be built to replace old ones, the money to come out of import and tonnage duties, and to auction off old ones.[42] He was authorized to grant patents to purchasers of land in the Northwest; and to fix the pay of assistant surveyors, chain carriers and axe men, provided the cost of surveying should not exceed three dollars per mile.[43] He was given various powers in relation to the Indians.[44] He was allowed to direct revenue officers, and officers of forts and revenue cutters to aid states in the execution of quarantine and health laws.[45] Finally, he was to appoint, direct and compensate (by not over fifteen thousand dollars) agents to investigate impressments of American sailors; and was empowered to appoint additional agents during the recess of the Senate.[46]

---

[37] Ibid., 442.
[38] Ibid., 444.
[39] Ibid., 450.
[40] Ibid., 452.
[41] Ibid., 454.

[42] Ibid., 462.
[43] Ibid., 468.
[44] Ibid., 471.
[45] Ibid., 474.
[46] Ibid., 477.

By far the most significant delegation [47] of this period was contained in a statute which may be set forth at length.[48] Section 1 provides " that the President of the United States be and he hereby is authorized and empowered, whenever in his opinion the public safety shall so require, to lay an embargo on all ships and vessels in the ports of the United States, or upon the ships and vessels of the United States, or the ships and vessels of any foreign nation, under such regulations as the circumstances of the case may require, and to continue or revoke the same, whenever he shall think proper. And the President is hereby fully authorized to give all such orders to the officers of the United States, as may be necessary to carry the same into full effect: *Provided,* The aforesaid authority shall not be exercised, while the Congress of the United States shall be in session: And any embargo, which may be laid by the President, as aforesaid, shall cease and determine in fifteen days from the actual meeting of Congress, next after laying the same." Section 2 provides " that this act shall continue and be in force until fifteen days after the commencement of the next session of Congress, and no longer."

An analysis of this law shows that the power granted is extremely broad, the limitations being first, those set by the nature of an embargo, and secondly, those of time. The President is given full discretion as to whether and when an embargo be laid; as to whether such embargo be laid on all vessels in the ports of the United States, or on American vessels only, or on foreign vessels only, and if the latter which ones; and as to regulations governing the embargo, the continuance or revocation of the same, and the enforcement thereof. He is authorized to proclaim an embargo, to issue regulations in regard to it, to issue orders for its enforce-

---

[47] However, a few of the preceding examples are of some importance; though on the whole the outstanding feature of the situation is the fact that administration was little developed, and that federal governmental problems were so few and relatively so simple that delegations were not frequently necessary or often broad in scope.

[48] 1 Stat. L. 372, 1794.

ment, and to revoke it. The only directions laid down as to the exercise of this great power are the very general phrases "whenever, in his opinion, the public safety shall so require," "under such regulations as the circumstances of the case may require," "whenever he shall think proper," and "all such orders . . . as may be necessary to carry the same into full effect." The limitations as to time are: (1) that he shall not exercise the authority while Congress is in session; (2) that any such embargo laid by him shall cease to operate fifteen days after the opening of the session of Congress next after its proclamation; and (3) that the act is to expire fifteen days after the beginning of the next session of Congress.

A comparison of this act with those passed by Congress during the War of 1917-1918 reveals the striking fact that the power here delegated is approximately as broad as in the later instances, with the single exception that the power here granted is to be exercised only when Congress is not in session, while in the war legislation of 1917 the plenary legislative authority is to be exercised regardless of the sittings of Congress. That this distinction is material is to be gathered from the fact that the earlier law provided for an emergency which the legislature would, because not in session, be unable to meet, while the later legislation is a frank delegation of discretion that the legislature might be expected to exercise. The delegations of the War with Germany are, therefore, more open to the accusation of constituting an abrogation by the law-making body of its legislative discretion. For it will be noted that one reason advanced for the permissibility of delegations to the other departments is that otherwise the legislature would be compelled to remain in continuous session.[49]

2. Already in the administration of Washington Congress had laid an embargo; and once it had, as we have

---

[49] As a matter of fact, however, the practical reasons that compelled delegations in 1917-1918 were just as real as those that compelled this delegation of 1794. It may be argued that the later delegations affected more 'fundamental' private rights.

just noted, authorized the President to do so during its recess. From the Presidency of Adams through the War of 1812, moreover, the European War absorbed a great deal of American thought, mainly because it interfered in annoying ways with our neutral commerce. Congress tried to meet the problem by retaliatory legislation, but policies depended upon the unpredictable actions of foreign governments, and to be effective they had to be put into operation quickly and without the undue delays that legislative debates would entail. The legislative branch might not even be in session. Hence it became, by the logic of the situation, necessary to leave to the Executive not only powers of fact finding, but also discretionary and, upon occasion, ordinance making authority. In this period, then, we have embargoes, non-intercourse acts, and alien, sedition, and alien enemy laws, in connection with many of which the President was given the right to issue both *Rechtsverordnungen* and *Verwaltungsverordnungen*. It may be added that this early practical construction of the Constitution by Congress and the President, at a time when incumbents in office were many of them men who had been members of the Philadelphia Convention or the ratifying State conventions, is the strongest argument [50] for the flexibility of the separation of powers as understood by the framers.[51] A few examples may be cited at this point:—

---

[50] The practice in 1917-1918 was incomparably more extended; but at least the constitutional construction of 1793-1815 showed that the rule against delegation was not absolute.

[51] The period began with a proclamation by President Washington that was taken on his own initiative and which called forth at the time strong opposition, not alone upon grounds of expediency but also because of the asserted lack of constitutional authority. At the outbreak of the war in Europe there were many French sympathizers in this country, especially among the followers of Jefferson. It will be remembered that in 1778 we had entered a treaty of alliance with France, and in 1793 there was a great deal of doubt about our obligations under that treaty. In the cabinet Hamilton opposed our siding with France, claiming that the French Revolution had relieved us from the obligations of the treaty. Jefferson was for helping her, correctly maintaining that a treaty is legally with a nation and is therefore not abrogated by a change in the government of that nation. It was claimed further by the opponents of participation that we were not bound to aid France in an aggressive war. Washington, in the face of a divided cabinet, decided to

June 13, 1798, an act was passed suspending commercial intercourse between the United States and France. This act in the third section provided that the President might grant passports to French vessels to enter the United States in all cases where it should be requisite for the purposes of any political or national intercourse. Section 5 declared that in the recess of Congress the President might by proclamation remit and discontinue the prohibitions and restraints of the act, if France disavowed and discontinued her depredations and thereby recognized our right to neutrality, if the same should be continued, the President " being well ascertained of the premises." [52]

June 22, 1798, Congress made the companies of volunteers authorized by a previous act subject to " such rules of training and discipline, as shall be thought necessary to prepare them for actual service, and which rules the President of the United States is hereby authorized to make and establish." [53]

In June, 1798, Congress passed an act entitled " An act to authorize the defence of the Merchant Vessels of the United States against French depredations." Section 3 of this act provided that no armed merchant vessel of the United States be permitted clearance without giving bond with several conditions, one of which was " that such owner or owners, and the commander and crew of such merchant vessel, shall, in all things, observe and perform such further instructions in the premises, as the President of the United States shall establish and order, for the better government of the armed

declare for our neutrality, and accordingly issued, April 22, 1793, his now famous proclamation of neutrality. This act raised a great deal of opposition and was defended by Hamilton under the nom de plume of " Pacificus." At the instigation of Jefferson, Madison replied under the name of " Helvidius." This Pacificus-Helvidius Debate, which appeared as letters in the press, threshed out the legality of the proclamation (see Foster, A Century of American Diplomacy; MacDonald, Documentary Source Book of American History, p. 243; Moore, Principles of American Diplomacy, p. 41; Works of Alexander Hamilton, J. C. Hamilton, ed., vol. vii, p. 76 ff; Writings of James Madison, G. Hunt, ed., vol. vi, p. 138 ff).

[52] 1 Stat. L. 565-566.
[53] Ibid., 569-570.

merchant vessels of the United States." The next section authorized the President to "establish and order suitable instructions to, and for, the armed merchant vessels of the United States, for the better governing and restraining the commanders and crews who shall be employed therein, and to prevent any outrage, cruelty or injury which they may be disposed to commit." [54]

The sixth section provided that whenever France should disavow and prevent her vessels from committing acts of depredation against our merchant vessels, "the President of the United States shall be, and he is hereby authorized to instruct" our merchant vessels "to submit to any regular search by the commanders or crews of French vessels, and to refrain from any force or capture to be exercised by virtue hereof." [55]

Another commercial act approved June 28, 1798, made it lawful for the President to cause the officers and crews of captured vessels and hostile persons found on board any recaptured vessel to be confined in any place of safety in such manner as he might think the public interest required, and all marshals and other officers were required to execute such orders as the President might issue for the said purpose. [56]

June 30, 1798, the President was empowered to regulate according to the rate of each vessel, the rank, pay, and substance of the officers of vessels got under the act, and the number of men to be engaged, and their pay, not exceeding the proportionable rates, etc., of the navy. The same law also granted him the power to increase or vary at his discretion the quotas of seamen, landsmen and marines on the frigates, and to permit a proportion of boys for them, and the other vessels of the navy, "according to the exigencies of the public service." [57]

A good example of what may be called the power of determining the incidentals in an enactment is the power given the President by an act of July 6, 1798, where it

---

[54] Ibid., 572-573.   [56] Ibid., 574-575.
[55] Ibid., 572-573.   [57] Ibid., 574-575.

was provided that certain arms should be deposited by his order at suitable places, to be sold to the state governments or the militia thereof " under such regulations, and at such prices as the President of the United States shall prescribe." [58]

The President approved, on June 25, 1798, " An Act concerning Aliens." This act authorized the President to order all aliens that he " shall judge dangerous to the peace and safety of the United States or shall have reasonable ground to suspect are concerned in any treasonable or secret machinations against the government thereof " to depart. But it was also provided that if an alien so ordered to depart should prove to the satisfaction of the President that his remaining would not endanger the United States, he might grant him a license to remain for such time and at such place as the President might direct. The license was made revokable at the will of the President; and the violation of such a license or the failure to obtain one after being ordered to depart was made punishable on conviction by imprisonment for a term not exceeding three years, and by the offender's never being able to become a citizen.

Section 2 authorized the President to deport any alien in prison in pursuance of this act, " whenever he may deem it necessary for the public safety," and to deport also aliens ordered to depart and who have not obtained a license, " in all cases where, in the opinion of the President, the public safety requires a speedy removal." " And if any alien so removed or sent out of the United States by the President shall voluntarily return thereto, unless by permission of the President of the United States, such alien on conviction thereof, shall be imprisoned so long as, in the opinion of the President, the public safety may require."

Section 4 provided that " all marshals and other officers of the United States are required to execute all precepts and orders of the President of the United States issued in pursuance or by virtue of this act." [59]

---

[58] Ibid., 576.   [59] Ibid., 570 ff.

The alien act was followed a week or two later by "An Act respecting Alien Enemies." Whenever there should be a declared war or an actual or threatened invasion proclaimed by the President, the subjects of the hostile nation being males fourteen and over should be liable to restraint as alien enemies. "And the President of the United States shall be, and he hereby is authorized, in any event, as aforesaid, by his proclamation thereof, or other public act, to direct the conduct to be observed, on the part of the United States, toward the aliens who shall become liable, as aforesaid; the manner and degree of the restraint to which they shall be subject, and in what cases, and upon what security their residence shall be permitted, and to provide for the removal of those, who, not being permitted to reside within the United States, shall refuse to depart therefrom; and to establish any other regulations which shall be found necessary in the premises and for the public safety." Provision is made, moreover, for reasonable time for them to recover, dispose of and remove their goods, and depart, according to our treaties; or, in the absence of treaty stipulations, "the President . . . may ascertain and declare such reasonable time as may be consistent with the public safety, and according to the dictates of humanity and national hospitality."

The alien enemy act further provided that, after any proclamation should be made as aforesaid, the courts should, upon complaint, have any alien enemy at large to the danger of the public safety, and contrary to the regulations of the President, be brought before the court, tried and removed, bonded, or otherwise restrained, "conformably to the proclamation or regulations which shall and may be established as aforesaid." [60]

July 9, 1798, was approved an act, "further to protect the Commerce of the United States," which authorized the President to instruct the commanders of the public armed vessels of the United States to capture any armed French vessels and to grant to private vessels of the United States special commissions gaining them the same rights of cap-

---

[60] Ibid.,577 ff.

ture as the public armed vessels had by law. They were made, in like manner, "subject to such instructions as shall be ordered by the President of the United States, for the regulation of their conduct. And the commissions which shall be granted, as aforesaid, shall be revocable at the pleasure of the President of the United States." Two conditions to be stipulated in the bonding of such vessels were that they should obey the instructions given for their conduct and deliver up their commissions when revoked by the President.[61]

As early as March 3, 1805, Congress enacted an act "for the more effectual preservation of peace in the ports and harbors of the United States." This act provided, inter alia, for the arrest of persons who should have committed treason and other specified crimes and who should have taken refuge on foreign armed vessels, upon warrants of a judge or justice; rules were laid down as to how the marshal should proceed, and it was stated that he should conform in all things to the instructions of the President or any other person authorized by him. Section 4 made it lawful for the President "either to permit or interdict at pleasure, the entrance of the harbors and waters under the jurisdiction of the United States to all armed vessels belonging to any foreign nation, and by force to repel and move them from the same, except" in specified cases; in which cases the commanding officer should conform to the rules of the collector issued in named matters under the authority and directions of the President, and not conforming thereto, should be required to depart from the country.

Section 5 enacted that the President might employ the forces of the nation to compel the departure of any armed vessel thus required to depart; "or if he shall think it proper, it shall be lawful for him to forbid, by proclamation, all intercourse with such vessel, and with every armed vessel of the same nation, and the officers and crew thereof; to prohibit all supplies and aid from being furnished them," and

---

[61] Ibid., 578-579.

also to instruct the collectors to refuse permission to make entry to the vessels and citizens of that nation, so long as the vessel remained in defiance of public authority. Violations of such a proclamation were made punishable by a fine not exceeding one thousand dollars, the offenders being also liable to be bound to their good behavior.

Section 6 aimed at retaliating for impressments and interferences with our neutral commerce by providing that whenever any officer of a foreign commissioned armed vessel committed a tort or trespass or spoliation on board an American vessel, or any unlawful interruption of trading vessels going to or from the United States, " it shall be lawful for the President of the United States, on satisfactory proof of the facts, by proclamation to interdict the entrance of the said officer, and of any armed vessel by him commanded within the limits of the United States, and if at any time after such proclamation is made, he shall be found within the limits of the United States," he was made liable to punishment, by fine and imprisonment, in any competent court, and part of his sentence should be deportation forever.

Section 7 authorized and required the President to " give as soon as may be, after the passage of this act, to the collectors of the respective districts, and to such other persons as he may think proper, the necessary instructions for carrying this act into effect, especially marking out the line of conduct to be observed by the marshal, and the several collectors in performing the duties enjoined by this act." [62]

In the latter part of December, 1807, Congress laid an embargo on all ships and vessels in the ports and harbors of the United States, not including public armed vessels of other nations; forbade clearances to any vessels except those under the direction of the President; and authorized him to give instructions to naval and revenue officers best adapted to carrying the embargo into effect.[63] We have here a good example of the delegation to the President of the authority to issue regulations to subordinate officers to govern them in

---

[62] 2 Stat. L. 339 ff.   [63] Ibid., 451-453.

executing and administering the law of the land, as distinguished from regulations which affect the persons or property of individuals outside of the administration.

The next March an act was passed supplementary to the embargo act of 1807, which in sec. 7 authorized the President to grant to citizens of the United States who had property of value without the jurisdiction of the United States, arising from property outside thereof prior to the embargo act, to send a vessel in ballast for such property, with certain enumerated conditions and under certain specified guarantees.[64]

Then in April the President was authorized to suspend, during the recess of Congress, in whole or in part, the embargo act and the act supplementary thereto, under such exceptions, restrictions, and security as the public interest and the circumstances required, if such peace or armistice or changes in belligerent measures affecting neutral rights as to render our commerce sufficiently safe, in his judgment, took place in Europe; provided, the suspension should not extend beyond twenty days after the next meeting of Congress.[65] Action taken under this act would clearly be in the nature of legislative action. An act to repeal an act is legislative as much as the original act, since it makes a change in the legal rights and obligations of those affected. That it removes certain restrictions instead of imposing them does not strip the act of the character of legislation.

Only three days later another law relative to the embargo was enacted, which in sections 6 and 11 forbade clearances to vessels going from any port of the United States to any other port or district of the United States adjacent to the territories of a foreign nation, without special permission of the President of the United States; and authorized the collectors of the customs to detain any vessel ostensibly bound with a cargo from one of our ports to another, whenever they thought the intention was to violate or evade any provisions of the embargo acts, until the President's decision should be had thereon.[66]

---

[64] Ibid., 473-475.   [65] Ibid., 490.   [66] Ibid., 499-501.

In January of 1809 Congress passed a law to enforce and make more effective the embargo.   Sec. 2 made it lawful for the collectors to refuse permission to put any cargo on any ship whenever there was in their opinion an intention to violate the embargo, or whenever they should have received instructions to that effect by direction of the President.   By section 4 the collectors were authorized, under such general instructions as the President might give to that effect, to grant general permits to coasting vessels.   But the act proceeded to lay down several conditions of its own, in regard to the granting of such general permits. Section 10 declared that the powers given the collectors of the customs to do certain acts to prevent violations of the embargo act " shall be exercised in conformity with such instructions as the President may give, and such general rules as he may prescribe for that purpose, made in pursuance of the powers aforesaid; which instructions and general rules the collectors shall be bound to obey; and if any action or suit be brought against any collector or other person acting under the direction of, and in pursuance of this act, he may plead the general issue, and give this act and the instructions and regulations of the President in evidence, for his justification and defense."   A court remedy was thereupon provided for.

Sections 11 and 13 dealt with the enforcement of the act by the President; while section 14 repealed the power of the President to grant permission to citizens having property outside the country to dispatch vessels for the same.[67]

The embargo was followed by non-intercourse acts directed against Great Britain and France.   March 1, 1809, is the date of an " act to interdict the commercial intercourse between the United States and Great Britain, and France, and their dependencies."   The eleventh section of this law provided that " the President of the United States be, and he hereby is authorized, in case either France or Great Britain shall so revoke or modify her edicts, as that they shall cease

[67] Ibid., 506 ff.

to violate the neutral commerce of the United States, to declare the same by proclamation "; after which trade may be renewed with the nation so acting. At the same time Congress repealed the embargo act except as to England and France (sec. 12).[68]

May 1, 1810, Congress enacted a law interdicting British and French armed vessels from the United States, with certain exceptions; in which cases, the commanding officer should conform to such regulations respecting health, repairs, supplies, stay, intercourse, and departure, as the collector should signify, under the authority and direction of the President, and not conforming thereto should be required to depart from the country. The fourth section also provided that, in case either England or France so modified her edicts as to cease to violate our commerce before the third of the next March, which fact the President should declare by proclamation, then, if the other did not also revoke or modify her edicts in like manner in three months, certain sections of the non-intercourse act should three months after the proclamation go into effect against the nation refusing or neglecting so to do; while the restrictions of the act of May 1, 1810, should cease in relation to the nation so revoking or modifying her edicts, from the date of the President's proclamation.[69] It was under this provision that the case of the Brig *Aurora*, discussed in another chapter, arose.

Finally, in June, 1812, after President Madison had laid the matter before Congress in a message, that body passed an act declaring war to exist between the United States and Great Britain; and that " the President of the United States is hereby authorized to use the whole land and naval force of the United States to carry the same into effect, and to issue to private armed vessels of the United States commissions or letters of marque and general reprisal, in such form as he shall think proper, and under the seal of the United States, against the vessels, goods and effects of the government of the United Kingdom." [70]

---

[68] Ibid., 528, 530-531. [69] Ibid., 605-606. [70] Ibid., 755.

In January of 1814 Congress authorized the President, in the existing war or any war in which the country might be engaged, to establish a post road between the headquarters of any army of the United States and any post office he might think proper.[71] Two months later it saw fit to authorize the President to retaliate against any violations of the laws and usages of war by the British, and against prisoners of war for any barbarities committed by the Indians in alliance with the British or acting in connection with them.[72]

II

In the second period delegations were not especially frequent or broad or centered around any single problem. We may cite at random a very few examples, however, in order to show that the practice, if not expanded, was yet not entirely abandoned. While the period is in general negative in respect to delegations, there were nevertheless certain problems that lent themselves to the procedure; and a few scattered illustrations may be set forth.

The President was in 1816 authorized to prescribe " forms of evidence " in regard to pensions.[73] Another act of that year provided " That licenses to trade with the Indians within the territorial limits of the United States shall not be granted to any but citizens of the United States unless by the express direction of the President of the United States, and upon such terms and conditions as the public interest may, in his opinion, require." [74]

In 1819 the President was " authorized and requested " " to employ so many of the public armed vessels as, in his judgment, the service may require, with suitable instructions to the commanders thereof, in protecting the merchant vessels of the United States and their crews from piratical aggressions and depredations." Sec. 2 authorized him to instruct

---

[71] Ibid., 790.
[72] Ibid., 829-830. See also 1 Stat. L. 577-578, 596-597, 570-572, etc.; 2 Stat. L. 426-430, 451-453, 528-533, 755, etc. See also 3 Stat. L. 88, 92, 114, 200, 230, etc.
[73] 3 Stat. L. 286. (See 1 Stat. L. 424-425; 2 Stat. L. 443, for delegations).   [74] Ibid., 332.

commanders of public armed vessels to seize and take to port vessels making piratical attempts and to retake unlawfully captured vessels of the United States.[75]

The Chief Magistrate was authorized to raise by volunteer or enlistment 600 mounted rangers "to be armed, equipt, mounted, and organized in such manner, and to be under such regulations and restrictions as the nature of the service may, in his opinion, make necessary." Details concerning such organization followed.[76]

The President was also "authorized to prescribe such rules and regulations as he may think fit, for carrying into effect the various provisions of this act, and of any other act relating to Indian affairs, and for the settlement of the accounts of the Indian department." [77]

It was provided by law that the Commission of Pensions " shall execute, under the direction of the Secretary of War, such duties in relation to the various pension laws as may be prescribed by the President." [78]

Another statute declared " That all pensions under this act shall be granted under such rules, regulations, restrictions, and limitations as the Secretary of War, with the approbation of the President of the United States, may prescribe."[79]

It was enacted in an act regulating the diplomatic and consular systems: " That the President be, and he is hereby authorized to define the extent of country to be embraced within any consulate or commercial agency, and to provide for the appointment of vice consuls, vice commercial agents, deputy consuls and consular agents, therein, in such manner and under such regulations as he shall deem proper; but no compensation shall be allowed for the services of any such vice consul, or vice commercial agent, beyond nor except out of the allowance made by this act for the principal con-

---

[75] Ibid., 510-513. See also ibid., 516-517, 568, 390.

[76] 4 Stat. L. 533; cf. ibid., 652. See also ibid., 564, 622, 713, for other delegations. See especially ibid., 632-635.

[77] Ibid., 738 (June 30, 1834).

[78] 5 Stat. L. 187 (March 3, 1837). See ibid., 32-33, 535-536.

[79] 9 Stat. L. 250. See ibid., 9-10, 59-66, especially secs. 6 and 21 of the Independent Treasury Act.

sular officer in whose place such appointments shall be made; and no vice consul, vice commercial agent, deputy consul or consular agent, shall be appointed otherwise than in such manner and under such regulations as the President shall prescribe, pursuant to the provisions of this act " (sec. 14).

Section 16 of the same act provided that the President might prescribe from time to time the rates of fees to be charged for official services and to define official services besides those expressly made so by law, and to adapt the same by such differences as necessary to each legation, consulate, or commercial agency.

Section 22 declared the President might provide at public expense all such stationery, etc., as he thought necessary for the several legations, etc., and when he thought there was sufficient reason therefor he might allow consuls general, etc., who were not allowed to trade, office rent not to exceed ten per cent. of their annual pay, and might " prescribe such regulations, and make and issue such orders and instructions, not inconsistent with the constitution or any law of the United States, in relation to the duties of all diplomatic and consular officers, the transaction of their business, the rendering of accounts and returns, the payment of compensation, the safe-keeping of the archives, and public property in the hands of all such officers, the communication of information, and the procurement and transmission of the products of the arts, sciences, manufactures, agriculture, and commerce, from time to time, as he may think conducive to the public interest." It was made their duty to conform to such regulations, orders and instructions.

Section 23 provided that the Secretary of State should cause passports to be granted, issued, and verified in foreign countries by such diplomatic or consular officers of the United States and under such rules as the President should designate and prescribe for or on behalf of the United States. Details as to the issuance thereof were, however, provided by the law itself.[80]

---

[80] 11 Stat. L. 57 ff. See Stat. L. 639. See also 11 Stat. L. 119-120 (August 18, 1856).

III

The outbreak of the Civil War produced an emergency that required immediate action or utter failure. Mr. Lincoln's prime object was to preserve the Union, and this he could do only by decisive action taken at once without waiting in all cases for Congress to debate proposed legislation. Hence, he called out 75,000 of the militia, in pursuance of a law that his predecessor had held, upon the advice of his attorney-general, did not give the power required by the existing emergency; he blockaded the Southern ports; he called for volunteers for, and increased the size of, the regular army and the navy; and he ordered arrests by the military, and the suspension of the writ of habeas corpus. That Mr. Lincoln doubted the constitutionality of his acts or some of them is shown by his statement to Congress, which met in extra session at his call on July 4, that " it is believed that nothing has been done beyond the constitutional competency *of Congress.*" But the call for the militia was based on a statute, and the blockade was later upheld by the Supreme Court. His increase of the army and his arrests were probably illegal; while the Chief Justice at the time held his suspension of the writ unconstitutional. At best, the powers assumed by the Executive before any declaration of war by the legislative branch were unprecedented and would have been a shock to the then existing constitutional opinion, had not Unionist emotion swept aside the legal scruples that up to that crisis had been so characteristic of the American people. But the political significance is even greater than the legal. " In the interval between April 12 and July 4, 1861," says Dunning, the leading authority on this subject, " a new principle thus appeared in the constitutional system of the United States, namely, that of a temporary dictatorship. All the powers of government were virtually concentrated in a single department, and that the department whose energies were directed by the will of a single man.[81] And of the psychological reaction upon Ameri-

---

[81] Dunning, Essays on the Civil War and Reconstruction, pp. 20-21.

can constitutional theory of the events of this crisis the same writer says: " This frank substitution of a ' popular demand ' for a legal mandate, as a basis for executive action, is characteristic of the times. The President's course was approved and applauded. Howe, of Wisconsin, proclaimed in the Senate that he approved it in exact proportion to the extent to which it was a violation of the existing law. The general concurrence in the avowed ignoring of the organic law emphasizes the completeness of the revolution which was in progress. The idea of a government limited by the written instructions of a past generation had already begun to grow dim in the smoke of battle." [82]   But at present we are not concerned with the validity of independent ordinance making on the part of President Lincoln, but rather with delegations made to him. We shall see, however, that Congress by retroactive delegation ratified his acts and proclamations,—a procedure which the Supreme Court in the Prize Cases upheld.

January 31, 1862, the Congress enacted: [83]

That the President of the United States, when in his judgment the public safety may require it, be, and he is hereby authorized to take possession of any or all the telegraph lines in the United States, their offices and appurtenances; to take possession of any or all the railroad lines in the United States, their rolling-stock, their offices, shops, buildings and all their appendages and appurtenances; to prescribe rules and regulations for the holding, using and maintaining of the aforesaid telegraph and railroad lines, and to extend, repair and complete the same, in the manner most conducive to the safety and interest of the Government; to place under military control all the officers, agents and employees belonging to the telegraph and railroad lines thus taken possession of by the President, so that they shall be considered as a post road and a part of the military establishment of the United States, subject to all the restrictions imposed by the rules and articles of war.

Sec. 2: . . . That any attempt by any party or parties whomsoever, in any State or District in which the laws of the United States are opposed, or the execution thereof obstructed by insur-

---

[82] Ibid., pp. 18-19. Not only was freedom of the person interfered with by military arrests, military trials and convictions, and suspension of the habeas corpus, but freedom of the press was also hampered by exclusion from the mails and even suppression by seizure (McPherson, History of the Rebellion, p. 188 ff.). On freedom of the press during the Civil War, see Carroll's article on the subject in the Virginia Law Review, May, 1923.

[83] 12 Stat. L. 334-335. Amended by 12 Stat. L. 625.

gents and rebels against the United States, too powerful to be suppressed by the ordinary course of judicial proceedings, to resist or interfere with the unrestrained use by Government of the property described in the preceding section, or any attempt to injure or destroy the property aforesaid, shall be punished as a military offence, by death, or such other penalty as a court-martial may impose.

Sec. 4: . . . That the transportation of troops, munitions of war, equipments, military property and stores, throughout the United States, shall be under the immediate control and supervision of the Secretary of War and such agents as he may appoint; and all rules, regulations, articles, usages and laws in conflict with this provision are hereby annulled.

Sec. 3 provided for a commission, to determine damages or compensation due to the telegraph and railroad companies, and to submit their award to Congress for action.

Sec. 5 fixed the rate of pay of the commissioners and said the provisions relating to operating and using the railroads and telegraphs " shall not be in force any longer than is necessary for the suppression of this rebellion."

On March 3, 1863, it was declared by Congress: [84]

That all able-bodied male citizens of the United States and persons of foreign birth who shall have declared on oath their intention to become citizens under and in pursuance of the laws thereof, between the ages of twenty and forty-five years, except as hereinafter excepted, are hereby declared to constitute the national forces, and shall be liable to perform military duty in the service of the United States when called out by the President for that purpose. . . .

Sec. 6: . . . That it shall be the duty of the provost-marshal-general, with the approval of the Secretary of War, to make rules and regulations for the government of his subordinates . . . to communicate to them all orders of the President in reference to calling out the national forces . . . and to perform such other duties as the President may prescribe in carrying out the provisions of this act.

Sec. 33: . . . That the President of the United States is hereby authorized and empowered, during the present rebellion, to call forth the national forces, by draft, in the manner provided for in this act.

Sec. 34: . . . That all persons drafted under the provisions of this act shall be assigned by the President to military duty in such corps, regiments or other branches of the service as the exigencies of the service may require.

Sec. 12: . . . That whenever it may be necessary to call out the national forces for military service, the President is hereby authorized to assign to each district the number of men to be furnished by said district; and thereupon the enrolling board shall, under the direction of the President, make a draft of the required

---

[84] Ibid., 731-737.

number, and fifty per cent in addition . . . the President . . . shall so make said assignment as to equalize the numbers among the districts of the several states, considering and allowing for the numbers already furnished as aforesaid and the time of their service.

Another statute provided: [85]

That, during the present rebellion, the President of the United States, whenever, in his judgment, the public safety may require it, is authorized to suspend the privilege of the writ of habeas corpus in any case throughout the United States, or any part thereof.

Sec. 4: . . . That any order of the President, or under his authority, made at any time during the existence of the present rebellion, shall be a defence in all courts to any action or prosecution, civil or criminal, pending, or to be commenced, for any search, seizure, arrest, or imprisonment, made, done, or committed, or acts omitted to be done, under and by virtue of such order, or under color of any law of Congress, and such defence may be made by special plea, or under the general issue.

Again, we find the following provision: [86]

That the President of the United States shall be authorized, whenever he shall deem it necessary, during the present war, to call for such number of men for the military service of the United States as the public exigencies may require.

Sec. 7: . . . And any person now in the military service of the United States, who shall furnish satisfactory proof that he is a mariner by vocation or an able or ordinary seaman, may enlist into the navy under such rules and regulations as may be prescribed by the President of the United States: Provided, etc. . . .

In an act of July 2, 1864, we read: [87]

Sec. 5: . . . That whenever any part of a loyal state shall be under the control of insurgents, or shall be in dangerous proximity to places under their control, all commercial intercourse therein and therewith shall be subject to the same prohibitions and conditions as are created by the said acts, as to such intercourse between loyal and insurrectionary states, for such time and to such extent as shall from time to time become necessary to protect the public interests, and be directed by the Secretary of the Treasury, with the approval of the President.

---

[85] Ibid., 755-758.

[86] 13 Stat. L. 6-11 (February 24, 1864). Cf. 13 Stat. L. 379, 402, 488.

[87] 13 Stat. L. 376-378. Other provisions which cannot be set forth in full are to be found in: 12 Stat. L. 255-258, 422-426, 326; 14 Stat. L. 46-47, 432-433, 177; 15 Stat. L. 243-244; 16 Stat. L. 419-429; 17 Stat. L. 14-15. The last named was an act to enforce the fourteenth amendment, passed April 20, 1871, and hence belonging in the Reconstruction Period. Several of the others were bills of indemnity. See the Prize Cases (2 Black 635).

Sec. 11: . . . That the Secretary of the Treasury, with the approval of the President, shall make such rules and regulations as are necessary to secure the proper and economical execution of the provisions of this act, and shall defray all expenses of such execution from the proceeds of fees imposed by said rules and regulations, of sales of captured and abandoned property, and of sales hereinbefore authorized.

IV

The fourth period was, with one or two great exceptions, not unlike the second. That is to say, there was no great crisis, like the Civil and German Wars, to call forth a shifting of the center of legislative gravity from Congress to the President. While delegations were probably more frequent and probably more often broad in scope, nevertheless any difference from the second period was in the main a matter of degree. Yet the acquisition of the Philippines and the Canal Zone called forth almost plenary delegations in respect to those possessions; while the development of co-legislation and sub-legislation by special administrative tribunals like the Interstate Commerce Commission is the outstanding feature of the period. It is this phase of the ordinance making power that in a later chapter will be shown to have latent potentialities for the re-adjustment of representative government to the needs of modern industrialism. It is not within the scope of this chapter, however, to trace historically this phase of the subject.

With reference to the Philippines, Congress enacted: [88]

All military, civil and judicial powers necessary to govern the Philippine Islands . . . shall, until otherwise provided by Congress, be vested in such person and persons and shall be exercised in such manner as the President of the United States shall direct, for the establishment of civil government, and for maintaining and protecting the inhabitants of said islands in the free enjoyment of their liberty, property and religion.

Later Congress enacted: [89]

---

[88] 31 Stat. L. 895. There were a few 'provisos' to this plenary delegation. These related mainly to franchises, the chief one prohibiting the sale or lease of public lands, timber thereon, or mining rights therein.

[89] 32 Stat. L. 691. Some details were, however, provided by Congress itself in this act. For example, sec. 5 dealt with the Bill of Rights.

That the action of the President of the United States in creating the Philippine Commission and authorizing said Commission to exercise the powers of government to the extent and in the manner, etc., . . . is hereby approved and ratified, and confirmed, and until otherwise provided by law the said islands shall continue to be governed as thereby and herein provided. . . .

Sec. 2: That the action of the President of the United States heretofore taken by virtue of the authority vested in him as Commander in Chief of the Army and Navy, . . . whereby a tariff . . . was to be levied and collected at all ports and places in the Philippine Islands upon passing into the occupation and possession of the forces of the United States, together with the subsequent amendments of said order, are hereby approved, ratified and confirmed. . . .

Sec. 3: That the President of the United States, during such time and whenever the sovereignty and authority of the United States encounter armed resistance in the Philippine Islands, until otherwise provided by Congress, shall continue to regulate and control commercial intercourse with and within said Islands by such general rules and regulations as he, in his discretion, may deem most conducive to the public interests and the general welfare.

Army Regulations were authorized in the following terms by 18 Stat. L. 337:

And the President is hereby authorized, under said section, to make and publish regulations for the government of the Army in accordance with existing law.

In 1914 Congress authorized the President to build an Alaskan railroad, and " to make and establish rules and regulations for the control and operation of said railroad or railroads." It also authorized him " to do all necessary acts and things in addition to those specially authorized in this Act to enable him to accomplish the purpose and objects of this act." [90]

At another time Congress enacted that: [91]

Whenever the President shall be satisfied that unjust discriminations are made by or under the authority of any foreign state against the importation to or sale in such foreign state of any product of the United States, he may direct that such product of such foreign state . . . as he may deem proper shall be excluded from importation to the United States.

Frequent provision was made for ordinances—especially

---

[90] 38 Stat. L. 305 ff.
[91] 26 Stat. L. 415; cf. 39 Stat. L. 799. For other delegations see 22 Stat. L. 88; 32 Stat. L. 830; 37 Stat. L. 434, etc.

executing ordinances—by department heads.   Examples are cited in the footnote. [92]

Illustrations cannot be given at greater length; but a few other references are given in the note below.[93]

V

Aside from all questions of the limitation of its war powers, Congress was in 1917 faced with a most serious practical problem.   The raising of a draft army and the economic mobilization of a nation were so complicated and so uncertain in their requirements that their minute and specific settlement by statute was impossible.   To have written the details into statutes would have been to put our war activities in a straight-jacket.   When defects were discovered in the details, they could have been remedied only by having Congress thresh out the pros and cons in the debating forum.   War is a time for action and not for talk.   Congress was forced, therefore, as were the legislatures of the other belligerent countries, in practically all its war measures to delegate to some administrative agency the power to settle the details and to determine, as the occasion demanded, the uncertainties.   The agency that was logically selected was the President, not solely because he was the personal leader of Congress and the nation, but also because the responsibility for the successful prosecution of the war rested upon him as the head of the executive department and the commander-in-chief of the army and navy.   At the same time

---

[92] We find in 14 Stat. L., for example, authorization of rules and regulations by the Secretary of the Navy (516, 567); by the Secretary of the Interior (542); by the Secretary of the Treasury (431, 547, 566).   See also 14 Stat. L. 394, etc.   An example is found in 18 Stat. L. 470 (March 3, 1875): "Sec. 3: That the Secretary of the Treasury shall have power to make such regulations, not inconsistent with law, as may be necessary to carry this act into effect."   See also 18 Stat. L. 6, 22, 24, 81, 45, 49, 50, 64, 82, 124, 127, 129, 130, 191, 196, 233, 272, 273, 304, 312, 335, 343, 412, 470, 461, 505, 506, 513, 517, 522, etc.

[93] 14 Stat. L. 1-2, 4; 15 Stat. L. 240-242; 16 Stat. L. 514, 261, 239, 171.   See also 15 Stat. L. 16; 18 Stat. L. 337; 19 Stat. L. 204; 21 Stat. L. 5-7; 20 Stat L. 38; 22 Stat. L. 121; 24 Stat. L. 80, 388-389; 25 Stat. L. 642, 1009, 527.   In 18 Stat. L. 252 (chap. 467) we seem to have legislative minutiae carried to the absurdity.

it was necessary to organize or to authorize the President [94] to organize special agencies, or else to empower the regular departments, to assist him in actually performing tasks which one man could at most merely supervise in a general fashion. Thus grew up an enormous administrative machine, some parts of which are described by Professor W. F. Willoughby in his work on Government Organization in War Time and After.[95] Personally or through such agencies the President exercised the many and broad powers of ordinance making which were delegated to him.

In carrying the practice of delegation to a pitch never before known in the history of American government,[96] Congress was faced with two obstacles. The first was the question of the political expediency of placing, even for a limited period, autocratic powers in the hands of one man; and the danger to our institutions which such a precedent might cause. The second was the doubtful constitutionality of granting broad powers of legislation to the Executive.

The first difficulty was voiced in the Congressional debates. A dictator, said Representative Young of Texas, in discussing the Food Control Bill, is now called an administrator.[97] On the whole, however, Congress, while not at all inclined

---

[94] " In almost no case did Congress attempt itself to prescribe the character of organization or the administrative methods that should be employed in enforcing the large volume of war legislation it enacted. Almost invariably it contented itself with providing that the President should take such action as in his opinion was wise to see that the provisions of those acts were properly carried out " (W. F. Willoughby, Government Organization in War Time and After, p. 6).

[95] See also Berdahl, War Powers of the Executive in the United States, part 3.

[96] The proclamations of various sorts from March 9, 1917, to March 4, 1919, comprise pp. 1645-1938 of 40 Stat. L. Pt. 2, or nearly 300 pages in all. Those from March 19, 1919, to March 3, 1921, comprise pp. 1741-1811 of 41 Stat. L. Pt. 2, or nearly 100 pages in all. Those from March 18, 1915, to Feb. 23, 1917, comprise pp. 1721-1818 of 39 Stat. L. Pt. 2, or nearly 100 pages in all. Those from March 30, 1911, to March 3, 1913, comprise pp. 1677-1781 of 37 Stat. L. Pt. 2, or slightly over 100 pages in all. Thus the bulk of the proclamations for all purposes was trebled in the war period; while many important ordinances were embodied not in proclamations but in executive orders.

[97] Congressional Record, vol. lv, p. 3802.

in ordinary times to grant arbitrary power to the Executive, saw the absolute necessity of so doing in the existing emergency. This came out in several speeches on the above-mentioned bill. Thus Senator Simmons declared: "There is but one condition under which I would vote to confer the power upon an administrative officer to arbitrarily fix the price of foods and of fuel. Unfortunately, Mr. President, that one condition exists today." [98]   Representative Langley stated, amidst applause, " So if the President needs the weapons of autocracy in this war with autocratic Germany, I am in favor of giving them to him." [99] Mr. Robbins characterized the bill " as the most extreme, arbitrary, and unlimited piece of legislation ever proposed in the American Congress." Yet he said he was going to vote for it because " our liberties are in much more danger from German aggression than from the President." [100]   Senator Johnson, who after the armistice insisted with characteristic vigor that the President be deprived of his powers under war legislation, remarked of this proposed law on the floor of the Senate: " Personally I have voted and will vote to give the autocratic powers requested without fear of ultimately affecting our democracy. I have an abiding optimism in the democracy of America, and a concentration of powers greater than those of any ruler on earth in a time of peril is a test of the courage and confidence of democracy in its own strength and virtue." [101]   From the final votes on the numerous war measures it is evident that views similar to these prevailed over the fears which many no doubt felt.

There was one great and outstanding contrast between the Presidential autocracy of Wilson and that of Lincoln.[102] In practically every [103] case the former was able to wait for Congress to delegate to him the authority which he needed

[98] Ibid., p. 4898.
[99] Ibid., p. 4019.
[100] Ibid., pp. 3901, 3902.
[101] Ibid., p. 4403.
[102] See Lindsay Rogers, " Presidential Dictatorship in the United States," in Quarterly Review, January, 1919.
[103] When he took over the railroads he acted under a statute passed during the ' preparedness movement ' of 1916.

to exercise in order to prosecute the war with effective energy. This was possible because the enemy was remote, and there was no immediate danger of invasion. With Lincoln the situation was different. He had either to act at once and without waiting for Congressional action, or else run the risk of disaster for his cause. To save the Union the President stretched to the limit his powers as Chief Executive and commander-in-chief, and actually usurped powers. Later, it is true, Congress ratified all his acts in a blanket bill of indemnity, a procedure which was not needed in the German War. But in the first instance the Chief Magistrate acted in important cases in excess of his constitutional authority.[104]

Equally significant was the point in which the two leading cases of Presidents turned law-givers were alike. Senator Johnson was justified in his belief that the almost plenary delegation of legislative powers would not destroy American democracy. He was justified because he had before him the previous case of a President's becoming a dictator, only to be followed by a President who was with difficulty able to maintain his constitutional position against a savagely hostile Congress. In part this was due to accidental matters like the personality and political views of the succeeding President; but in large part it was due to a natural reaction from a Presidential predominance which was ill suited to American predilections. That this was so was shown when President Harding followed President Wilson, not by accident, but by a deliberate choice of the party leaders. In that choice the leaders were partly influenced by the fact that he was a mild-mannered man and not one who would expand the powers of his office. If it be said that the alternative candidate was also a less powerful personality than the war President, this again shows the trend of the times. Congress finally took away the war-time delegated powers of legislation, and the Presidency, in a manner strikingly like that after the Civil War, once more subsided to its normal proportions.[105] Yet it must not be overlooked that such

---

[104] See Dunning, Essays on the Civil War and Reconstruction. chap. 1.
[105] The President himself in the main followed the policy of

an experience must leave its mark upon our institutions. Just as the constitutional powers of the President were permanently enlarged by their exercise in the War of Secession, so also will the practice of delegation be given an impetus by the precedents and examples of the war acts of Congress in the War of 1917-1918.

The second of the obstacles mentioned above to the delegation by Congress of its war powers to the President was the doubtful constitutionality of such a procedure. There had been cases which had upheld delegations, to be sure.[106] Yet in some of the acts of 1917 Congress granted discretion so broad in scope as to amount almost to a transfer of its legislative discretion to the Executive. Necessity demanded that the bills be enacted, though the constitutional questions received some attention in Congress.[107] In the Selective Draft Cases [108] the validity of one of these major acts of delegation was upheld. One wonders what would have been the decision of the court in a case arising under legislation such as that rashly proposed by Mr. Parker of New Jersey in the following terms: [109]

"As I say, I am for the principle of this bill, and I would that it were shortened and that it simply said that the Congress of

---

removing the harness from business soon after the armistice. Says Mr. W. F. Willoughby in his work referred to above: "Among our allies in Europe the feeling was general that the necessity for controlling both industry and trade would continue with little abatement until the period of readjustment to peace conditions had been effected. This was not the opinion of the Administration at Washington. The President in his address to Congress upon its convening in December, 1918, stated, in effect, that in his judgment there was no need for setting up any elaborate machinery for handling reconstruction problems; that all that was required was that industry and trade should be relieved of the restrictions that had been imposed upon them and that they should reconstruct themselves. . . . The same position was taken by him in dealing with foreign Governments. . . . This policy of the President prevailed both inside and outside Congress . . ." (Government Organization in War Time and After, p. 114).

[106] See chap. vi.

[107] See Congressional Record, vol. lv, part 4, p. 3951 ff., for discussion of the constitutionality of the delegations of the Food Control Bill.

[108] 245 U. S. 366.

[109] Congressional Record, vol. lv, part 4, 3878.

the United States recognizes and confirms the absolute power which exists in the Commander in Chief to protect this Nation in time of war, and that if he thinks it necessary, if he declares a state of siege, he may seize, commandeer, and control all of our energies and all of our lives for that purpose. (Applause)."

In the part of this work dealing with constitutional construction we shall attempt to show that legally there is a vast difference between such a blanket delegation [110] and those contained in the war acts in the late war.[111]

To attempt to enumerate the many delegations to President Wilson would require too much space, as it would be unnecessary. Instead of that, therefore, we shall summarize the main powers granted in several of the most important of the war acts. In so doing it will be necessary to omit the limitations thrown around the powers given, as also to omit some of the details and the verbiage of the enactments.

---

[110] A 'blanket' delegation involving 'skeleton legislation' is valid or not according to whether it *transfers* legislative power relative to a given topic to the President or whether it blocks out a *general policy* for a limited and reasonably definite subject and merely leaves it to the President to *concretize* a legislative abstraction.

[111] For a reference to the Fuel Administrator's famous 'heatless days' order,—an illustration of the scope of executive legislation in the war,—see McMaster, The United States in the World War, pp. 422-424. The following Executive Orders are summarized from Mr. W. F. Willoughby (they are taken at random): (1) Executive Order of June 22, 1917: it established an Export Council as advisory body in administering the system of control of exports and vested actual administration in the Secretary of Commerce (p. 127); (2) Executive Order of May 28, 1918: "I hereby establish the War Industries Board as a separate administrative agency to act for me and under my direction. . . . The functions, duties and powers of the War Industries Board, as outlined in my letter of March 4, 1918, to Bernard M. Baruch, Esquire, its Chairman, shall be and hereby are continued in full force and effect " (p. 77; see p. 74); (3) Executive Order of April 6, 1917, directing Secretary of Navy to control all means of radio communication—under Act to Regulate Radio Communication, 1912; (4) April 28, 1917: Executive Order "prohibiting all telegraph, telephone and submarine cable companies, from transmitting messages to points outside the United States and from delivering messages received from such points except as permitted under rules and regulations to be established by the Secretary of War for telegraph and telephone lines and by the Secretary of the Navy for submarine cables. Both the War and Navy Departments framed such regulations and each appointed an officer to act as censor " (pp. 41-42). (5) Oct. 12, 1917: Executive Order was " the organic act, as it were, under which these bodies have operated." It sets forth " in detail the

With these omissions we may summarize a few of the more salient delegations to President Wilson as follows: [112]

1. To take over and operate enemy vessels for use in the war.

2. To draft the National Guard and National Guard Reserves, an additional force of 500,000 men, and, in his discretion, an additional force of 500,000 men for training, and to recruit training units to maintain each at maximum strength, and if necessary the men needed to raise and maintain the Regular Army at maximum strength.

3. To make regulations governing the prohibition of alcoholic liquors in or near camps and to officers and men.

4. To proclaim certain places prohibited for the purposes of the espionage act, title I.

5. To regulate and prohibit exports.

6. To regulate priorities in transportation.

7. To regulate by a licensing system the importation, manufacture, storage, mining or distribution of any necessaries.

8. To requisition foods, feeds, fuels and other supplies necessary for any public use connected with the national defense, and to requisition storage facilities therefor.

9. To purchase, store, provide storage facilities for and sell for cash at reasonable prices, wheat, flour, meal, beans and potatoes.

---

manner in which the several powers conferred by that Act (the Trading with the Enemy Act) should be exercised. It thus defined the duties of certain heads of departments in respect to the exercise of certain powers, and created and defined the duties of a Censorship Board and the office of Alien Property Custodian, in addition to making provision for the exercise of control over imports and exports and of trading with the enemy. In respect to the latter features, . . . the order made provision for two new bodies, to be known as the War Trade Council and the War Trade Board, which should supersede and take over the duties of the Exports Council and the Exports Administrative Board and in addition exercise control over imports and the trading with the enemy features of the act " (p. 129).

[112] (1) 40 Stat. L. 75; (2), (3) 76 ff.; (4), 219; (5), 225; (6), 272; (7), 277; (8), 279; (9), (10), 279-280; (11), 280; (12), 281; (13), 282; (14), (15), 284-285; (16), 287; (17), 411 ff.; (18), 413; (19), 414; (20), (21), (22), (23), 415; (24), 420-421; (25), 426; (26), 451-452; (27), 454; (28), (29), 455; (30), 456; (31), 458; (32), 556.

10. To take over any factory, packing house, oil pipe line, mine or other plant, or any part thereof, in or through which any necessaries were produced, and to operate the same, prescribing necessary regulations for the control and compensation of employees, etc.

11. To regulate or prohibit practices and transactions in any board of trade, exchange or similar institution, in order to correct or remove certain evil practices.

12. To fix a reasonable guaranteed price for wheat based upon a statutory minimum; to increase the import duty on wheat so as to keep the importation of wheat at a low price from increasing the government's liabilities under the price guarantee; and to purchase any wheat of which the price was guaranteed, and resell or use the same.

13. To limit, regulate or prohibit the use of foods, fruits, food materials or feeds in the production of malt or vinous liquors for beverage purposes, or reduce the alcoholic content allowable in them, or prevent their importation, except under license.

14. To commandeer distilled spirits for redistillation.

15. To fix the price of coal and coke and to regulate the method of production, sale, shipment, distribution, apportionment or storage thereof; to take over and operate the plant of any producer or dealer who failed to conform to his prices and regulations or conducted his business inefficiently or in a manner prejudicial to the public interest, prescribing regulations for the employment, control and compensation of the necessary employees. Or, to require producers to sell only to an agency designated by the President, such agency to regulate the resale thereof, the prices, the methods of production, etc.

16. To procure necessary nitrate of soda and to dispose of the same for cash at cost.

17. To license:

(a) Trade between residents of the United States and any enemy or ally of enemy or any person acting in behalf of the same.

(b) The immigration and emigration of enemies and allies

of enemy, and the transportation by American vessels of the same.

(c) The transmission out of the United States of any letter, or other writing, book, map, plan or other paper, picture, or any telegram, cablegram, or wireless message, or other form of communication for any enemy or ally of enemy.

(d) The conducting of business by any enemy or ally of enemy and enemy or ally of enemy insurance company within the United States.

(e) The changing of the name of any enemy and ally of enemy, and enemy and ally of enemy partnerships.

18.   To establish censorship of communications between the United States and any foreign country or carried by any means of transmission touching any port, place or territory of the United States and bound to or from any foreign country.

19.   To prohibit or license business in the United States by any or all foreign insurance companies.

20.   To suspend the provisions of the Trading with the Enemy Act so far as they applied to an ally of enemy.

21.   To order the postponement of the performance of any act for not over 90 days pending investigation by him, if he believed such an act violated sec. 3 of the Trading with the Enemy Act.

22.   To regulate or prohibit by rules, licenses, etc., any transactions in foreign exchange, export or ear-markings of money or bullion, and transfers of credit (unless purely domestic), transfers of evidences of indebtedness or of ownership of property between United States and any foreign country or between foreigners, by any person in the United States, and to require complete information under oath.

23.   To prescribe the duties of the Alien Enemy Custodian.

24.   To license the use of an enemy or ally of enemy machine, manufacture of composition, design, trade-mark, print, label or copyright during the war.

25.   To permit publications in a foreign language.

26.   To make an agreement with common carriers taken over by him as to their compensation (limitations).

27. To determine rate of dividends to be paid by said common carriers.

28. To use a revolving fund of $500,000,000 to run the railroads, and to operate inland and coastwise transportation.

29. To approve the issuance of railroad securities by the carriers and purchase them for the United States.

30. To initiate rates, fares, charges, classifications, regulations and practices, with review of their justness and reasonableness by the Interstate Commerce Commission.

31. To relinquish federal control of all railroads at any time.

32. To redistribute functions among executive agencies, for war efficiency; for this purpose to utilize, coordinate or consolidate any executive agencies, or to transfer duties and personnel from one agency to another; to create an agency for aircraft control; to recommend the abolition of agencies.

VI

For a foretaste of what we may expect from the period on which we have just entered we may content ourselves with the citation of two delegations, one of a power to change tariff rates and thus to affect the interests of private persons by ordinance, the other of a power to regulate the making of the budget and hence to issue material ordinances. The first is very significant, but is too long for full quotation.[113] The following parts of the Budget and Accounting Act, 1921,[114] may appropriately be quoted:

The Assistant Director shall perform such duties as the Director may designate. . . . The Bureau, under such rules and regulations as the President may prescribe, shall prepare for him the Budget, the alternative Budget, and any supplemental or deficiency estimates, and to this end shall have authority to assemble, correlate, revise, reduce or increase the estimates of the several departments or establishments.

The Director, under such rules and regulations as the President may prescribe, shall appoint and fix the compensation of attorneys and other employees and make expenditures for . . . etc. . . ., within the appropriations made therefor.

---

[113] 42 Stat. L. 858. See W. M. McClure, " A New Commercial Policy for the United States," in Columbia University Studies in History, Economics and Public Law, vol. cxiv, No. 2, 1924.

[114] Ibid., pp. 20-27.

Under such regulations as the President may prescribe, (1) every department and establishment shall furnish to the Bureau such information as the Bureau may from time to time require, and (2) the Director and the Assistant Director, or any employee of the Bureau when duly authorized, shall, for the purpose of securing such information, have access to, and the right to examine, any books, documents, papers or records of any such department or establishment.

The head of each department and establishment shall designate an official thereof as budget officer therefor, who, in each year under his direction and on or before a date fixed by him, shall prepare the departmental estimates.

Such budget officer shall also prepare, under the direction of the head of the department or establishment, such supplemental and deficiency estimates as may be required for its work.

The departmental estimates and any supplemental or deficiency estimates submitted to the Bureau by the head of any department or establishment shall be prepared and submitted in such form, manner and detail as the President may prescribe.

The Comptroller General shall prescribe the forms, systems and procedure for administrative appropriation and fund accounting in the several departments and establishments, and for the administrative examination of fiscal officers' accounts and claims against the United States.

All officers and employees of the General Accounting office, whether transferred thereto or appointed by the Comptroller General, shall perform such duties as may be assigned to them by him.

The Comptroller General shall make such rules and regulations as may be necessary for carrying on the work of the General Accounting office, including rules and regulations concerning the admission of attorneys to practice before such office.

VII

We may conclude this chapter with the quotation of a few delegations contained in the permanent laws of the United States:

The President may prescribe such regulations as he may think fit for carrying into effect the various provisions of any act relating to Indian affairs, and for the settlement of the accounts of Indian affairs.[115]

The Commissioner of Pensions shall perform, under the direction of the Secretary of the Interior, such duties in the execution of the various pension and bounty-land laws as may be prescribed by the President.[116]

The President is authorized to prescribe such regulations, and make and issue such orders and instructions, not inconsistent with the Constitution or any law of the United States, in relation to the duties of all diplomatic and consular officers, the transaction of their business, the rendering of accounts and returns, the payment of compensation, the safe keeping of the archives and public property in the hands of all such officers, the communication of

---

[115] Rev. Stat. 465.   [116] Ibid., 471.

information, and the procurement and transmission of the products of the arts, sciences, manufacture, agriculture, and commerce, from time to time, as he may think conducive to the public interest. It shall be the duty of all such officers to conform to such regulations, orders, and instructions.[117]

The President may by regulations, which he may modify from time to time, prescribe the procedure, including modes of proof, in cases before courts-martial, courts of inquiry, military commissions and other military tribunals: Provided, That nothing contrary to or inconsistent with these articles shall be so prescribed: Provided, further, That all rules made in pursuance of this article shall be laid before the Congress annually.[118]

Under such regulations as the President may prescribe, and which he may from time to time revoke, alter, or add to, the commanding officer of any detachment, company, or higher command may, for minor offenses not denied by the accused, impose disciplinary punishments upon persons of his command without the intervention of a court-martial, unless the accused demands trial by court-martial.

The disciplinary punishments authorized by this article may include admonition, reprimand, withholding of privileges, extra fatigue and restrictions to certain specified limits, but shall not include forfeiture of pay or confinement under guard. . . .[119]

The President is authorized to prescribe such regulations for the admission of persons into the civil service of the United States as may best promote the efficiency thereof, and ascertain the fitness of each candidate in respect to age, health, character, knowledge and ability for the branch of service into which he seeks to enter; and for this purpose he may employ suitable persons to conduct such inquiries, and may prescribe their duties and establish regulations for the conduct of persons who may receive appointments in the civil service.[120]

---

[117] Ibid., 1752.

[118] Ibid., 1342, amended, 39 Stat. L. 656.

[119] Ibid., 1342; amended, 39 Stat. L. 667.

[120] Ibid., 1753. See also ibid., 1547, 2058, 2132, 4228, 2071, 2114, 463, 465 2110, etc.

PART III

CONSTITUTIONAL CONSTRUCTION

CHAPTER V

THE CONSTITUTION AND THE ORDINANCE MAKING POWER:
GENERAL VIEW

The law of England is divided into three parts, common law, statute law, and custom; but the king's proclamation is none of them.

The king by his proclamation cannot create any offence which was not one before.

—COKE.[1]

The statesmen of the Convention . . . made an enlarged copy of the State Governor, or to put the same thing differently, a reduced and improved copy of the English king.

—VISCOUNT BRYCE.[2]

The founding fathers struck off the Constitution in 1787, but in so doing they merely made application to the peculiar problem [3] with which they were faced of their experience as modified or enforced by their reading.[4] In creating the

---

[1] 12 Co. Rep. 74, 76.

[2] The American Commonwealth (1912 edition), vol. i, p. 39.

[3] That problem is most brilliantly discussed in Fiske, The Critical Period of American History. For an entirely different approach see Beard, Economic Interpretation of the Constitution of the United States. The truth lies in a synthesis of these two views. The men who organized the movement for the 'revision' of the Articles of Confederation saw clearly that the growing anarchy and interstate friction made the thirteen struggling States a prey which, with continued disunion, some foreign aggressor would seek to devour. They were a group of conservatives who wisely desired to secure stability, protect private property, and organize national preparedness. To these ends a stronger central government was an essential means; and this meant among other things the creation of a real national Executive. Such an Executive must have adequate power without the opportunity of becoming a tyrant; must, in the apt phrase of the Federalist, be at once " vigorous and safe " (No. 70). The statesmen of 1787 were faced by a condition rather than a theory, and sought the middle course between autocracy and mobocracy.

[4] Every reader of the Federalist papers has direct evidence that at least some of the statesmen of the time knew Blackstone and

Presidency they drew upon their experience with executive power as wielded by king, colonial governor and state governor, and their experience without executive power in the prior steps toward union. Likewise they drew upon their reading about political theories, about ancient or foreign executives, and about English law and history. This was no less so with reference to the President's ordinance making powers than with reference to his other powers; though of course they did not think of his ordinance making powers as such. Throughout the range of executive powers the mental image which formed the ideal of the framers was primarily a composite picture of the Crown shorn of its mediaeval prerogatives and of the state governor freed from legislative domination.[5] The product was an Executive at

---

Montesquieu. The debt of Jefferson to Locke is obvious, and is illustrated by the fact that the phrase of the Declaration of Independence " when a long train of abuses," is taken bodily from the Second Treatise. That they kept their eyes closely upon the new state constitutions is manifest from a comparison of the federal constitution with those documents. In a reply to Mason's objections to the Constitution Iredell said: " It seems to have been wisely the aim of the late Convention, in forming a general government for America, to combine the acknowledged advantages of the British Constitution with proper republican checks to guard as much as possible against abuses " (Ford, Pamphlets on the Constitution Published During Its Discussion by the People, 1787-1788, p. 351). In considerable measure, however, this English influence came indirectly through the then very recent state constitutions (Bryce, The American Commonwealth, vol. i, p. 30). On this whole question of the origin of the Constitution see ibid., chap. iii. There was little of Rousseau, much of Locke, in the American political theory of the time (Merriam, American Political Theories, pp. 91-92). It is interesting to note that they read something of English constitutional development in Blackstone, Cooley's edition, p. 406 ff. Lord Bryce remarks that they thought of the English constitution in terms of the legal theory of it as set forth in Blackstone. They did not understand fully the beginnings of the modern cabinet system which in their own day was not thoroughly developed. Like language, law and political systems were, by being cut off from the main current of British life, turned into a new course; and the Americans either developed peculiar modes of expression and peculiar institutions of their own or retained the older English ways of language and politics after they had been outgrown in the mother country.

[5] Bryce, The American Commonwealth, 1912 edition, vol. i, p. 39. See on this whole problem C. C. Thach, " The Creation of the Presidency, 1775-1789," in Johns Hopkins University Studies in Historical and Political Science, Series xl, No. 4, passim.

once vigorous and safe.[6]   Colonial experience and the ideas of the Revolution produced a President with powers distinctly narrower than those of the English king;[7] while the danger to vested rights and order[8] which resulted from mobocracy acting through too powerful legislatures produced a President with position and power distinctly broader than those of any single state governor. The lesson taught by this latter danger was emphasized by the situation which had existed in the earlier central organization of the Confederation. In this respect as in others the government under the Articles showed the men of the Philadelphia Convention what not to do.[9]

The legal significance and practical advisability of turning to extrinsic evidence for the contemporaneous construction of the Constitution will be discussed in a later chapter.[10] Such evidence will itself be introduced in connection with different constitutional problems as they arise. It will be convenient, however, to sum up at this point certain basic principles embodied in the Constitution, principles which hold true whether we seek in that instrument the intent of the framers or the meaning which practice and judicial interpretation have read into it. In a word, for the purpose of getting a bird's eye view we may give emphasis to certain undisputed aspects of the product of the Federal Convention of 1787.

A fundamental principle is that the President has no inherent powers, but is a mere agent to whom is delegated in the Constitution all the authority which he possesses.[11]

---

[6] The Federalist, No. 70.

[7] In the convention debates Mr. Wilson, while supporting the monarchical idea of a single instead of a plural executive, "did not consider the Prerogatives of the British Monarch as a proper guide in defining the Executive powers. Some of these prerogatives were of a Legislative nature. Among others that of war & peace, &c." (Farrand, Records of the Federal Convention, vol. i, pp. 65-66).

[8] Thach, chap. i. Cf. Wilson, Division and Reunion, p. 12; cf. also the Federalist, Nos. 2-8.

[9] Cf. The Federalist, Nos. 14, 21, 22.

[10] Chap. vi.

[11] Thus, as Professor Willoughby has said: "In republics the principle is fundamental that all powers of the government are

In this respect his position is exactly opposite to that of the Prussian monarchy in the period before 1918.[12]   Prussia had a constitution and the rule of law; but the theory was that the king was sovereign, and that the constitution was only an emanation of the will of the king,[13] a self-imposed limitation by which out of the plenitude of his legal omnipotence he granted participation in certain governmental functions to legislative or other organs, which were thus created by his volition.   By this theory, while the executive granted to the legislature the practically important function of determining the contents of bills, it was still the volitional act of the sovereign himself in promulgating such bills which gave such legislatively determined content the force of law.[14] Also, the monarch had the legal right, even when he lacked the actual power, to repeal or retract the constitution; between which and ordinary statutory law there was not, in the absence of special provision to that effect in the instrument itself, any legally important distinction.[15]

Such a theory is untenable with reference to the Presidency, whatever view we take of the controversy which developed over the nature and source of the Constitution.   Whether we consider that document as the creation of the peoples

---

derived by grant from the people. This principle . . . is . . . not inconsistent with the maintenance of monarchical rule. It is inconsistent only with the doctrine that the King rules by reason of an original personal right, and that he possesses other than delegated powers " (Prussian Political Philosophy, p. 94; see all of chap. v). He proceeds to cite the Belgian government as one having at its head a monarch while at the same time having it specifically stated in its constitution that " All powers emanate from the people," and that " They shall be exercised in the manner established by the constitution."

[12] Borgeaud, Adoption and Amendment of Constitutions, p. 43; Garner, Introduction to Political Science, p. 547.

[13] Cf. the wording of the preambles of the old Prussian and the Japanese constitutions with the Bills of Rights of our state constitutions and the preamble of the Constitution of the United States.   Both the first two have governments of law, but the régime of law is by edict of the sovereign (Willoughby, Prussian Political Philosophy, chap. v).

[14] Von Rönne, quoted by Willoughby, ibid., chap. v.

[15] Laband, Staatsrecht des deutschen Reiches, quoted by Borgeaud, p. 68.

of the several states by contract with each other,[16] or whether we look upon it as the will of the people of the United States considered as one body politic,[17] there can be no room for the idea that the President in any way inherited the sovereignty of the Crown. For both the theory of states' rights and the theory of national supremacy assume popular sovereignty, which is the major premise of American political philosophy and constitutional law.[18] The Virginia Bill of Rights set forth the doctrine " That all power is vested in, and consequently derived from, the people ; that magistrates are their trustees and servants, and at all times amenable to them." [19] The federal Constitution likewise purported to emanate from " We the people " [20] of the several States ; it was ratified by specially chosen conventions representing the people; and to it were early added the ninth amendment, which states that " The enumeration in the Constitution of certain rights shall not be construed to deny or disparage others retained by the people," and the tenth amendment, which declares that " The powers not delegated to the United States by the Constitution, nor prohibited by it to the States, are reserved to the States respectively or to the people." Consequently the powers of all organs of the central government are derivative, coming from the States or from the people. About this matter at least there has never been serious dispute.

There is another question, however, with which this one has at times been confused. Granted that the delegations of the Constitution are the sole source of federal authority,

---

[16] See McLaughlin, " Social Compact and Constitutional Construction," in American Historical Review, vol. v, pp. 467-490.

[17] Works of Daniel Webster (5th ed.), vol. iii, p. 321.

[18] The theories of popular sovereignty and autocracy are primarily political theories, for in the strict meaning of jurisprudence sovereignty is vested neither in the people nor in the monarch, but in the state conceived abstractly as the omni-competent legal person which has the authority to command obedience of all other legal persons (Willoughby, Nature of the State, chap. ix). But both doctrines have in a real sense affected juristic theory.

[19] Sec. 2. Cf. the Revolutionary Constitution of Pennsylvania (Poore, Charters and Constitutions, p. 154).

[20] Preamble.

there still remains the problem what rule of interpretation to apply to such delegations. While the state legislatures do not in strictness have inherent powers,[21] the state constitutions are interpreted as giving them the residuum of all governmental powers not placed elsewhere nor denied to them. The presumption is thus always in favor of a legislature's having a given power. Obviously no other organ of government can also be in this same position. All other governmental agencies in the United States have only those powers which are delegated to them; and the presumption is against the possession of a given power. Nevertheless, express statements may be in general terms, as notably when the Constitution of the Union vests "the executive power" in the President. In such cases the question arises whether such statements are grants of general executive power, or mere summations of the specific executive powers which follow. Similar clauses have received the latter construction in at least some state decisions. With reference to the President, we may say that under the tenth amendment a grant of general executive power must of course be interpreted to apply to power only in connection with the execution of the Constitution, laws and treaties of the United States.[22] The question whether the President has such general executive power under the Constitution will be taken up in a later chapter.

There is another matter of which we may dispose at this point. Did the framers mean to give the President the prerogative powers of the Crown as implied in his "executive power?" Assuming for the moment that he has general executive power, we may yet deny without fear of serious contradiction that it includes the royal prerogatives. Two early state constitutions in so many words provided that their chief executives should not have prerogatives under any Eng-

---

[21] In governments based upon the premise of popular sovereignty no organ of government has 'inherent' powers.

[22] Under our federal system he clearly has nothing to do with the execution of state law as such.

lish law.[23]   If the President were by general grant of the
Constitution given all the prerogatives, the clauses delegating such of the prerogatives to him as the right to act as commander-in-chief of the army and navy would be superflu-
ous.[24]   It is a general rule of construction that the drafters
of an instrument did not use unnecessary words.   Other prerogative powers are specifically delegated to Congress [25] or
else fall clearly within the reserved powers of the States.[26]
This fact shows that the executive power was not meant to
include the prerogatives in toto.   Finally, we may mention
as evidence the fact that in the Philadelphia Convention the
opinion was expressed that some of the prerogatives were
legislative in nature; and that the powers of the Crown could
not be used in all respects as a model.[27]   The true principle
of construction in this matter has been forcibly put by the
Supreme Court in the following words: [28]

It is true that most of the states have adopted the principles of
English jurisprudence, so far as it concerns private and individual

---

[23] Virginia and Maryland (Poore, Charters and Constitutions, pp.
825, 1910-1911).

[24] Cf. the reasoning by which constitutional lawyers argue against
the claim that 'due process of law' necessarily requires a grand
jury indictment.   Other prerogative powers specifically conferred
upon the President are the power to receive ambassadors and the
power of veto.

[25] E. g., the prerogatives of issuing letters of marque and reprisal
and of declaring war.

[26] For example, the power of erecting courts other than to deal
with matters specially by the Constitution placed in the scope of
the jurisdiction of the federal judiciary; or, the establishment of
public marts; or the power of granting corporate charters (except
in regard to the carrying out of special federal powers).

[27] In the debate of June 1, "Mr. Wilson preferred a single
magistrate, as giving most energy dispatch and responsibility to the
office.   He did not consider the Prerogatives of the British Monarch
as a proper guide in defining the Executive powers.   Some of these
prerogatives were of a Legislative nature.   Among others that of
war & peace, &c." (Farrand, Records of the Federal Convention,
pp. 65-66).

[28] Fleming v. Page (9 How. 603).   The principle set forth in
United States v. Wilson (7 Pet. 150), that where a power has by
the Constitution been conferred upon the President, the interpretation of its meaning may be sought in the meaning of the corresponding power of the Crown, is not inconsistent with Fleming v.
Page.   In the Wilson case the meaning of the pardoning power
was involved.

rights. And when such rights are in question, we habitually refer to the English doctrine, not only with respect, but in many cases as authoritative. But in the distribution of political powers between the great departments of government, there is such a wide difference between the power conferred on the President of the United States, and the authority and sovereignty which belongs to the English crown, that it would be altogether unsafe to reason from any supposed resemblance between them, either as regards conquest in war, or any other subject where the rights and powers of the executive arm of the government are brought into question. Our own Constitution and form of government must be our only guide.

In the first three Articles the framers blocked out the separation of powers by creating a legislature, an Executive, and a judiciary, and vesting the three classic functions of government in these three independent and coordinate departments.[29] Although they did not follow the example of Massachusetts and other States in placing in the document a distributing clause which prohibited the exercise by any department of powers belonging within the functions of the others, they accomplished precisely the same result by positively vesting the three functions in the three separate branches.[30] For, in accordance with the principle *expressio unius est exclusio alterius,* this allotment of power implies a corresponding negative prohibition. And this arrangement cannot of course be altered except by constitutional amendment. Thus by giving to Congress " All legislative powers herein granted " the supreme law precluded the President in general terms from the exercise of legislative powers.

The Constitution, however, confers upon him a number of powers in express terms; and we shall therefore have to analyze these to see whether any of them are, or involve in their very essence, ordinance making powers as we have defined those powers.[31] For of course the general principle of the separation of powers must give way before the pres-

---

[29] Cf. Kilbourn v. Thompson (103 U. S. 168).

[30] Goodnow, Principles of the Administrative Law of the United States, p. 32.

[31] It may well be that certain powers which the framers conferred upon the President for political reasons—to make him a ' strong ' Executive—fall within our technical definition of ' ordinance.' They may even be ' legislative ' in the usage of the framers.

ence of a specific power of ordinance conferred upon the Chief Magistrate in the Constitution itself. While that document makes the President primarily the head of a department the business of which is to carry out the law and not to make it, and while for this reason the President is prima facie without legislative power, nevertheless an explicit exception made to this principle by the Constitution must be accepted as being as valid as any other part of the instrument.[32] Madison admitted in the Federalist that the separation of powers could not be written into a constitution in absolute terms and without exceptions;[33] and nothing is clearer about the work of the framers than that they conferred upon the President not merely powers of law enforcement, but certain additional powers outside that narrow sphere. They believed in a strong Executive, and in the later stages [34] of the Convention they conferred these special powers for political ends rather than theoretical reasons. In a later chapter we shall endeavor to demonstrate by historical evidence that some of these powers included, both in the minds of the framers and in practical construction under the Constitution, powers which we should term ordinance making.

Are there any other sources of Presidential ordinance making power? It seems permissible to say that the President has legislative powers not only when they are expressly delegated to him by the Constitution, but that he has such powers in an incidental way to the extent that they are essential to the exercise of his given powers or necessary to protect himself from encroachments by the other departments of government. Yet if one admits this broad principal one opens the way to the utter destruction of the separation of powers. The Constitution itself confers upon Con-

---

[32] See the discussion of the separation of powers in Willoughby, Constitutional Law of the United States, vol. ii.

[33] Nos. 47 and 48.

[34] The point is brought out by Farrand that these powers were conferred late in the convention when the delegates were tired (The Framing of the Constitution, pp. 160-161, 163-164, 171-173, 185, 186).

gress the power to pass all laws necessary and proper not only for carrying out its own powers, but also the powers of all other departments and officers of the government. This precludes the President from the exercise of legislative powers as a means of carrying out his own powers,[35] as distinguished from legislative powers which are part and parcel of his express powers. The latter, we have seen, he can exercise. And it would appear that he is limited to this, except where the Congress delegates to him ordinance making powers. He is given the duty to see that the laws are faithfully executed; and it is under this clause, as we shall see, that he can issue regulations under statutory authority.[36]   This question, however, was never squarely faced by the statesmen of the period of adoption; and such bits of evidence as we have of their views must be postponed for a later chapter.

---

[35] See chap. ix below.   There are, to be sure, exceptions sometimes made to the absolute statement in the text that one department may not perform powers which come within the range of the powers of another department (see Goodnow, Principles of the Administrative Law of the United States, pp. 37-41, for state cases).   But these exceptions cannot be safely built into a generalization.   They are special exceptions based at bottom on common sense; and for our purposes may be ignored, except where they involve ordinances.

[36] When it is said that the exercise of legislative powers by the President is excluded from our constitutional system, it must be remembered that this means legislative powers as the term was understood in 1789.   Thus while it is perfectly clear that Congress has no right under our system to transfer its legislative discretion to the President, the question arises whether the term legislative powers *necessarily* implied the enactment by Congress itself of every detail, or whether it meant *either* the laying down of detailed regulations, *or* the enactment of general principles and provision for the concretizing thereof by the Executive, as the one or the other method should in each case appear to the legislature as best. In a later chapter we shall argue that the term has only the latter implication.   Congress can delegate discretion as to subordinate premises (not full discretion in the premises) under the 'necessary and proper' clause; the President can act under such delegations under the 'faithful execution' clause (See chap. vi).

CHAPTER VI

CONSTITUTIONAL BASIS AND SCOPE OF THE DELEGATED ORDINANCE MAKING POWERS OF THE PRESIDENT

The Constitution of the United States is not a mere lawyers' document: it is a vehicle of life, and its spirit is always the spirit of the age. Its prescriptions are clear and we know what they are; a written document makes lawyers of us all, and our duty as citizens should make us conscientious lawyers, reading the text of the Constitution without subtlety or sophistication; but life is always your last and most authoritative critic.

As the life of the nation changes so must the interpretation of the document which contains it change, by a nice adjustment, determined, not by the original intention of those who drew the paper, but by the exigencies and the new aspect of life itself.

—WOODROW WILSON.[1]

We must never forget, that it is *a constitution* we are expounding.
—CHIEF JUSTICE MARSHALL.[2]

Whatever the logical difficulties, the fact remains that there is a broad twilight zone between the field of what is distinctly and exclusively legislative and what is necessarily executive in character; that courts have recognized that matters within this 'no man's land' may be expressly authorized by statute for administrative action; and if neither of these steps is taken such action has been, under some circumstances, assumed as an inherent executive or administrative power.

—FAIRLIE.[3]

It will not be contended that Congress can delegate to the courts, or to any other tribunals, powers which are strictly and exclusively legislative. But Congress may certainly delegate to others powers which the legislature may rightfully exercise itself.

The line has not been exactly drawn which separates those important subjects, which must be entirely regulated by the legislature itself, from those of less interest, in which a general provision may be made, and power given to those who are to act under such general provisions to fill up the details.

It is, undoubtedly, proper for the legislature to prescribe the manner in which those ministerial offices shall be performed, and this duty will never be devolved on any other department without urgent reasons.

But, in the mode of obeying the mandate of a writ issuing from a court, so much of that which may be done by the judiciary, under

---

[1] Constitutional Government in the United States, pp. 69-70. Cf. pp. 157-158, 169-170, 192, 193, and chap. vii.
[2] McCulloch v. Maryland, 4 Wheat. 407.
[3] "Administrative Legislation," in Michigan Law Review, January, 1920.

the authority of the legislature, seems to be blended with that for which the legislature must expressly and directly provide, that there is some difficulty in discerning the exact limits within which the legislature may avail itself of the agency of its courts.

—CHIEF JUSTICE MARSHALL.[4]

Contemporanea expositio est optima et fortissima in lege.

Consuetudo est optimus interpres legum.

That Congress cannot delegate legislative power to the President is a principle universally recognized as vital to the integrity and maintenance of the system of government ordained by the Constitution.

—MR. JUSTICE HARLAN.[5]

The maxim that a legislature may not delegate legislative power has some qualifications, as in the creation of municipalities, and also in the creation of administrative boards to apply to the myriad details of rate schedules the regulatory police power of the state. The latter qualification is made necessary in order that the legislative power may be effectively exercised.

—MR. CHIEF JUSTICE TAFT.[6]

The true distinction is between the delegation of power to make the law, which necessarily involves a discretion as to what it shall be, and conferring authority or discretion as to its execution, to be exercised under and in pursuance of the law. The first cannot be done; to the latter no valid objection can be made.

—JUDGE RANNEY.[7]

I

We may now turn to an examination in detail of the legal aspects of our subject. The first question that arises in this connection is the constitutional authority by which the legislative department may make delegations of rule-making powers to the President. In view of the provision of the fifth amendment that no person shall " be deprived of life, liberty, or property, without due process of law," of the fundamental constitutional principle *delegata potestas non potest delegari,*[8] and of the basic constitutional doctrine of

---

[4] Wayman v. Southard (10 Wheat. 1). The quotation was mere dictum, however.

[5] Field v. Clark, 143 U. S. 649.

[6] Wichita R. R. & Light Co. v. Public Utilities Commission of Kansas, 260 U. S. 48.

[7] Cincinnati, Wilmington, etc., Railroad v. Commissioners, 1 Ohio St. 88; cf. 21 Penn St. 188, 202; 72 Penn. St. 491, 498.

[8] The maxim occurs also in the following forms: (1) delegatus

the separation of powers, is Congress acting within the scope of its legitimate authority when it confers upon the Executive powers of a legislative nature?

Let us first consider the bearing of the due process clause upon the matter. In the first place, where the regulations which the President is authorized to make have to do solely with the functioning of the administration, and not in any direct way with private rights of individuals, such administrative ordinances being enforceable only by removal from office and not by criminal penalties for disobedience, there is no deprivation of life, liberty, or property in the constitutional sense. It is clear, then, that the clause in question does not operate to prevent ordinary Presidential *Verwaltungsverordnungen.*

In the second place, with regard to authorizations of *Rechtsverordnungen,* we must bear in mind that the term due process is a broad generalization which the Supreme Court of the United States has in more than one case interpreted as not necessarily requiring the historical procedural methods embodied in our particular system of the common law.[9] Among the jurists of this generation in America there is noticeable a division into two schools of thought with respect to constitutional interpretation. The one school holds that while specific provisions are subject to judicial enforcement in accordance with the meaning which they had at the time the Constitution was adopted, general expressions like the fifth amendment must be reinterpreted in terms of the conditions and ideas of each generation.[10] According to this view, to limit Congress to what was considered due process in 1789 would be to place our system in a 'straightjacket'[11] and to ignore the fact that institutions must

---

non potest delegare; and (2) vicarius vicarium non habet (See Bouvier's Law Dictionary, vol. i, pp. 819-825).

[9] Hurtado v. California (110 U. S. 516); Twining v. New Jersey (211 U. S. 78).

[10] Cardozo, The Nature of the Judicial Process. pp. 76-77, 82-83, Lecture iii. See especially the book review by Felix Frankfurter, in Harvard Law Review, April, 1924, p. 783.

[11] Cf. Woodrow Wilson, Constitutional Government in the United States, pp. 192, 193.

change and develop in a manner analogous to the evolutionary process of organic life. An extreme form of this way of thinking leads to the assertion that the due process issue is as much a ' political question ' as is the question whether a state has a republican form of government,[12] and should accordingly be left to Congress. At the least, any process is ' due ' which is in its nature reasonable as applied to the circumstances not of a past age, but of the ever changing present.[13] On the other hand, the more conservative school holds that with reference to almost all parts of a written constitution judicial construction is final and authoritative, and that such construction must in all cases be made in the light of the political ideas of the men who framed and adopted the instrument. The logic of this attitude rests on the principle of interpretation that the intent of the legislator is the cardinal consideration.[14]

This issue is clear-cut and fundamental, and since it is involved in several of the legal problems connected with the ordinance making powers of the President, we may at this point set forth our opinion upon it in some detail. The Constitution was adopted in the eighteenth century, an age when men thought in static rather than evolutionary terms.[15] To introduce the more liberal rule of construction mentioned above might, therefore, be considered a legally revolutionary act. Yet we find that the statesmen of that era did as a matter of fact recognize, if not evolution in the sense of the famous Spencerian definition, yet at any rate a necessity for change due to changed conditions or to the more thorough understanding that comes from experience. Else they would not have placed an amending clause in the Constitution. Were this not so, however, practical considerations would require the more liberal interpretation of blanket clauses

---

[12] Pacific States Tel. and Tel. Co. v. Oregon, 223 U. S. 118.
[13] See the dissenting opinion of Mr. Justice Holmes in Lochner v. New York, 198 U. S. 45; cf. Noble State Bank v. Haskell, 219 U. S. 104; Cardozo, Nature of the Judicial Process, pp. 112-115.
[14] Blackstone, Commentaries (Cooley, ed.), vol. i, p. 58, n. 14.
[15] Pound, "Juristic Science and the Law," in Harvard Law Review, vol. xxxi, pp. 1047-1048.

even if this entailed a break in the legal continuity of the system. Fortunately, it is possible to preserve our traditional legalistic rule of construction without unduly cramping such construction in practice.

To do this we start with the cardinal principle of construction of a law that we must seek the intent of the legislators. But to assert this is not to assert that we must necessarily limit the content of their generalizations to the ideas of their own time. In connection with the meaning of the commerce clause the Supreme Court from the early case of Gibbons v. Ogden [16] down has held that commerce is not limited to the instrumentalities of trade known in 1789.[17] This is cited to show that Marshall did not hold to the theory that the framers meant to place future generations in the straight-jacket of their own ideas. In this spirit we maintain that, while we must preserve the conception that the intent of the framers is the guide, we need not hold that it was their intent to crystallize their ideas as the supreme law for future generations. The rule must thus be applied in a more elastic form in the case of an organic act than in the case of an ordinary statute.[18] We must assume that the framers intended that their generalizations should mean what they meant to them as that should be modified or added to by the experience and needs of later times. All that is required of the men of such later times in construing the instrument, is to do so in the spirit of the framers,[19] in the sense of giving an interpretation which those framers would

---

[16] 9 Wheat. 1. Fulton invented the steamboat between 1789 and 1824, when Marshall wrote the opinion.

[17] Cf. Pensacola Telegraph Co. v. Western Union Telegraph Co., 196 U. S. 1.

[18] See the words of Marshall in McCulloch v. Maryland, quoted at the beginning of this chapter.

[19] Woodrow Wilson, quoting an English judge, distinguishes between "those extensions of the meaning of law by interpretation which are the product of insight and conceived in the spirit of the law itself, and those which are the product of sheer will, of the mere determination that the law shall mean what it is convenient to have it mean." He adds: "Marshall's interpretations were the products of insight" (Constitutional Government in the United States, p. 159).

probably have given had they written the Constitution in such later times.   In practice, then, the task of the jurist becomes a balancing of historical usage against insistent present needs of change.[20]

In this process the words of the instrument are the primary evidence of the intent of the framers.[21]   Yet terms will be used which are more or less technical, and in such event extrinsic evidence is permissible.   This is so because of the proper adaptation to constitutional construction of the parole-evidence rule of the common law.[22]   By such adaptation we assert that any extrinsic evidence is admissible which tends to show the mutual meaning of the parties.   And the first question is, who are the parties to the adoption of the Constitution?

Whether that document be conceived as a compact between the people considered as thirteen bodies politic, or as one, it differs from a will in that it is not uni-lateral, but multi-lateral.   Hence we must seek the mutual meaning of the parties to the covenant.   It is usually assumed that it is the will of the framers which is to be sought; but it is rather the will of the adopting people or peoples.[23]   It is the meaning of the latter which is embodied in the instrument.   The framers bear the same relation to the adopters as the lawyer who draws up a will bears to his client.

What evidence is admissible?   Properly all which tends to show the meaning of the adopters.   This includes even statements of one party in which it cannot be proved that the other parties concurred if and only if there is reason to

---

[20] See Cardozo's discussion of the methods of philosophy (logic), evolution (history), tradition (customs), and sociology (social welfare, justice) in The Nature of the Judicial Process.

[21] Said Marshall in Gibbons v. Ogden (9 Wheat. 1): "We know of no rule for construing the extent of such powers, other than is given by the language of the instrument which confers them, taken in connection with the purposes for which they were conferred."

[22] As set forth in Greenleaf on Evidence (16th edition), chap. xxi, as the chapter has been re-written by the editor, Professor Wigmore.   See also Thayer, Preliminary Treatise on the Law of Evidence, pp. 215, 390, 413-414, 435.

[23] Cf. The Federalist (Ford, ed.), No. 40 (39).

believe that they embodied the common meaning of the times. Where there are so many persons concerned, as here, it is practically impossible to establish a special and peculiar meaning of a term different from that of the times. It becomes necessary, therefore, to assume that the ordinary contemporaneous meaning of the period of adoption was in all cases intended.[24] Such meaning is to be sought in the historical connotations which terms and phrases had taken on and in the expressions of their signification which occur in contemporaneous practice and writings. Neither the debates of the Philadelphia Convention of 1787, nor those of the state conventions which adopted the document are, therefore, on a superior plane to other evidence, unless indeed in rare cases they show a unanimity of opinion on some one point.[25]

What authority should be given to positive contemporaneous evidence? From the principles above set forth we deduce first of all that any method which is historically the very antithesis of due process or some other abstract or general expression should be excluded except in unusual cases. By the same token we should accept as due process any method which is historically connoted by the term. Moreover, we must give weight to evidence which tends to prove, though it does not conclusively do so, that a given process is historically, or in the view of 1789, ' due ' or not. Yet it is not necessary to confine ourselves to the latter sort of evidence. Consideration should also be given to what is reasonable in present circumstances. The test of the reasonableness is in part historical and in part a present balancing of the interests of the individual against those of the community.[26]

---

[24] Cf. Blackstone, Commentaries (Cooley, ed.), vol. i, pp. 59-60.

[25] The debates in such conventions are recognized by the leading authorities to be at best evidence, not conclusive proof, even of the intent of the convention. For it is pointed out that those members who voted without expressing themselves may have voted upon entirely different grounds from those stated by the members who talked (see Cooley, Constitutional Limitations, 7th ed., p. 101; Willoughby, Principles of the Constitutional Law of the United States, sec. 16 ff.).

[26] Cardozo describes the ' judicial process ' of interpretation as a balancing of the several considerations which he mentions, now

Thus it is not a conclusive but at best a rebuttable argument against the validity of the delegation of rather broad discretionary powers that such delegations are contrary to the traditional [27] though not the invariable [28] practice of Anglo-Saxon peoples before the rise of capitalistic industry. In rebuttal, it is easy to demonstrate the advisability if not absolute necessity of leaving at least the details of our complex social and industrial legislation to that branch of government which rubs elbows with the actual problems and can deal with them in a more direct and more flexible way than the legislature can.[29]   Under existing economic conditions executive justice,[30] where subject to the definition of legislative enactment [31] in the first instance and to the checks of judicial review [32] in the second, is more truly a due process than is the traditional legislative justice.[33]   That the fifth amendment does not prohibit the delegation, within reasonable limits to be defined later, of regulative powers does not, however, prove that it is consistent with a delegation that virtually amounts to a transfer of full legislative discretion. The latter would seem to be entirely out of consonance with

---

giving greater weight to one, now to another (The Nature of the Judicial Process, pp. 112-115, 160.   Cf. p. 167 ff.).

[27] Cf. Lowell, Government of England, vol. i, pp. 20, 363 ff.   See also the very concrete and detailed emergency legislation of the several States in the Revolutionary Period, collected in Emergency Legislation Passed Prior to December, 1917, Dealing with the Control and Taking of Private Property for the Public Use, Benefit, or Welfare (collected by J. Reuben Clarke, Jr., under the direction of the Attorney General).

[28] The early delegations to the President, contained in 1 and 2 Stat. L., save the practice from being the 'historical antithesis' of 'due process of law,' or for that matter of the separation of powers discussed below (see chap. iv).   Less clearly in point are Stubbs, Constitutional History of England, vol. ii, p. 619; McIlwain, The High Court of Parliament and Its Supremacy, pp. 331-332. For these instances may not have been known to the framers.

[29] Cf. Freund, "The Substitution of Rule for Discretion in Public Law," in American Political Science Review, November, 1915.

[30] The phrase is that of Dean Pound.   See his Introduction to the Philosophy of Law, p. 136.

[31] See sec. v of this chapter.

[32] See chaps. vii and xi.

[33] Albertsworth, "Judicial Review of Administrative Action by the Federal Supreme Court," in Harvard Law Review, December, 1921.

the spirit of our institutions and the theory of a rigid constitution,—and hence an undue and unreasonable procedure.

II

Both the other two constitutional principles flow logically from the fundamental idea of the Constitution that it is " the supreme law of the land " in which the sovereign people has delegated to the several governmental agents the powers which they possess. It follows that this distribution of powers may not be altered by those agents, but only by that authority which can amend the Constitution. Thus, when the document delegates to Congress " all legislative powers herein granted," the principle of agency [34] that a delegate may not re-delegate his powers is clearly applicable. For that principle is fundamental to public as to private law.[35]

---

[34] Story on Agency, sec. 13. This limitation does not, however, apply to the legislation of Congress with reference to the Philippines. See 206 U. S. 370; 34 Stat. L. 636, ch. 3912; Willoughby, Constitutional Law of the United States, vol. i, sec. 158 ff.

[35] That a delegate may not re-delegate his powers is a principle applicable to public law wherever a rigid constitution has delegated certain powers to a given organ of government. Thus recently in France constitutional writers like Esmein and Berthélemy have denied the right of Parliament to delegate legislative power to the President; and M. Esmein's reasoning on this subject is so lucid as to justify quotation. He says, in part: " C'est qu'en effet, sous nos constitutions nationales et rigides, les divers pouvoirs constitués ne tirent leur existence et leurs attributions que de la Constitution elle-même. Ils n'existent qu'en vertu de cette Constitution, dans la mesure et dans les conditions qu'elle a fixées. Le titulaire d'aucun de ces pouvoirs n'en a la disposition, mais seulement l'exercice. Par cela même que la Constitution a établi des pouvoirs divers et distincts, et reparti entre diverses autorités les attributs de la souveraineté, elle interdit implicitement mais nécessairement que l'un des pouvoirs puisse se décharger sur un autre de sa tache et de sa fonction; de même qu'un pouvoir ne saurait empiéter sur un autre, il ne saurait même momentanément abdiquer en faveur d'un autre. Ce serait substituer momentanément pour la durée de la délégation, une Constitution nouvelle à la Constitution existante. Ce serait contraire, en même temps, au principe de la souveraineté nationale, tel qu'il se traduit dans nos constitutions écrites, et au principe de la séparation des pouvoirs. Ce serait sortir de la Constitution et par suite entrer dans la Révolution " ("De la délégation du pouvoir législatif," in Revue politique et parlementaire, 1-2, 1894. See also Berthélemy, "Le pouvoir réglementaire du Président de la République," in Revue politique et

The analogy to the common law rule must not perhaps be pressed; but that the legislature may not delegate to any other authority its legislative powers is set forth, though with exceptions, by Cooley.[36] As there stated, the prohibition is not confined to the delegation of legislative powers to a coordinate branch of the government. The responsibility of exercising the powers granted rests upon the agent, and it may devolve that responsibility no more upon the heads of departments or administrative commissions or private individuals or the people than upon the President himself.

A more limited aspect of the same basic principle is the separation of powers, a political dogma which, as we have noted before, has been embodied in our federal constitutional law.[37] It is more limited because it forbids the delegation of legislative powers not to any authority, but only to a coordinate department of the government.[38] And yet the sepa-

---

parlementaire, 15-16, 1898, pp. 1-15, 322-335). This is now the accepted theory in France, although it was formerly held by all that legislative power was delegated to the President by the Chambers (Raiga, Le pouvoir réglementaire du Président de la République). Esmein's contention on this particular point has not, however, been accepted by the Conseil d'Etat (Esmein, Eléments de droit constitutionnel français et comparé, sixième édition, pp. 681 ff.).

[36] Constitutional Limitations, p. 137 ff. Says the learned jurist: "One of the settled maxims in constitutional law is, that the power conferred upon the legislature to make laws cannot be delegated by that department to any other body or authority. Where the sovereign power of the State has located the authority, there it must remain; and by the constitutional agency alone the laws must be made until the constitution itself is changed. The power to whose judgment, wisdom and patriotism this high prerogative has been intrusted cannot relieve itself of the responsibility by choosing other agencies upon which the power shall be devolved, nor can it substitute the judgment, wisdom and patriotism of any other body for those to which alone the people have seen fit to confide this sovereign trust." See also the *dictum* to the same effect in Field v. Clark, 143 U. S. 649.

[37] Goodnow, Principles of the Administrative Law of the United States, chap. iv.

[38] The President himself is the Executive Department. Yet the heads of departments also come within the narrower rule of the separation of powers because, in practice and under certain decisions of the courts, they are really an integral part of the "executive power" which is vested primarily in the President (see Wilcox v. Jackson, 13 Pet. 498, and Wolsey v. Chapman, 101 U. S. 755; also Harrison, This Country of Ours, pp. 69, 70, 168, 107, 189; see

ration of powers is not explicitly stated in a distributing clause, but is implied from the same premises from which the rule against delegation of vested power flows. From the fact that the three basic functions of government are respectively vested in three separate departments in general terms, it follows from the nature of the Constitution that none of these departments may exercise powers which functionally come within the scope of the other departments.[39] The only exceptions are where the Constitution itself explicitly provides for " partial mixtures of powers," [40] or where a constitutional power on logical analysis, if not by historical connotation, is or involves a power of ordinance making. It is obvious that the exercise by the President of legislative powers which could not be brought within these exceptions would violate the theory of the constitutional allotment of powers as much when he acted under attempted delegations from Congress as when he usurped the powers in question.[41]

It appears at first blush that these principles forbid the delegation of any ordinance making powers to the Executive. Dean Pound has referred to " the perennial struggle of American administrative law with nineteenth-century constitutional formulations of Aristotle's three-fold classification

---

chap. viii, below). The heads of departments thus come at least within the spirit of the rule. Whether all administrative agencies do or do not is a mere academic question; because they come within the broader principle anyway. It is this which justifies the courts in making no distinction on this score in the cases. Thus the Supreme Court cited Field v. Clark, 143 U. S. 649, in Buttfield v. Stranahan, 192 U. S. 470, and the latter in Arver v. United States, The Selective Draft Cases, 245 U. S. 366.

[39] Kilbourn v. Thompson, 103 U. S. 168.

[40] The Federalist, No. 47. See also Willoughby, Constitutional Law of the United States, sec. 743.

[41] When Madison proposed to the Philadelphia Convention of 1787 that the President be given in the Constitution the power " to execute such other powers as may be from time to time delegated by the national Legislature," Pinckney suggested that the words " not legislative nor judiciary in their nature " be inserted, on the ground that " improper powers might otherwise be delegated." It is significant that Madison did not even require a vote on the suggestion, but incorporated it into his motion without recorded protest (Farrand, Records of the Federal Convention, vol. i, pp. 62 ff.).

of governmental power." [42]   Theory and practice seem to collide; and we are faced by a dilemma which it is highly important to resolve.[43]   For to ignore the foundation theory of our written Constitution were nothing less than a legal revolution; while to allow the application of that theory to exclude all delegations of rule-making powers were to clog the free operation of twentieth century government. It is equally improper to dismiss the separation of powers by calling it a political maxim not entirely workable in practice, and to fail to realize the practical necessity of the tendency toward administrative co-legislation and executive justice. The Supreme Court has never held unconstitutional an attempted delegation of discretionary power; and hence it may be said that the practice has become fixed in our constitutional system. Yet the Court has never formulated the reasoning of its decisions in a manner to resolve the dilemma which we have stated. It becomes necessary, therefore, to attempt to do so at this point.

Let us first state the distinction which we shall attempt to justify. In the leading case of Field v. Clark,[44] the court stated that the power delegated was not legislative " in any real sense." It was legislative in the sense in which that term is technically defined in a previous chapter. However, we are here concerned with the meaning of the term as used in the first Article of the Federal Constitution. But even so, the statement of the Court, if not carried further, is a mere begging of the question. Furthermore, it may be argued that, since Congress has only legislative powers, any power which it delegates to another organ must of necessity be legislative in nature.[45] The logic of such an argument is flawless, but it is with the unreality of such formal logic that we disagree. The very nature of government is such that the legislature cannot always decide every detail. It becomes

---

[42] An Introduction to the Philosophy of Law, p. 15.
[43] Ibid., chap i.   The reference to Aristotle as the author of the theory, in its modern form, at least, is incorrect.
[44] 143 U. S. 649.
[45] Fairlie, The National Administration, p. 23.

necessary, therefore, for the courts to distinguish between what it must do to fulfill its function and what it may either do or leave to the administrative department in connection with its execution of the law.[46] Herein is no denial that Congress alone has all legislative power under the Constitution; but the exercise of that power must often consist of blocking out the primary rights and duties of a regulation and providing for the determination of details by executive officials. Though Congress may go into such detail as it sees fit, it may with equal propriety and in complete discharge of its constitutional responsibility prescribe a general policy and then define with reasonable clearness the subordinate discretion which it leaves to the Executive. Such subordinate exercise of discretion, when it results in rules of conduct, is indeed legislative in the sense of general jurisprudence. It is not necessarily legislative in the sense that the delegation thereof involves the transference to another authority of the legislative power of Congress or a redistribution by Congress of the allotment of powers as determined and fixed in the fundamental law. Congress may make such delegations under the 'necessary and proper' clause, and the President may act under them by virtue of his 'faithful execution' power. Such a distinction is premised upon the idea that the framers were not so theoretical and so unpractical as to intend to make their constitutional allotment on the basis of the intrinsic nature of the power without any regard to its scope. If we approach the matter from that angle we make of the above-quoted statement of the Supreme Court a practical principle and not a mere side-stepping of the issue; and at the same time we have a sufficient answer for those who speak in terms solely of logic and not of government in action.

---

[46] Only thus can the legislative function be "effectively exercised." See dictum of Mr. Chief Justice Taft in Wichita R. R. & Light Co. v. Public Utilities Commission of Kansas, 259 U. S. 1092. Cf. the language of Marshall in Wayman v. Southard, 10 Wheat. 1; and that of Mr. Justice Harlan in Boske v. Comingore, 177 U. S. 459.

It must be confessed that the Constitution does not expressly make this distinction, which is sometimes referred to as a distinction between legislative and administrative discretion.[47] That document emphasizes rather the contrast between legislative and executive powers.[48] Yet general constitutional terms like ' legislative powers ' are subject to a somewhat more flexible interpretation than narrower and more specific terms like pardon, ex post facto law, or bill of attainder.[49] Extrinsic evidence, in the form of historical or contemporaneous evidence of the signification attached to a word in 1789, is permissible, whether introduced to support the contention that delegations are legitimate or that they are not. We may check such bits of contemporaneous and historical evidence as are obtainable against present needs. If they agree, the matter is settled. If not, a balance must be struck as best it may.

III

The first evidence to be examined will be historical and contemporaneous. The former is significant legally in so far as it shows practice crystallizing out in an idea; and it is further important for contemporaneous construction in so far as it can be demonstrated that historical ideas were accepted by the generation which adopted the Constitution.

Locke, to whom the statesmen of that age owed many of their political ideas, states in his Two Treatises of Civil Government that " The legislature neither must nor can transfer the power of making laws to anybody else, or place it anywhere but where the people have." [50] This is not true in Locke's country today; though it is not certain whether the framers clearly understood parliamentary supremacy in its

---

[47] Cf. In re Kollock, 165 U. S. 526.

[48] Goodnow, Principles of the Administrative Law of the United States, p. 73.

[49] Cf. book review by Frankfurter, in Harvard Law Review, April, 1924, p. 783. See South Carolina v. United States, 199 U. S. 437; United States v. Wilson, 7 Pet. 150.

[50] Sec. 142 of the Second Treatise.

absolute sense.[51]   Moreover, the statement may be meant in a political rather than a legal sense, and at the most it refers in terms to a transfer of legislative power, which this treatise does not claim to be constitutional in the United States.   Stubbs [52] tells us of delegations aimed to limit the prerogative powers of the Crown, though the framers may not have known of his examples.   Blackstone seems to say that the law can leave a discretionary power of proclamation to the king; [53] and he more than once mentions delegations, including the transfer of legislative power contained in the famous Statute of Proclamations.[54]   The latter he condemns as improper, though perhaps he does not mean to call it illegal.   It may not be without some significance that the framers were probably familiar with this governmental process in the mother country.   Nevertheless, that does not prove that they understood it to be permissible in a system in which the legislature was a limited organ acting under a written constitution and its rigid enactment of the separation of powers; and at best the practice of delegations was not extensive in the England of their day.

Likewise in the Revolutionary emergency legislation of the States we find that the statutes went into the most minute details; and that for the most part such delegations as they made were to the justices of the peace.[55]   That is not an analogous case, for it is admitted by the leading authorities that the rule against delegation has an exception in the case of delegations to local officers of police ordinance making powers.[56]   However, delegations of that period would not

---

[51] This general question has been recently raised again—though in a different connection—by the publication of McIlwain, The American Revolution.

[52] Constitutional History of England, vol. i, p. 619.

[53] Commentaries, vol. i, book i, pp. 270-271.

[54] Ibid., vol. i, book i, p. 271; book iv, p. 431.   For Blackstone's influence on the Americans see Goodnow, Principles of Constitutional Government, p. 4 ff.   The first volume appeared in 1765, the other three in the next four years.   Thus in 1789 this treatise was a standard work that had been out twenty years.

[55] Emergency Legislation Passed Prior to December, 1917 (J. Reuben Clarke, compiler).

[56] Cooley, Constitutional Limitations (5th ed.), pp. 139-140.

prove our case, because it was a time of stress, and also because the principle of a written constitution unamendable by the ordinary legislature was but in its inception.[57]

One searches in vain the records of the Constitutional Convention of 1787 for more than one incident, and that one is inconclusive, at least if taken by itself. That incident is recorded by Mr. Madison, who says: [58]

Mr. (Madison)—(thought) it would be proper, before a choice shd. be made between a unity and a plurality in the Executive, to fix the extent of the Executive authority; that as certain powers were in their nature Executive, and must be given to that departmt. whether administered by one or more persons, a definition of their extent would assist the judgment in determining how far they might be safely entrusted to a single officer. He accordingly moved that so much of the clause before the Committee as related to the powers of the Executive shd. be struck out & that (after the words) "that a national Executive ought to be instituted" (there be inserted the words following) viz, "with power to carry into effect the national laws. to appoint to offices in cases not otherwise provided for, and to execute such other powers ("not Legislative nor Judiciary in their nature") as may from time to time be delegated by the national Legislature." The words ("not legislative nor judiciary in their nature") were added to the proposed amendment, in consequence of a suggestion by Genl Pinkney that improper powers might (otherwise) be delegated.
(Mr. Wilson seconded this motion)

Mr. Pinkney moved to amend the amendment by striking out the last member of it; viz. "and to execute such other powers not Legislative nor Judiciary in their nature as may from time to time be delegated." He said they were unnecessary, the object of them being included in the "power to carry into effect the national laws."
Mr. Randolph seconded the motion.

Mr. Madison did not know that the words were absolutely necessary, or even the preceding words. "to appoint to offices, &c. the whole being perhaps included in the first member of the proposition. He did not however see any inconveniency in retaining them, and cases might happen in which they might serve to prevent doubts and misconstructions.

(In consequence of the motion of Mr. Pinkney, the question on Mr. Madison's motion was divided; and the words objected to by Mr. Pinkney struck out; by the votes of Connecticut. N. Y. N. J. Pena. Del. N. C. & Geo: agst. Mass. Virga. & S. Carolina the preceding part of the motion being first agreed to; Connecticut divided, all the other states in the affirmative.)

The fact that Madison did not protest when Pinckney

---

[57] Cf. Clarke's Compilation at pp. 896-899, with Poore, Charters and Constitutions, p. 1620 n.
[58] Farrand, Records of the Federal Convention, vol. i, pp. 66-67.

amended his original motion by having inserted the words "not Legislative nor Judiciary in their nature" shows that Madison did not mean to allow the delegation of legislative power when he made the motion. Yet it must be assumed that he had something in mind. His motion was voted down; for after the insertion of the above-mentioned phrase Pinckney still opposed it as being unnecessary, since included in the power to execute the laws, which appeared earlier in Madison's motion. This is the only reason Madison records as given for the adverse vote. He admitted that the power he desired to confer might be included in the power of execution, but he desired to avoid ambiguity. It thus appears, for aught that we are told, that Madison and those who voted with him, and also Pinckney and those who opposed, intended the President to have the power to carry into execution such other powers, not legislative nor judicial in their nature, as Congress might delegate to him.

But what did that include? In all probability it included at least those military and political powers, of an executive nature from the historical point of view, which were embodied in the later drafts, but not yet specified.[59] From practice just before and especially just after the adoption of the Constitution we may perhaps infer that it also included the delegation of ministerial powers and particular acts of discretion, and also limited rule-making powers which served to carry into execution the laws.

In the debates of the era of adoption we find at least one bit of evidence which runs counter to our contention. It occurs in the discussion in the Federalist of the proper location of the pardoning power. In arguing against requiring the concurrence of one or both houses in the exercise of this power by the President in the case of treason, the writer says: [60]

If it should be observed that a discretionary power, with a view

---

[59] Ibid., vol. i, pp. 20, 236; vol. ii, pp. 590, 419, 185-186; vol. iii, pp. 427 ff, 502; Farrand, The Framing of the Constitution, pp. 163-164, 171-173, 160-161.

[60] No. 74.

to such contingencies, might be occasionally conferred upon the President, it may be answered in the first place, that it is questionable whether, in a limited Constitution, that power could be delegated by law.

Aside from the apparent uncertainty on the point at issue, it is clear that this opinion militates against just such delegations as have in practice been made and upheld by the courts. For if the power of pardon or amnesty cannot be delegated, how can we justify the delegation of the power to lay an embargo [61] or to suspend the privilege of the writ of habeas corpus? [62] To draw distinctions calculated to do away with the significance of this opinion would be entirely unwarranted by the circumstances. But it must be remembered that individual expressions of opinion by members of the Convention, even when contained in writings that were so widely read and that exerted so potent an influence as those of Publius, are at best only evidence, not conclusive proof, of the intent of those who adopted the Constitution as the supreme law of the land.[63] In view of the evidence which we have on the other hand, we would adopt a false perspective if we allowed the whole question to be settled by this unelaborated and hesitating statement of an argumentative epistle.

The strongest and most positive contemporary evidence in favor of our contention is to be found in legislative, executive and judicial construction of the Constitution during that period of our constitutional history which immediately followed the adoption of the instrument. In interpreting technical terms of the Constitution it is fitting to turn to the practice of the early years of its operation, when many of the framers and members of the adopting conventions were actually in responsible positions in the several branches of the government,[64] and when in fact all federal officials had

---

[61] 1 Stat. L. 372.
[62] This was done by Congress in the Civil War. The two sorts of delegations are not strictly on all fours with each other; but the point is, that doubt as to the constitutionality of the practice of delegation was expressed in the Federalist.
[63] Cooley, Constitutional Limitations (7th ed.), p. 101.
[64] Willoughby, Constitutional Law of the United States, sec. 11.

been, at least by representation, parties to the act of adoption. *Contemporanea expositio est optima et fortissima in lege.* Some of the Congressional delegations of this era have been set forth in a preceding chapter. The fact that the Presidents signed the bills in which they were embodied and often acted under them adds executive to legislature sanction of the constitutionality of the procedure. While the delegations were not numerous, and appeared as exceptions to the customary congressional practice of detailed legislation, it must be borne in mind that the total legislative output of those days was extremely small.[65]   The outstanding fact is this: even though tradition and precedent dictated, and circumstances suggested that for the most part a minimum of discretion be allowed to the Executive, the peculiar nature of our foreign commercial problems necessitated in this early time occasional departures from accepted methods.[66]   But when once it is admitted that the rule against delegation and the separation of powers do not absolutely prohibit all delegations, the issue is reduced to one of degree and not of principle. The best proof that the men who framed the Constitution did not mean to have us carry logic to the absurdity of choking the free operation of government is that they themselves refused in practice to do so. For our purpose, then, it matters little whether they considered the matter from the standpoint of theory in 1787-1789, or what their theoretical opinion might have been, if, immediately after 1789, they gave a certain interpretation through their conduct. And if this interpretation could be given by them in the one case where it was acutely needed, it can with entire propriety be given by us today in other cases. After all, the evidence of their ' government in action ' is more eloquent than ' government in their books.' [67]

---

[65] Each of the earlier volumes of the statutes-at-large covered a period of ten years, while a volume is now required for each two-year period.

[66] For example, see 1 Stat. L. 521, 555, 558 ff., 565, 566, 569-570, 570 ff., 572-573, 574-575, 578-579, 604-605, 673, 721-722, 753-754; and 2 Stat. L. 339 ff., 451-453, 490, 528, 530-531, 605-606, 755 ff.

[67] Cf. the phrases of Dean Pound—law in action and law in books

Contemporaneous construction is not entirely confined to the political departments of the government. The cases of the Brig *Aurora* [68] and Wayman v. Southard [69] throw some light upon the matter. In the period of commercial warfare with England and France, during the Napoleonic Wars, one of our non-intercourse acts conferred upon the President, in case either France or England so revoked or modified her edicts as to cease to violate our neutral commerce, the power to proclaim the fact, whereupon in three months certain restrictions should be revived against the other nation unless she also revoked her edicts. The President proclaimed that France had so revoked or modified her edicts as to cease to violate our commerce; and, after the three months' period had elapsed, the Brig *Aurora,* an English ship, was captured under the revived act, and condemned. When the case reached the Supreme Court, the claim was advanced, but denied by the Court, that the statute conferred legislative power upon the President. This case, decided in 1813, was cited as a precedent in the leading case of Field v. Clark.[70] While it indicates that in that period it was understood that the operation of a statute might be made dependent upon a determination of the President, it is not a precedent, except by way of anticipation, for the delegation to the President of determinations which involve evaluation of so subjective a character as to render his action discretionary in a strict sense. It is a case where action is on the border line between fact-finding and discretion.

—in an article by that title in American Law Re·.·w, vol. xliv, p. 12 ff.

[68] 7 Cr. 382.

[69] 10 Wheat. 1.

[70] In that case the authority of the *Aurora* case was impeached by counsel upon the following grounds:

1. It was decided before the principles of the Constitution had been adequately considered.

2. The bare conclusion is offered, without any exposition of the basis on which it was made.

3. It is not in point: it was almost a war power, and was not a taxing power; and "while it involved a certain amount of judgment it was not such an abdication of legislative functions as that in section 3 of the Tariff Act." The court, however, considered it a case in point.

The other case was decided in 1825, and the opinion was
written by Chief Justice Marshall, who had been a member
of the Virginia Convention that ratified the Constitution.[71]
It involved the delegation to the courts themselves of rule-
making power in regard to judicial procedure. The Process
Act had adopted the state laws regulating the modes of
procedure in suits at common law in the federal courts, " subject, however, to such alterations and additions as the said
courts respectively shall, in their discretion, deem expedient,
or to such regulations as the Supreme Court of the United
States shall think proper, from time to time, to prescribe
to any circuit or district court concerning the same." In
answering the argument that this was a delegation of legislative power to the courts, Marshall drew the distinction between subjects which are " strictly and exclusively legislative " and subjects where the power may be delegated " to
fill up the details " of a " general provision." But he did
not draw any logical line of demarcation between the two;
on the contrary he said that what the courts might be allowed
to regulate is " so blended with that for which the legislature must expressly and directly provide " that there is
" difficulty in discerning the exact limits " of the former.
For our purposes at the present moment, however, the significance of the opinion lies in the admission at this early period
by the highest judicial tribunal of our system that the delegation of discretionary power is, within limits, permissible.
As the opinion itself tersely puts it:

The difference between the departments undoubtedly is, that the
legislature makes, the executive executes, and the judiciary con-
strues the law; but the maker of the law may commit something to
the discretion of the other departments, and the precise boundary
of this power is a subject of delicate and difficult inquiry, into
which a court will not enter unnecessarily.

IV

If it be claimed that the above is merely circumstantial
evidence, and that the matter is still in doubt, we can offer
other arguments. Where the intent of the framers is doubt-

[71] Beveridge, Life of John Marshall, vol. i, p. 318.

ful, great weight is by the Courts properly given to legislative construction. *Consuetudo est optimus interpres legum.* The mere passage of a statute by Congress establishes for the courts every presumption in favor of the validity of the statute; [72] and this is rightly so, for the reason that Congress is a coordinate branch of the government, all of whose members are equally with the members of the courts sworn to support the Constitution. " The presumption of constitutionality," says an eminent authority, " which attaches to an act of Congress, is increased when legislative interpretation has been frequently applied during a considerable number of years or when it dates from a period practically contemporary with the adoption of the Constitution, or when based upon a confidence in its correctness, many and important public and private rights have been fixed." [73]   In point of fact, all three of the factors mentioned lend support to the interpretation here advocated. Legislative construction is favorable for the entire period of our constitutional history. A few instances are given in Field v. Clark. We have already seen that these delegations date from the first years of the government. And to take only the most outstanding examples of the rights affected, many of the war acts of President Lincoln would have made his subordinates liable for damages but for the Congressional act of indemnity,[74] which was in effect a retroactive delegation of the power to act; while almost all of the war activity of the government in the last war would be invalid if such delegations were unconstitutional.[75]

---

[72] Willoughby, Constitutional Law of the United States, sec. 9. In the United States v. Gettysburg Electric Railway Company the Court said: " In examining an act of Congress it has been frequently said that every intendment is in favor of its constitutionality. Such an act is presumed to be valid unless its invalidity is plain and apparent; no presumption of invalidity can be indulged in; it must be shown clearly and unmistakably. This rule has been stated and followed by this court from the foundation of the government " (160 U. S. 668).

[73] Willoughby, Constitutional Law of the United States, vol, i, p. 25.

[74] See the Prize Cases, 2 Black 635.

[75] The acts delegating the extensive powers conferred upon President Wilson in the war with Germany may be found in 40 Stat. L., passim.

It is conceded that Congressional practice should not be sanctioned if clearly in violation of the Constitution. The principle is analogous to that stated in an old English decision that " no degree of antiquity can give sanction to a usage bad in itself." [76] It is emphatically recognized in the case of Fairbank v. United States,[77] where a careful review of the previous decisions leads to the conclusion that the argument is to be relied upon only in case of doubt. Yet in regard to the matter under consideration, the issue was sufficiently doubtful for legislative practice to be the chief argument relied upon by the Supreme Court in the leading case of Field v. Clark. The Court said that the provision upheld is " not entirely a new feature of the legislation of Congress, but has the sanction of many precedents in legislation. While some of these precedents are stronger than others in their application to the case before us, they all show that, in the judgment of the legislative branch of the government, it is often desirable, if not essential, for the protection of the interests of our people, against unfriendly or discriminating regulations established by foreign governments, in the interests of their people, to invest the President with large discretion in matters arising out of the execution of statutes relating to trade and commerce with other nations. If the decision in the case of the Brig *Aurora* had never been rendered, the practical construction of the Constitution, as given by so many acts of Congress and embracing almost the entire period of our national existence, should not be overruled, unless upon a conviction that such legislation was clearly incompatible with the supreme law of the land."

In case of doubt it is also entirely permissible to adopt the more efficient interpretation, the one more conducive to

---

[76] Money et al. v. Leach, iii Burr. 1742-1767.

[77] 181 U. S. 283. "We have no disposition," said Mr. Justice Brewer in his opinion, " to belittle the significance of this matter. It is always entitled to careful consideration, and in doubtful cases will, as we have shown, often turn the scale; but where the meaning and scope of the constitutional provision are clear, it cannot be overthrown by legislative action, although several times repeated and never before challenged."

the smooth working of the system. If such interpretation were contrary to the letter or spirit of any portion of the Constitution, the argumentum ab inconveniente would not hold. But that is the point at issue, and if our evidence has not positively proved that ours is the correct interpretation, it has at least negatively demonstrated that it is not clearly in conflict with the Constitution. Hence it is in order to point out the practical necessity of delegations under modern conditions as a reason for resolving the doubt in favor of an interpretation which would allow such delegations. This has been done by the Supreme Court in more than one case. In Field v. Clark the Court quoted with approval the famous statement of Locke's Appeal: [78]

The legislature cannot delegate its power to make a law; but it can make a law to delegate a power to determine some fact or state of things upon which the law makes, or intends to make, its own action depend. *To deny this would be to stop the wheels of government.* There are many things upon which wise and useful legislation must depend which cannot be known to the law making power, and, must, therefore, be a subject of inquiry outside of the halls of legislation.

In Buttfield v. Stranahan [79] the Court declared:

Congress legislated on the subject as far as it was reasonably practicable, and from the necessities of the case was compelled to leave the executive officials the duty of bringing about the result pointed out by the statute. To deny the power of Congress to delegate such a duty would, in effect, amount but to declaring that the plenary power vested in Congress to regulate foreign commerce could not be efficaciously exerted.

Finally, in Mutual Film Co. v. Industrial Commission [80] the decision reads, in part, as follows:

While administration and legislation are quite distinct powers, the line which separates exactly their exercise is not easy to define in words. It is best recognized in illustrations. Undoubtedly the legislature must declare the policy of the law and fix the legal principles which are to control in given cases; but an administrative body may be invested with the power to ascertain the facts and conditions to which the policy and principles apply. If this could not be done there would be infinite confusion in the laws, and in an effort to detail and to particularize, they would miss sufficiently both in provision and execution.

---

[78] 72 Pa. 491. (Italics author's.)
[79] 192 U. S. 470.
[80] 236 U. S. 230.

It is thus that the fortunate use of broad generalizations in the Constitution introduces a flexibility which makes the instrument adaptable to the needs of successive generations. The interpretation which we desire may be stated as the proposition that the legislative powers granted to Congress include the power, as being a necessary and proper means of carrying them into execution, to delegate to the Executive the function of issuing ordinances which concretize the legislative enactments. It thus comes within the terms of the text; and since it cannot be shown to be invalid, but on the contrary is supported by evidence that tends to render it valid, we may with perfect legal propriety adopt it on the ground of its expediency.

As a present problem of constitutional law the validity of the delegation of discretionary power is settled for all practical purposes by the line of decisions beginning with Field v. Clark, decided in 1892. It is of course possible that the Court might reverse all of these decisions; because the rule of stare decisis is not a principle of law, but a policy usually but not always followed by the courts.[81] But both because there have been so many decisions upholding delegations, and because of the necessity for this practice, it is unthinkable that the Court will change its opinion. Not all of the cases referred to have involved delegations to the President; but in respect to the permissibility of the practice the Court has made no distinction between him and the heads of the departments. It is indisputable that such cases as the Brig *Aurora* v. United States,[82] Field v. Clark,[83] Buttfield v. Stranahan,[84] the Interstate Commerce Commission v. Goodrich Transit Co.,[85] St. Louis I. M. & S. R. Co. v. Taylor,[86] Intermountain Rate Cases,[87] First National Bank v. Fellows,[88] Brushaber v. Union Pacific R. Co.,[89] Arver v.

---

[81] Lile, Some Views of the Rule of Stare Decisis, Annual Address Before the Alabama State Bar Association, July, 1916.

[82] 7 Cr. 382.
[83] 143 U. S. 649.
[84] 192 U. S. 470.
[85] 224 U. S. 194.
[86] 210 U. S. 281.
[87] 234 U. S. 476.
[88] 244 U. S. 416.
[89] 245 U. S. 366.

United States and other cases (Selective Draft Cases),[90] taken together, practically affirm that both the President and cabinet officers and administrative commissions may be granted, at least with reference to some topics and to a certain extent, discretionary and even rule-making power with regard to the elaboration, or execution, or bringing into operation of the rules of statutes.

V

It is next requisite to examine the limitations on the scope of the power that may be delegated to the Executive. Here we pass to a problem where no exact distinctions are possible. It would be expected that if any jurist could draw with precision the line of demarcation it would be the author of the acute decision in Brown v. Maryland.[91] We have seen that, in Wayman v. Southard, Marshall had to admit that " the precise boundary of this power is a subject of delicate and difficult inquiry." [92] While we can gather some principles from the dicta of the decided cases, for the very reason that none of them declares any delegations unconstitutional, we can, at best, only surmise the extreme limits to which the practice may go. It might, indeed, be claimed that, because no cases enforce the rule against delegation, it is only a political maxim and not a principle of law, except to the extent that it forbids Congress to transfer its legislative power to the executive. With this statement we cannot entirely agree. In all probability one reason no law has been declared invalid on this score is the fact that Congress has never overstepped certain limits which we shall proceed to discuss. It is not true, therefore, that this constitutional limitation is political rather than legal in character; though it is true that the amount of discretion as to subordinate premises which may be granted without violating the rule as understood by the Supreme Court is very broad.

---

[90] 240 U. S. 1.
[91] 12 Wheat. 419.
[92] See the quotation at the beginning of this chapter.

The fundamental limitation has to do with the scope of the discretion that may be delegated. All students of the subject will admit that Congress could not, if it would, transfer in toto to the President or any other agency all or any of its enumerated powers. Thus a statute in general terms that the President be given authority to pass regulations regarding interstate or foreign commerce, would without doubt be held invalid. Nor can Congress delegate the power to regulate even one whole field of interstate commerce. Surely it would not be legitimate for it to authorize the President to pass reasonable regulations with reference to the interstate railroad problem. Yet Congress has granted the Interstate Commerce Commission the power to fix maximum railroad rates, provided they be reasonable; [93] and all admit that this is constitutional.[94] What is the distinction? Essentially the quantitative one of the scope of the discretion.

Thoughtful examination will reveal the fact that this is a very proper, if not a very precise, criterion. To grant the power to regulate interstate commerce or the instrumentalities thereof would not be to define a single, definite problem; for the subject includes whole fields, involving numerous problems. The President would be left to determine not the concrete rules to make effective a Congressional policy, but the policy itself, and even for what problem among the many involved he should establish a policy. This would mean that there would be only the vaguest sort of objective standards to guide the President's action. On the other hand, when Congress delegates the power to fix minimum and maximum railroad rates, it singles out one problem, which has unmistakable limits. It leaves to the Commission a power which does, indeed, involve subjective evaluation, but yet evaluation of a defined situation, and with certain more or less objective standards as a guide. The narrower scope of the power alters its character from a dele-

---

[93] United States Compiled Statutes (1918), sec. 8583.
[94] Willoughby, Principles of the Constitutional Law of the United States (students' edition), p. 550.

gation of ' free determination' to a delegation of the power by scientific analysis to make effective the general policy set forth in the law. If it be asked how this distinction can be made precise, the answer is that it is unwise to attempt any such thing. As in so many matters in the law, it is better to state the principle in general terms, and leave it to the courts to apply that principle in each case as it arises. By this method " lines are pricked out by the gradual approach and contact of decisions on the opposing sides ";[95] and the law in action is made conformable to social and industrial facts.

Congress has proceeded with great restraint in times of peace in regard to the scope of its delegations. It has not gone very far, except with reference to special problems, such as the international complications that arose out of the Napoleonic Wars, foreign commercial relations generally,[96] and certain other subjects.[97] But in the crises of the Civil and German Wars it was found necessary in the interest of quick and flexible action for Congress to delegate in many cases almost full discretion in the premises. The argument has been advanced that this is justifiable under the war power; though the courts have not always put those wartime delegations which they have upheld upon this special basis.[98] Upon principle we may say that if the Constitution is the supreme law of the land in war as in peace, the war powers of Congress may be interpreted only as giving that body a greater quantum of power, not as giving it the legal right to violate any fundamental constitutional limitations,

---

[95] Mr. Justice Holmes in Noble State Bank v. Haskell, 219 U. S. 104.

[96] Field v. Clark, 143 U. S. 649.

[97] See Albertsworth, "Judicial Review of Administrative Action by the Federal Supreme Court," in Harvard Law Review, December, 1921.

[98] But see the language of the opinion in Dakota Central Telephone v. South Dakota, 250 U. S. 163, 1919. Cf. Arver v. United States (Selective Draft Cases), 240 U. S. 1. At any rate, Mr. Cecil T. Carr is wrong when he implies that Congress used the practice first in the late war with Germany (See his Delegated Legislation, p. 26).

whether expressed or implied.[99]   Thus in a war Congress
may, in conformity with the doctrine of implied powers, extend federal control over matters which aside from war only
the States could regulate.   This war time extension of federal control is merely an application of recognized principles
of constitutional construction.   Similarly, since the delga-
tions of rule-making power to the President are based upon
the presumed recognition in 1789 of their practical expediency, the scope of such delegations might conceivably be
enlarged because of the necessities of war; though in point
of fact some delegations of peace go in scope almost as far
as those of war.   But even if war might justify in law the
increase of the quantum of a delegation, Congress could not
even then transfer its legislative power to the Executive;
for that would be a violation of a principle rather than the
extension of a recognized one.   This must be so unless we
accept the theory of the wartime ' sovereignty ' of Congress
which was proclaimed during the Civil War, and is a logical
result of many definitions of the ' war power '.   Whether
under certain circumstances it would not be morally justifiable for Congress to violate the Constitution in a crisis is
an entirely different question.   But to maintain that Congress, in the absence of express provisions in that document
for the emergency abrogation of some or all of its provisions, could legally do so, is a contradictio in adjecto [100]

---

[99] In Ex parte Milligan, 4 Wall. 141, the majority and the minority
of the Court differed as to whether Congress could have authorized
the action which in the absence of such authorization the case
held the Executive had illegally taken.   Whatever our opinion upon
the particular point, we may agree with the principle there set
forth that: " The Constitution of the United States is a law for
rulers and people, equally in war and in peace, and covers with the
shield of its protection all classes of men, at all times, and under
all circumstances.   No doctrine, involving more pernicious consequences, was ever invented by the wit of man than that any of its
provisions can be suspended during any of the great exigencies of
government."   See Dunning, Essays on the Civil War and Reconstruction, pp. 18, 21, 58-59, but especially pp. 48-49.

[100] It might be urged that the Constitution in granting without
limitation to Congress the power to declare war implied a theory of
inter arma leges silent.   This seems to the present writer a mere
begging of the question.

which is made possible only by the confusion on the part of its proponents of the elementary distinction between law and ethics.

State decisions have in some cases indicated that the legislature must prescribe more or less definite standards for the guidance of the Executive in the exercise of its rule-making discretion.[101] Certainly the scope of the delegation must be narrowed down to one rather definite problem, and the purpose of the legislature must be in some way either express or implied. Is more than this necessary? In Yick Wo v. Hopkins [102] the ratio decidendi was that the discretion delegated to the board was administered in a discriminatory manner; but the opinion went further than the facts required and in a dictum declared that the city ordinance which granted the authority of the board was invalid because " the power given to them is not confined to their discretion in the legal sense of that term, but is granted to their mere will." It is true that the ordinance did not mention any criteria by which the board was to be guided; but it is not to be implied from that fact alone that arbitrary power was meant to be conferred. Still less is this to be implied where a rule-making discretionary power is conferred. The only absolute requirement in this regard is that the totality of effect must imply, if the statute does not express, a reasonable and just policy and purpose which an honest board can use as a norm for its decisions. If the rules then prescribed are ' unreasonable,' the courts should hold them invalid.

This particular issue was not, it is true, raised in all cases. But the Court has frequently upheld delegations in which the criteria laid down were mere legislative abstrac-

---

[101] Harmon v. Ohio, 66 Ohio St. 249. It is worthy of note that numerous state decisions have declared particular delegations void as being a delegation of legislative power (See 153 S. W. 769; 92 Wis. 73; 166 Pa. 72; 103 N. W. 1021; 145 N. W. 425). Other state decisions declare the delegations in question do not delegate legislative power, and are therefore constitutional. The Supreme Court of the United States has held ordinances void as being ultra vires (e. g., Merritt v. Welsh, 104 U. S. 694); but it has never declared a delegation by Congress unconstitutional.

[102] 118 U. S. 356.

tions. Thus in Field v. Clark they were "reciprocally unequal and unreasonable"; in Buttfield v. Stranahan, "purity, quality and fitness for consumption." It is hardly to be disputed that, in the light of these cases, Congress can delegate to the President or heads of departments the power to concretize such legislative abstractions. In other cases the statute merely provided for the fixing of a standard, without defining even by generalization what that standard was to be. In the St. Louis I. M. & S. R. Co. v. Taylor [103] the law had declared that the American Railway Association or the Interstate Commerce Commission should designate "the standard height of drawbars for freight cars, measured perpendicular from the level of the tops of the rails to the centers of the drawbars, for each of the several gauges of railroads in use in the United States, and shall fix a minimum variation from such standard height to be allowed between drawbars of empty and loaded cars." This differs from the above cases in that the objects for which the discretion was to be exercised were not designated even in general terms. That was not necessary, because those objects were easily implied.

In Mutual Film Co. v. Industrial Commission [104] the state law in question had laid down criteria in the form of legislative abstractions; but an Ohio case [105] was cited to the Court to prove that this was not enough, that the statute had to make some attempt to define its general terms. The Court remarked without explanation that the case could be distinguished; then it immediately used an argument which, if too broad to be considered the ratio decidendi of its decision, is yet one which should be the basis for the decision of future cases. Speaking for the Court, Mr. Justice McKenna said:

The objection to the statute is that it furnishes no standard of what is educational, moral, amusing or harmless, and hence leaves decision to arbitrary judgment, whim and caprice; or, aside from

---

[103] 210 U. S. 281.
[104] 236 U. S. 230.
[105] Harmon v. Ohio, 66 Ohio St. 249.

those extremes, leaving it to the different views which might be entertained of the effect of the pictures, permitting the "personal equation" to enter, resulting "in unjust discrimination against some propagandist film," while others might be approved without question. But the statute by its provisions guards against such variant judgments, and its terms, like other general terms, get precision from the sense and experience of men and become certain and useful guides in reasoning and conduct. . . . If this were not so, the many administrative agencies created by the state and national governments would be denuded of their utility and government in some of its most important exercises become impossible.

The Justice then quotes the terse remark of another court that "it would seem next to impossible to devise language that would be at once comprehensive and automatic." This line of reasoning has implicit in it the principle which is here asserted as the correct one; namely, that no criteria, whether abstract or concrete, are needed if only the scope and purpose are sufficiently expressed or implied. Whether this is the case is a matter which can only be determined in each case by considering all the attendant circumstances and concluding in the light of them whether or not the total effect is one of clarity.

To this suggested general principle I would, however, make a single exception in regard to the matter of fixing the sanction of the regulations. There are no cases upon the subject, because Congress has not attempted to leave this matter to the Executive.[106] Perhaps if Congress prescribed a punishment of, let us say, "from ten to fifty thousand dollars fine, or from one to three years imprisonment, or both," it might leave it to the President to determine which punishment might be meted out, in particular cases,[107] or even uniformly for all. Again, it might prescribe a specific punishment and leave to the Executive the determination of whether future conditions which it could not foresee

---

[106] But see 1 Stat. L. 570 ff. The length of time of imprisonment seems there to have been left to the President. Even so, however, the exceptional circumstances in which this discretion would be allowed would preclude the objection that due process was wanting. The general rule as stated is not affected by such an instance.

[107] It has often left this to the courts.

warranted making the prohibited action a crime punishable by such penalty. But be that as it may, it is here claimed that it would be deprivation of life or liberty or property without due process of law for Congress to enact that a certain course of action was criminal, and then to leave it to the Executive to prescribe a ' reasonable ' penalty.[108] This is so clearly the teeth of legislation, and has in history so obviously been such,[109] that it is altogether on a different plane from the determination of a ' reasonable ' freight rate by the Executive. There is, moreover, no such practical need [110] for executive determination of penalties as there is, under modern industrial conditions, for executive determination of substantive rights and duties.

Are there any limitations upon the power of Congress in regard to delegations that have to do with the nature of the subject to be regulated? This cannot be answered from the decided cases; no Supreme Court cases have, for any reason, held delegations void. It will be noted that many of the cases upholding delegations deal with importation and other matters where there is no fundamental right involved; [111] with matters like the regulation of the use of property, and not the deprivation thereof; [112] with matters which have to

---

[108] It may be mentioned that this limitation is confined to the penal sanction. Congress may no doubt do what it did in the embargo delegation of 1794, when it authorized President Washington to issue orders for the administrative enforcement of the embargo in case he saw fit to establish the same (1 Stat. L. 372).

[109] Evidence of this is that Congress has never attempted to delegate any such power to the President. The rule of our law that an indictment must state a violation of the law carries with it the idea that the law must itself prescribe the punishment. This idea is so closely linked with the historical conception of legislative justice that it is part and parcel of the term due process of law. We may not be confined entirely to all historical forms of justice in interpreting due process; but on accepted rules of construction we cannot escape from a historical form which was and is undoubtedly thought of as an essential element of the concept (see also Ilbert, Legislative Methods and Forms, p. 310; Carr, Delegated Legislation, p. 54, n. 2).

[110] We have seen that the practical need carries great weight in interpreting ' due process.'

[111] Field v. Clark, 143 U. S. 649; Buttfield v. Stranahan, 192 U. S. 470.

[112] St. Louis I. M. & S. R. Co. v. Taylor, 210 U. S. 281.

do merely with the methods of carrying out the will of Congress; [113] with matters where a privilege is granted by way of exception to the general prohibition of the law,[114] or where the regulations prescribe the conditions upon which a privilege may be obtained, etc.   In none of these cases is the due process provision applicable.   Are there others which future judicial construction might hold to involve more fundamental rights that can be regulated or taken away only by the legislative department itself, or only in case of governmental necessity?

This question is obviously of the utmost importance; because upon the answer to it depends whether the delegation of ordinance making power is an exceptional practice or whether it is one which may be employed in all phases of governmental activity.

The former view is naturally held if we regard delegations as exceptions to the separation of powers and permissible only in cases of absolute necessity.   But with this point of view the present writer is in disagreement.   The attempt has been made above to prove that the delegation of a limited ordinance making power to the Executive is a proper exercise by Congress of its legislative powers.   It is beyond dispute an appropriate means to the end of enforcing the legislative policies of the legislative department.   It is shown above to be prohibited neither by the letter nor by the spirit of the Constitution.   This being so, it is not necessary that it be the only possible means to the end in question.   It is not requisite that it be an absolutely necessary means to the end.   It is for Congress and for Congress alone to decide, in its legislative discretion, when it is a proper method.   Any other principle is contrary to the cardinal constitutional doctrine of McCulloch v. Maryland.[115]

---

[113] Interstate Commerce Commission v. Goodrich Transit Co., 224 U. S. 194.

[114] Intermountain Rate Cases, 234 U. S. 476; First National Bank v. Fellows, 244 U. S. 416.

[115] 4 Wheat. 316.   The reasonable relationship of delegations in general (within the limits herein set forth) as 'means' to the 'end' of efficient execution of the laws of Congress is abundantly

The opinion is advanced that Congress can delegate the determination of substantial rights, within the limits hereinbefore set forth, with regard to all subjects which Congress itself has the power to regulate. Due process prevents Congress itself from passing some regulations affecting the ' natural rights ' which our Constitution is supposed to protect. It is fundamental that Congress can delegate only such powers as come within the sphere of its own competence.[116] But there is no reasonable ground for holding that due process is wanting merely because it is the Executive that issues the regulation, when the Executive is acting upon the authority of, and within the limits that must be set forth by the Congress, and when adequate appeal to the courts for the determination of at least whether those limits have been overstepped, is reserved. There are no cases the rationes decidendi of which are in conflict with this position; and it is a much more tenable legal position than one based upon the assumption that delegations are prima facie illegal.

It may be doubted whether the statesmen of 1789 contemplated a power of delegation of so broad a scope as here defined. They gave scant consideration to the problem, and to its scope scarcely any at all. However, we have evidence in their practice that they realized the power might be broad. The embargo delegation of 1794 is proof of this fact, though it is not as broad as our theory. A contemporary, as Chief Justice of the Supreme Court, handed down the opinion that to decide where the power " to fill up the details " may be given is " a subject of delicate and different inquiry." [117] Thus the evidence suggests that, in so far as they considered the matter at all, they sensed the fact that it does not bear exact definition, and sub-consciously realized the truth that such a definition is attempted at the risk of frustrating

attested by the practical universality of the existence of executive ordinance making, either by delegation or constitutional authority, in modern constitutional governments (see Nakano, The Ordinance Power of the Japanese Emperor, p. 41). Its universality strongly suggests its necessity.

[116] Cf. City of Evansville v. Miller, 146 Ind. 613.

[117] Chief Justice Marshall in Wayman v. Southard, 10 Wheat. 1.

the efficiency of the practice. They wisely left the scope of the power to be worked out in practice. In granting Congress all the legislative powers, and in limiting it to appropriate ("necessary and proper") means of carrying these powers into execution, they made it clear that the power may never be a cloak for the transfer or devolution of legislative power. The rest we may assume them to have left to be determined by the needs of government in action.[118] This seems a reasonable interpretation of the Constitution; but here again, if there is still doubt, it may be resolved in favor of the efficient construction.

VI

It may be in point to present some sample delegations which have been upheld by the Supreme Court in decided cases. In a previous chapter we have given the delegations in the Brig *Aurora* case and in the leading case of Field v. Clark. Buttfield v. Stranahan [119] involved section 3 of the tea inspection act of March 2, 1897,[120] which declared:

That the Secretary of the Treasury, upon the recommendation of the said board, shall fix and establish uniform standards of purity, quality and fitness for consumption of all kinds of teas imported into the United States. . . . All teas, or merchandise described as tea, of inferior purity, quality and fitness for consumption to such standards shall be deemed within the prohibition of the first section hereof.

---

[118] It is worthy of mention that not only did the framers give to Congress legislative powers and the power to employ the necessary and proper means of making these powers effective; but they gave to the President the power and duty of taking care that the laws are faithfully executed, thus furnishing the constitutional basis for his action in performing the ordinance making powers entrusted to him and in supervising the performance of such powers when entrusted to his subordinates. They may not have had this in mind in drafting the 'necessary and proper' and 'faithful execution' clauses; but the practice comes easily within the terms they used, and hence will only be excluded if it be shown they would have excluded it specifically, had it been called to their attention. See on this point Dartmouth College v. Woodward, 4 Wheat. 518.

[119] 192 U. S. 490.

[120] 29 Stat. L. 604.

This clearly involved the formulation of a rule by a process involving some degree of subjective evaluation.

In the Intermountain Rate Cases [121] the following delegation was declared constitutional: [122]

Provided, however, That upon application to the Interstate Commerce Commission such common carrier may in special cases, after investigation, be authorized by the Commission to charge less for longer than for shorter distances for the transportation of passengers or property; and the Commission may from time to time prescribe the extent to which such designated common carrier may be relieved from the operation of this section; Provided, further, . . .

Section 18 of the river and harbor act of March 3, 1899,[123] was in the case of Union Bridge Co. v. United States [124] and Monongahela Bridge Co. v. United States[125] upheld as not delegating " strictly legislative or judicial power." The section enacted:

That whenever the Secretary of War shall have good reason to believe that any railroad or other bridge now constructed, or which may hereafter be constructed, over any of the navigable waters of the United States, is an unreasonable obstruction to the free navigation of such waters on account of insufficient height, width of span, or otherwise, or where there is difficulty in passing the draw opening or the draw of such bridge by rafts, steamboats, or other water craft, it shall be the duty of the said Secretary, first giving the parties reasonable opportunity to be heard, to give notice to the persons or corporations owning or controlling such bridge, so to alter the same as to render navigation through or under it reasonably free, easy and unobstructed; and in giving such notice he shall specify such changes, recommended by the Chief of Engineers, that are required to be made, and shall prescribe in each case a reasonable time in which to make them. . . .

Each of these last two statutory provisions delegated a degree not to be sure of discretion in the premises, but of subordinate discretion or discretion as to subordinate premises. But both of them granted power to act in individual cases and after investigation or hearing. They are thus delegations of ' sub-legislative ' rather than of ' legislative '

---

[121] 234 U. S. 476.
[122] 24 Stat. L. 380, chap. civ, as amended by 36 Stat. L. 547, sec. 4.
[123] 30 Stat. L. 1121, 1153, chap. 425.
[124] 204 U. S. 364.
[125] 216 U. S. 177.

power,[126] while action taken under them is judicial, not in its essential nature, but in respect of the required procedure. Now if power to act in particular cases can be conferred, it can also be conferred with reference to the formulation of a uniform rule with regard to the same matter.

Section 11(k) of the Federal Reserve Act [127] gives the Federal Reserve Board authority to " grant by special permit to national banks applying therefor . . . the right to act as . . . under such rules and regulations as the said board may prescribe." In the First National Bank v. Fellows [128] this was declared valid. The rules and regulations were ordinances, but they set forth only the conditions on which the permit could be obtained.

In St. Louis, I. M. & S. R. Co. v. Taylor [129] the Court upheld sec. 5 of the safety appliance act of March 2, 1893,[130] which provides:

> That within ninety days from the passage of this act the American Railway Association is authorized hereby to designate to the Interstate Commerce Commission the standard height of drawbars for freight cars, measured perpendicular from the level of the tops of the rails to the centers of the drawbars, for each of the several gauges of railroads in use in the United States, and shall fix a maximum variation from such standard height to be allowed between the drawbars of empty and loaded cars. Upon their determination being certified to the Interstate Commerce Commission, said Commission shall at once give notice of the standard fixed upon to all common carriers, owners or lessees engaged in interstate commerce in the United States, by such means as the Commission may deem proper. But should such Association fail to determine a standard as above provided, it shall be the duty of the Interstate Commerce Commission to do so, before July first, eighteen hundred and ninety-four, and immediately to give notice thereof as aforesaid. And after July first, eighteen hundred and ninety-five, no cars, either loaded or unloaded, shall be used in interstate traffic which do not comply with the standard above provided for.

The prescription of the standard height and maximum variations therefrom would be a concrete ordinance. Unlike an ' executive order ' it would be a ' uniform rule.'

---

[126] As those terms are technically defined in chap. ii.
[127] 38 Stat. L. 251, 262, chap. 6.
[128] 244 U. S. 416.
[129] 210 U. S. 281.
[130] 27 Stat. L. 531, chap. 196.

In the Selective Draft Cases the Court declared: [131] " We think that the contention that the statute is void because investing administrative officers with legislative discretion has been so completely adversely settled as to require reference only to some of the decided cases." The dismissal of the contention in this summary manner must not cause us to overlook the importance of the decision. This is seen from an examination of the provisions of that law. The President is thereby authorized: [132] (1) To raise the Regular Army in accordance with the National Defense Act; (2) To draft the members of the National Guard and the National Guard Reserves; (3) To draft, as therein provided, organize and equip an additional force of 500,000 enlisted men and provide the necessary officers by any of several mentioned methods; (4) To raise in like manner, in his discretion and at such time as he may determine, another " additional force " of 500,000 men; (5) To draft, organize, equip and officer as above provided, such recruit training units as he may deem necessary to keep each of the above forces at the maximum strength; (6) To raise such number of ammunition batteries and battalions, with such numbers and grades of personnel as he may deem necessary; (7) To raise and maintain by voluntary enlistment not over four infantry divisions.

If and whenever the President decides that the enlisted men required to raise and maintain the Regular Army and maintain the National Guard draftees at the maximum legal strength cannot be effectually secured by voluntary enlistment, they are to be raised by selective draft. The draft is to take place and be maintained under such regulations as the President may prescribe not inconsistent with the terms of the act. No person exempted for religious scruples shall be exempted from service in any capacity that the President shall declare to be noncombatant. The President is authorized to exclude or discharge from the draft, or to draft for partial military service only, county and municipal officers,

---

[131] 240 U. S. 1.   [132] 40 Stat. L. 76.

etc., and such other persons employed in the service of the United States as the President may designate.

The President is authorized, in his discretion, to create and establish local boards; their members to be chosen from the locality where the board has jurisdiction, under the rules and regulations prescribed by the President. They are to hear questions of exceptions, which shall be made under Presidential regulations. The President is authorized to establish district boards to review, under the rules and regulations prescribed by the President, decisions of the local boards and to hear claims not within the jurisdiction of the local boards. The act was thus honeycombed with delegations.

CHAPTER VII

OTHER CONSTITUTIONAL ASPECTS OF THE DELEGATED ORDINANCE MAKING POWERS OF THE PRESIDENT

As a general rule, the courts may not on these writs consider or review questions of fact or expediency which have been decided on by the administrative authorities. This is one of the most important general principles affecting the use of the writs and lies at the basis of nearly all the cases.

—GOODNOW.[1]

We agree that the courts of the United States, in determining what constitutes an offence against the United States, must resort to the statutes of the United States, enacted in pursuance of the Constitution. . . . The criminal offence is fully and completely defined by the act and the designation by the Commissioner of the particular marks and brands to be used was a mere matter of detail.

—MR. CHIEF JUSTICE FULLER.[2]

I

We have seen that Congress may delegate to the President subordinate discretion, and have examined the scope of the power that it may grant him in this regard.[3] In this chapter[4] we shall consider certain other legal aspects of the delegated ordinance making power. And first of all it is necessary to inquire whether Presidential regulations fall within the category of ' ordinance ' in the formal sense of that term,—in a word, whether they have the criteria which material laws and material ordinances have in common.

These criteria may be summarized as follows: (1) whether final discretion be vested in the issuing officers; (2) whether that discretion relate to the creation of legal rights and duties either of private persons or of governmental organs or officers; (3) whether such rights and duties be of uniform application in the case of material laws or relate to general duties

---

[1] Principles of the Administrative Law of the United States, p. 433, referring to the prerogative writs.

[2] In re Kollock, 165 U. S. 526.

[3] See above, chap. vi.

[4] In chap. xi, below, private remedies will be considered in connection with political safeguards.

in the case of material ordinances; (4) whether to such rights and duties there be attached administrative, judicial, or penal sanctions or some combination of these three sorts. We may with propriety ask if the ordinances of the President fulfill all these conditions of formal ordinances.[5]

While judicial process is not always necessary to due process,[6] nevertheless it is fundamental that appeal may be taken to the courts, collaterally if not directly, from practically every act of the executive department, in order to test, at the minimum, whether there has been an excess or utter lack of jurisdiction.[7] This, however, is true in the American system with reference to legislative as well as executive or administrative acts; and hence is not something which marks off ordinances from statutes. A more searching inquiry is this: into what *other* questions will the courts go, in passing upon the validity of ordinances which are challenged before them? And the chief issue is whether the courts will accept as law every ordinance in the issuance of which there has been no excess of jurisdiction, or whether, on the contrary, they will inquire into the wisdom or motives of the action which produced the ordinance in question. In other words, will the judiciary presume, in the name of due process of law, to go behind the ordinance considered as the governmental product of the exercise by the Executive of a discretionary choice?

---

[5] That is to say, do the ordinances the President may be given authority to issue conform to the definition of the term ordinance as set forth above?

[6] Willoughby, Principles of the Constitutional Law of the United States (student's edition), p. 532.

[7] A court of law will inquire even whether a court martial had jurisdiction of a case decided by such court martial (see Willoughby, Principles of the Constitutional Law of the United States, student's edition, p. 496). The court of one state need not give full faith and credit to a judicial decision of a court of another state if it finds the latter did not have jurisdiction (ibid., p. 79). These facts are cited, not as being strictly in point, but as illustrative of the general principle that in rendering judgment a court will always inquire into the jurisdiction of the court or official upon whose acts it is passing. The rationale of this principle is the fact that under Art. III final determination of jurisdiction is essentially a judicial question.

In Buttfield v. Stranahan [8] the Court say:

> Whether or not the Secretary of the Treasury failed to carry into effect the expressed purpose of Congress and established standards which operated to exclude teas which would have been entitled to admission had proper standards been adopted, is a question we are not called upon to consider. The sufficiency of the standards adopted by the Secretary of the Treasury was committed to his judgment, to be honestly exercised, and if that were important there is no assertion here of bad faith or malice on the part of that officer in fixing the standards, or on the part of the defendant in the performance of the duty resting on him.

In this case, however, there was really no question of due process of law involved, because the denial of the right to import is not a constitutional deprivation of property.[9]

In a very recent case decided by the Supreme Court, Dakota Central Telephone v. South Dakota,[10] there was called into question the right of the President to control the telephone lines under the power conferred upon him by Congress under its war power. In the decision upholding the action of the President under this delegation, the Court said:

> The proposition that the President, in exercising the power, exceeded the authority given him, is based upon two considerations: First, because there was nothing in the conditions at the time the power was exercised which justified the calling into play of the authority; indeed, the contention goes further and assails the motives which it is asserted induced the exercise of the power. But as the contention at best concerns not a want of power, but a mere excess or abuse of discretion in exerting a power given, it is clear that it involves considerations which are beyond the reach of the judicial power. This must be, since, as the court has often pointed out, the judicial may not invade the legislative or executive departments so as to correct alleged mistakes or wrongs arising from asserted abuse of discretion.

With reference to this case, however, it might be claimed that there is special immunity for Presidential action because of the ' political ' character of his determination, or because here was an instance of ' emergency ' action in time of war.

Other cases in point are Martin v. Mott,[11] and Luther v. Borden,[12] where the Court discussed the power of decision

---

[8] 192 U. S. 470.
[9] This point appears to be made by the Court in the opinion.
[10] 250 U. S. 163, 1919.
[11] 12 Wheat. 19.
[12] 7 How. 1.

of the President that the militia be called out.   In both these cases, however, that same ' political ' element was present and frankly recognized by the Supreme Court to be present.   In fact, it seems clear from these cases that the decision of a ' political question ' by the ' political department ' having jurisdiction is not subject to review or question by the judicial department.   Nor could the ' due process ' issue well be raised here.

At the other extreme is the opinion, delivered as late as 1920, in the Ohio Valley Water Company v. Ben Avon Borough et al.[13]   This case may be extreme, but it is cited to show a tendency to distinguish between political and industrial matters in regard to the finality of the discretion.

The opinion in the Ben Avon case has been severely criticized as contrary to the established principle that the courts will not review discretion.[14]   The relation of rate-fixing to the fair valuation of a public utility is called a question of ' policy ' and " not of exact fact or of law ";[14] and on that basis it is contended that it violates due process for a court to review de novo a rate determination on the ground that it may not be based on a fair valuation.

There are, however, other instances where, whether wisely or not, courts have, in exceptionally clear cases, gone behind a particular discretionary determination.   Thus in case of gross and obvious abuse or fraud, at least where this is admitted, the courts may depart from the seemingly absolute rule above stated, and exercise a control over administrative action.   Though decided in a state court, Dental Examiners v. the People[15] is indicative of the attitude the courts of this country are apt to take in clear cases of arbitrary abuse of discretion as to a particular situation.   In ordering by mandamus the State Board of Dental Examiners to grant a license to the relator to practice dentistry on the ground

---

[13] 253 U. S. 473.
[14] See the criticism of this case in Cheadle, "Judicial Review of Administrative Determinations," in Southwestern Political and Social Science Quarterly, June, 1922.
[15] 123 Ill. 227, 1887.

that their refusal was admitted on demurrer to be through malice, the Supreme Court of Illinois, speaking through Mr. Justice Magruder, said:

> In the People ex. rel. Sheppard v. State Board of Dental Examiners, 110 Ill. 180 . . . the mandamus was refused on the general ground that the writ will not be issued to compel the performance of acts or duties, which necessarily call for the exercise of judgment and discretion on the part of the officer or body at whose hands their performance is required.
> But if a discretionary power is exercised with manifest injustice, the courts are not precluded from commanding its due exercise.

The writ of mandamus does not lie against the President,[16] to be sure, but this limitation would not apply to a cabinet officer. Even so, however, the case is not entirely in point, because the power to issue a uniform rule is less susceptible of exercise in a malicious manner than is a particular determination; and also because a rule can be questioned in the process of its enforcement in particular cases, whereas a particular act or omission is itself a step in enforcement, and must be attacked, or the individual has no later redress. The dental case is thus cited to bring out the point, that while particular discretion may in clear cases be attacked for motive, discretion as to a rule can rarely if ever be.

Our conclusions relative to this first criterion of 'formal ordinances' may now be drawn: It is a general principle that the legislature may vest final discretionary (including rule-making) authority in the Executive, and that this precludes judicial interference. In such cases executive justice is clearly more 'due' than judicial justice;[17] only the courts

---

[16] See below, chap. xi.

[17] If Congress can relieve itself of this discretionary responsibility at all, why can it not vest it finally and exclusively in the Executive? It is certainly due process for decision of what the law shall be to be made by the political departments without judicial interference. For the court to go into the wisdom of a law of Congress would be for it to violate the principle of the separation of powers. Why should not the same principle apply to judicial review of 'administrative legislation'? Is executive exercise of discretion as to concrete details less 'due' than legislative? In point of fact, it is more so, in these days, at least. However, traditionally the courts have tended to exercise greater checks on executive than on legislative action; and it will of course be admitted that they

may always inquire whether the officer was within his jurisdiction,[18] and perhaps whether the ordinance was on its face
unreasonable.[18] This rule limiting judicial action is absolute
in the case of 'political' discretion; but it is weakened in
the case of discretion relative to vested interests, and perhaps
personal liberty, where there are at least some fairly definite
objective criteria to guide decision.[19] Between these extremes
there is a group of cases where, in general, the rule holds
good. Perhaps it ought to hold good in all cases, except
where there is patent fraud or gross abuse of power.[20]

We should contrast the attitude of our courts on this
subject with that of the Council of State in France. The
practice of that body of holding administrative acts null and
void as involving a misapplication of power (détournement de
pouvoir) is claimed by M. Duguit to mean the doing away
with discretion. The act may be held to have 'an ulterior
motive,' or to be for a purpose other than that for which
the power conferred by law upon the administrative officer
was intended to be exercised.[21]

II

Valid ordinances of the President have a legal status as
juristic acts which the courts must accept as authoritative.
This status they share with all other authorized acts of government, whether or not they are legislative in character.
In this sense an administrative finding of an objective fact
'has the force of law' in the same sense as a statute or
ordinance. There is this basic difference, however, that the

---

should exercise at least as much. Perhaps, after all, the Ben Avon
case reveals scarcely more meddling with administrative discretion
than the Lochner case revealed with reference to legislative discretion.

[18] See, on the decisions reviewing questions of fact, law, mixed
fact and law, and discretion, Albertsworth, "Judicial Review of
Administrative Action by the Federal Supreme Court," in Harvard
Law Review, December, 1921. On 'reasonableness,' see City of
Clinton v. Phillips, 58 Ill. 102, dealing with a city ordinance.

[19] Such as, rate-fixing by public utilities commissions.

[20] See the opinion of the writer in note 17 above.

[21] "The French Administrative Courts," in Political Science Quarterly, September, 1914.

administrative act is issued in pursuance of law while the statute or ordinance is creative of law.   An administrative determination may finally and authoritatively establish a fact, but an ordinance creates rights and duties.   In the case of *Verwaltungsverordnungen,* these rights and duties are of a sort that relate to the internal affairs of the administration and are enforceable mainly through the President's power of removal.   In the case of *Rechtsverordnungen,* the rights and duties which are created relate to private interests, whether by way of imposing private duties, or of granting private rights or privileges.   The second criterion is thus satisfied.

III

With reference to the third criterion a solution may easily be given.   It is true that we have affirmed the legislative character of discretionary rules and denied the legislative character of particular acts of discretion.   Does this mean that the latter sort of action is permissible where the former would not be under the due process clause?   On the contrary, quite the reverse is the case.   Uniformity means equality of treatment, and, as between discretion displaying this characteristic, and that which is particular and cannot find its place in the régime of law, the former is prima facie more due or reasonable.   It might be possible to argue that the delegation of discretion of any sort is both a delegation of legislative power and a taking without due process of law. We have seen that this is not necessarily so; but it is sounder to argue that it is so than to claim that a delegation is less reasonable when it authorizes uniform rules, equally and impartially applicable to all in the same class, than when it authorizes subjective determination of particular cases.   The technical distinction between legislative and sub-legislative discretion has no significance for American constitutional law, unless the delegation of the former be considered more apt to be constitutional.   Whether it is or not, depends upon the nature of the subject to be dealt with.[22]

[22] It should be made clear that the thesis of this paragraph is

IV

In the first chapter it is set forth that the sanction of legislation, while an essential criterion, is not necessarily confined to the penal sanction. Any legal means of enforcing a rule may properly be described as a sanction.[23] Thus when in 1794 Congress delegated to President Washington the power not only to establish an embargo during the recess of that body, but also to issue the necessary orders for its enforcement, it was delegating to him the authority to provide what is best described as an administrative sanction. Naval vessels, acting under an order of the President issued in pursuance of such a delegation, might legally restrain vessels which sought to violate the embargo. This is strictly a more direct means of enforcing obedience than is the method of punishing violations of a rule. Then there is what we may term the judicial sanction, which is equally

---

that where Congress can vest sub-legislative discretion it can a fortiori vest co-legislative discretion to the same extent. It is not claimed that a delegated power to exercise discretion in a series of particular cases involves the power to issue uniform rules having the force of law, in the absence of express statutory authorization. Logically this might be so; but actually the courts will go behind such rules and seek the reasonableness of their application in each individual case unless the said rules are expressly authorized by law. How far it will go behind particular determinations again depends on whether or not the legislature delegates particular discretion to the administration. If it does not, it is the court that has final decision as to the conformity of the individual action with an abstract legislative rule. In general jurisprudence we make a distinction between rule-making and particular discretion. But in American constitutional law an administrative official has power finally to exercise either sort only when that power is specially granted by statute. In case it is granted, discretion as to a rule seems prima facie more reasonable than discretion as to a particular situation. At any rate, both sorts are delegated and upheld by the courts.

[23] It may be said, however, that in the case of the 'sanction' of removal, as a disciplinary measure in administration, the President is not bound to exercise his power in a given case unless he so desires; while in the case of a penal sanction, it is enforced by the courts, which may not refrain from enforcement. Furthermore, civil service rules (Verwaltungsverordnungen) cannot be enforced by injunction issued by a court of equity to prevent their violation (White v. Berry, 171 U. S. 366). Contrast the rule in France (Garner, "Judicial Control of Administrative and Legislative Acts in France," in American Political Science Review, November, 1915).

consistent with due process of law and equally effective in many cases. The outstanding examples are the prerogative writs of injunction and mandamus. These also are more direct than is the penal sanction. And certainly judicial action is " due process " par excellence.

What about the penal sanction itself? It was maintained in Chapter VI, that Congress cannot leave to the Executive the determination, in his discretion, of a ' reasonable ' penalty for the violation of statutes or of ordinances. But can Congress itself make the violation of executive ordinances issued under its authority a crime, and provide a punishment therefor? In the United States v. Grimaud [24] an affirmative answer was given. Let us examine the facts of the case.

The forest reserve acts authorized the Secretary of Agriculture to "make provisions for the protection against destruction by fire and depredations upon the public forests and forest reservations . . . and he may make such rules and regulations and establish such service as will insure the objects of such reservations; namely, to regulate their occupancy and use, and to preserve the forests thereon from destruction; and any violation of the provisions of this act or such rules and regulations shall be punished " as prescribed. Regulation 45 of the Secretary issued under this act June 12, 1906, reads as follows: " All persons must secure permits before grazing any stock in a forest reserve, except the few head in actual use by prospectors, campers, and travelers, and milch or work animals, not exceeding a total of six head, owned by bona fide settlers residing in or near a forest reserve, which are excepted and require no permit." The defendants were indicted for grazing sheep on the Sierra Forest Reserve without having obtained a permit as required by Regulation 45. They demurred, their several demurrers were sustained, and the government appealed to the Supreme Court. This case was United States v. Grimaud. The counsel for the defendants in error claimed that the act was unconstitutional " for the reason that it does not

_____
[24] 220 U. S. 506.

sufficiently define, or define at all, what acts done or omitted to be done, within the supposed purview of the said act, shall constitute an offense or offenses against the United States. . . . It is not within the power of Congress, under the Constitution of the United States, to delegate to the Secretary of the Interior, or the Secretary of Agriculture of the United States, or any other person, authority or power to determine what acts shall be criminal; and the act in question is a delegation of legislative power to an executive officer to define and establish what shall constitute the essential elements of a crime against the United States."

This contention was denied by the Court. It was admitted that Congress cannot delegate its legislative power, " but," said the Court, " the authority to make administrative rules is not a delegation of legislative power, nor are such rules raised from an administrative to a legislative character because the violation thereof is punished as a public offense." And again the Court declared:

The Secretary of Agriculture could not make rules and regulations for any and every purpose. . . . As to those here involved, they all relate to matters clearly indicated and authorized by Congress. The subjects as to which the Secretary can regulate are defined. The lands are set apart as a forest reserve. He is required to make provisions to protect them from depredations and from harmful uses. He is authorized to " regulate their occupancy and use and to preserve the forests thereon from destruction." A violation of reasonable rules regulating the use and occupancy of the property is made a crime, not by the Secretary, but by Congress. The statute, not the Secretary, fixes the penalty. . . . The offense is not against the Secretary, but, as the indictment properly concludes, " contrary to the laws of the United States and the peace and dignity thereof."

Essentially the same situation was involved in the more recent case of McKinley v. United States.[25] This case involved the constitutionality of sec. 13 of chapter 15 of an act of May 18, 1917, which provides:

That the Secretary of War is hereby authorized, empowered, and directed during the present war to do everything by him deemed necessary to suppress and prevent the keeping or setting up of houses of ill fame, brothels, or bawdy houses within such dis-

[25] 249 U. S. 397, 1919.

tance as he may deem needful of any military camp, station, fort, post, cantonment, training, or mobilization place, and any person, corporation, partnership, or association . . . who shall violate any order, rule, or regulation issued to carry out the object and purpose of this section shall, unless otherwise punishable under the Articles of War, be deemed guilty of a misdemeanor and be punished by a fine of not more than $1,000 or imprisonment for not more than twelve months, or both.[26]

Plaintiffs in error were indicted, convicted and sentenced upon indictment in a District Court for violation of a regulation of the Secretary of War made under the authorization of this act. The indictment charged that they did unlawfully keep and set up a house of ill fame within the distance designated by the Secretary of War, under the act, to wit, within five miles of a certain military station of the United States. They contended that Congress had no constitutional authority to pass the act. In a memorandum opinion Mr. Justice Day said:

Congress having adopted restrictions designated to guard and promote the health and efficiency of the men composing the Army, in a manner so obvious as that embodied in the statute under consideration, may leave details to the regulation of the head of an executive department and punish those who violate the restrictions. This is also well settled by the repeated decisions of this court.

Mention may be made in passing of a case decided earlier than these two, which involved the same principle, except that the subject on which the administrative agent was delegated rule-making powers (namely, the marks and brands which packages of oleomargarine were to bear) was distinctly narrower than in the cases given above. That was the case of In re Kollock.[27] By an act of Congress retail dealers in oleomargarine were required to " pack the oleomargarine sold by them in suitable wooden or paper packages, which shall be marked and branded as the Commissioner of Internal Revenue, with the approval of the Secretary of the Treasury, shall prescribe." Fine and imprisonment were denounced on " every person who knowingly sells or offers for sale, or delivers or offers to deliver, any oleomargarine in any other

---

[26] 40 Stat. L., 76, 83.   [27] 165 U. S. 526, 1897.

form than in new wooden or paper packages as above described, or who packs in any package any oleomargarine in any manner contrary to law, or who falsely brands any package or affirms a stamp on any package denoting a less amount of tax than that required by law." Kollock was convicted, in the words of the Court, "as a retail dealer in oleomargarine, of knowingly selling and delivering one-half pound of that commodity, which was not packed in a wooden or paper package bearing thereon any or either of the marks or characters provided for by the regulations and set forth in the indictment." Before the Supreme Court it was argued for Kollock that the statute was invalid because it did not "define what act done or omitted to be done shall constitute a criminal offense," and delegated the power to " determine what acts shall be criminal" by leaving the stamps, marks and brands to be defined by the Commissioner.

Mr. Chief Justice Fuller, who delivered the opinion of the Court, said:

We agree that the courts of the United States, in determining what constitutes an offense against the United States, must resort to the statutes of the United States, enacted in pursuance of the Constitution. But here the law required the packages to be marked and branded; prohibited the sale of packages that were not; and prescribed the punishment for sales in violation of its provisions; while the regulations simply describe the particular marks, stamps, and brands to be used. The criminal offense is fully and completely defined by the act and the designation by the Commissioner of the particular marks and brands to be used was a mere matter of detail. . . . We think the act not open to the objection urged, and that it is disposed of by previous decisions.

Prior to these cases was the decision in United States v. Eaton,[28] which is easily distinguished from them. To realize the true meaning of the Eaton case it is necessary to have a clear understanding of the terms of the oleomargarine act of August 2, 1866, under which the indictment was returned, and of the regulation issued under the delegation of that act. Sec. 5 of the act required manufacturers of oleomargarine to keep such books and render such returns as the Commissioner of Internal Revenue, with the approval of

[28] 144 U. S. 677.

the Secretary of the Treasury, might, by regulation, require. No part of the act specifically imposed this same duty upon wholesale dealers in oleomargarine. In fact, Congress later imposed such a duty upon them, but provided no penalty. But sec. 20 authorized the Commissioner, with the approval of the Secretary, generally to make "all needful regulations" to carry the act into effect; and sec. 18 provided punishment for the failure to do anything "required by law in the carrying on or conducting of his business." A regulation issued under sec. 20 required wholesale dealers to keep books and make a monthly return. Eaton, a wholesale dealer, was indicted under sec. 18 for a violation of this regulation. The Supreme Court sustained Eaton's demurrer; but from the opinion it is clear that the Court did not rest its decision upon the thesis that Congress could not make the violation of a regulation a crime, but distinctly upon the basis that, in view of the fact that under our system the benefit of the doubt in criminal cases is given to the accused, it was not clear that Congress had make the violation of this particular sort of regulation a crime. The combination of circumstances which made this doubtful was: (1) that the act prescribed punishment for the omission to do something prescribed by law without mentioning the omission to abide by the regulations issued under the law; (2) that the very thing required by the regulation of wholesale dealers had been specifically by the law required of manufacturers without any mention of wholesale dealers; while later Congress did require this of wholesale dealers, but without penalty. The court argued, therefore, that while the regulation might be valid as a requirement under the delegation, what is required is not a thing so "required by law" as that its violation is a crime under sec. 18. The case is thus clearly distinct from the others; though it is important in that it signifies the intention of the Court, while admitting the power of Congress to make the violation of an ordinance a criminal offense, to apply the rule of strict construction in deciding whether it has so done.

It is thus equally evident that Congress can delegate a power of regulation for defined purposes and provide for the punishment of violations of the resulting ordinances, and that it must be made clear by Congress that the violation of the particular type of ordinance in question is meant to be punished. The point which is not certain is just how clear this must be made. In the Kollock case the penal clause spoke of selling oleomargarine " in any other form than in new wooden or paper packages as above described." Thus here no mention was made of the regulations by name; yet the words " as above described " obviously referred to them, as the statute left the brands on such wooden or paper packages to be determined by such regulations. Between this case and the Eaton case there is a series of possibilities where the absence of cases makes it possible only to conjecture. Thus it is not likely that the absence of the statutory requirement that manufacturers keep books and make reports would have altered the situation in the Eaton case, as long as the penal section spoke of the requirements of law only. And it is likely that if the penal section had specifically mentioned regulations, the Court would have held that the omission, from the clause requiring manufacturers to report, of all reference to wholesale dealers excluded an ordinance requiring reports of the latter from the range of regulations punishable under sec. 18.

Thus the mere fact of making criminal the violation of executive ordinances does not of itself render them legislative in the sense that the delegation of power to issue them is unconstitutional. Nor is the punishment of an individual for the violation of such an ordinance a deprivation of liberty or property without due process of law. Here again, however, the question arises whether this applies only to ' executing ' ordinances, ordinances which regulate the exercise of a privilege, ordinances which regulate a mere minor detail, ordinances which prohibit activities which the individual has no right to carry on, ordinances which are calculated to prevent fraud in the conduct of private business, etc. Might it be made to apply equally to important ordinances regulating private action in accordance with a broadly worded delegation and in regard to a matter affecting personal liberty or vested rights? We have seen that where the government could regulate such matters at all, it was a due process to delegate to the Executive, within the limits set forth in the preceding chapter, a power of ordinance in regard thereto. And similarly it would seem that where the government can regulate the subjects, and where the Executive can be granted a limited discretion in the regulation thereof, it is wholly unreasonable to hold that the Executive's share of the regulation cannot be made effective by legislatively imposed penal sanctions.

V

To what extent, if any, must the Executive in the issuance of ordinances act in accordance with a certain procedure? In so far as special procedure is requisite it is clear that to that extent the ordinance making power differs from the law making power. The methods [29] of legislation (except as to specific constitutional requirement) as well as its products (except with reference to jurisdiction) are beyond the control of the courts.

In this respect there seems to be a distinction between political and industrial discretion. Notice and hearing are, in cases of emergency action, neither required by the courts [30] nor desirable in point of policy. In the case of administrative tribunals set up to decide matters of industrial relations, there is a tendency in legislation in this country to make notice and hearing requisite. Mr. Taft, in his book on the Presidency, noted with approval this tendency; [31] and it is not with surprise that we find him uttering the following significant dictum in Wichita R. R. & Light Company v. Public Utilities Commission of Kansas: [32]

---

[29] Cf. Commonwealth v. Sisson, 189 Mass. 247.
[30] Cf. Martin v. Mott, 12 Wheat. 19.
[31] Our Chief Magistrate and His Powers, p. 82.
[32] 260 U. S. 48.

The maxim that a legislature may not delegate legislative power has some qualifications, as in the creation of municipalities, and also in the creation of administrative boards to apply to the myriad details of rate schedules the regulatory police power of the state. The latter qualification is made necessary in order that the legislative power may be effectively exercised. In creating such an administrative agency the legislature, to prevent its being a pure delegation of legislative power, must enjoin upon it a certain course of procedure and certain rules of decision in the performance of its function. It is a wholesome and necessary principle that such an agency must pursue the procedure and rules enjoined and show a substantial compliance therewith to give validity to its action. When, therefore, such an administrative agency is required as a condition precedent to an order, to make a finding of facts, the validity of the order must rest upon the needed finding. If it is lacking, the order is ineffective.

It is pressed upon us that the lack of an express finding may be supplied by implication and by reference to the averments of the petitioner invoking the action of the Commission. We can not agree to this. . . .

This case merely enforced with strictness the requirements of the statute; but it raises the interesting possibility that, in industrial ordinance making, due process may make notice and hearing essential.[33] Such an interpretation of due process would be altogether desirable. The situation is entirely different from that involved in the issuance of ordinances to meet a wartime or other crisis. Since the justification of delegations is that they lend opportunity for a more scientific approach than is found in regulation by the popular assembly, it is in conformity with the essential idea of executive legislation that the executive department be required to observe certain procedure in exercising its discretion. This is furthermore a matter upon which the courts are entirely competent to check up. It is utterly unlike the situation with reference to judicial interference with discretion proper, judicial review of the expediency of the substantive part of an ordinance. This last is a matter about which the administrative officer is presumably competent, the judge essentially incompetent, wisely to decide. But with reference to

---

[33] The Interstate Commerce Commission is required by statute to give notice and a hearing in rate-fixing, though its orders may be issued to a single road and are not necessarily uniform, except in relation to those who use the roads.

procedure the courts can review administrative action without usurping policy-determining functions.

Here also, there seems to be a class of cases between the extremes, where notice and a hearing are desirable, but probably not essential.

Administrative hearings held by the ordinance making authority precede issuance.[34] For the most part, judicial hearings relate to the enforcement rather than the issuance of ordinances. Judicial process is essentially the process furnished an individual in respect to his private rights and interests. Such process is essential to 'due process,' at some stage, for review of administrative action with reference, at the minimum, to jurisdiction and regularity of forms and procedure. It may precede enforcement, as where the administrative officers have to get the courts to enforce their regulations;[35] or it may come after summary action, as where a ministerial officer is sued in damages.[36] Whether it shall be anterior or posterior to the enforcement of the ordinance depends upon the urgency of the need for action.[37]

Still another question is the forms of action by which the judicial process is put into motion. This is closely related to subjects already discussed, such as the questions into which a court will go; the procedure which the ordinance making or ordinance administering authority must observe; and the necessity for some sort of judicial process to inquire at least whether action has been ultra vires. The form of action may have some bearing upon the question as to what the court will inquire into.[38] However, with reference to

---

[34] But of course administrative hearing may be again requisite in connection with the enforcement of an ordinance. This, however, is in itself a broad question of administrative law in which the same rules should apply that apply in connection with the enforcement of a statute. Nor can we here go into hearings in connection with particular, as distinguished from ordinance making, discretionary action.

[35] United States v. Grimaud, 220 U. S. 506.

[36] See chap. xi.

[37] Lawton v. Steele, 119 N. Y. 236.

[38] That is to say, in considering what questions a court will go into in passing upon the validity of an ordinance, one must have defi-

the above topics of inquiry we have attempted to state the
general rule in broad terms, rather than to distinguish
individual cases.   Consideration of the problem from the
point of view primarily of the forms of action will be made
in a later chapter.[39]

VI

There are other important legal matters which demand
our attention.   The Constitution enjoins the President to
" take care that the Laws be faithfully executed."   In
Anglo-Saxon countries this is the primary executive duty;
and it includes not only the obligation to take all steps
within his legal competence to put into motion the administrative machinery necessary to enforce the enactments of
the legislature, but also the obligation to make such determinations of fact and to exercise such discretion as the said
enactments may impose upon him.   The question arises
whether statutory provisions delegating such authority to
the President are, or may be, mandatory.   As a matter
of fact, they are in numerous cases so worded as to make it
clear that the discretion includes not only the determination of the content of the ordinance, but also the decision
whether the circumstances call for its issuance at all.   In
other cases, however, the meaning is not clear; or else it
is specifically made the duty of the Chief Executive to issue
the regulations in question.   Perhaps in case of doubt the
will of the legislature can be ascertained from the character and general purpose of the enactment.   Where it is
unquestionable that the delegation is meant to be mandatory, it would seem that, under the duty of law enforcement
in its broadest sense, the President is bound, by constitutional morality, to carry out the legislative instructions.
But the obligation is not strictly legal.   It is the better rule

---

nitely in mind the form of action—whether it is a civil suit against
an official or a criminal prosecution, etc.—involved in the case under
discussion. For the two questions are by no means unrelated, even
though some general principles seem to run through the cases
relating to all forms of action.
   [39] Chap. xi.

that the President is not subject to judicial process; [40] and, therefore, there are no legal means, by mandamus or otherwise, to compel him to act.

In Dunlap v. United States [41] the plaintiff had sued in the Court of Claims for rebate under a statute of Congress providing that a manufacturer using alcohol in the arts " may use the same under regulations to be prescribed by the Secretary of the Treasury," and get a rebate if he complied with such regulations. The Secretary had not issued any regulations under the act, but instead reported to Congress that the enforcement of the regulations which he contemplated would cost at least half a million dollars annually, for which no appropriation was available, and that therefore he could not execute the section until Congress took further action in the matter. The Supreme Court, sustaining the decision of the Court of Claims, held that the right to rebate was not " a right granted *in praesenti* to all persons who might, after the passage of the law, actually use alcohol in the arts . . . to a rebate or repayment of the tax paid on such alcohol, but that the grant of the right was conditioned on use in compliance with regulations to be prescribed, in the absence of which the right could not vest so as to create a cause of action by reason of the unregulated use." In support of this view, though not necessary to it, was the opinion expressed by the Court that Congress " may reasonably be held to have left it to the Secretary to determine whether or not such regulations could be framed, and if so, whether further legislation would be required." Said the opinion:

If the duty of the Secretary to prescribe regulations was merely ministerial, and a mandamus could, under circumstances, have issued to compel him to discharge it, would not the judgment at which he arrived, the action which he took, and his reference of the matter to Congress, have furnished a complete defense? But it is insisted that by reason of the exercise of discretionary power necessarily involved in prescribing regulations as contemplated the Secretary could not have been thus compelled to act. We think the argument entitled to great weight, and that it demonstrates the intention of Congress to leave the entire matter to the Treasury

---

[40] See ibid.   [41] 173 U. S. 65.

Department to ascertain what would be needed in order to carry the section into effect.

The doctrine of the decision seems to be that where Congress gives a privilege which is to be exercised in conformity with executive ordinances, such a privilege does not vest as a right until such ordinances have been issued. But there are suggested by the opinion the further principles, which we hold to be true, that where Congress had not made their issuance explicitly mandatory, the Executive is relieved from even the moral responsibility to issue them, at least in cases where he can furnish such a valid excuse as here, and that a mandamus will not lie to compel even a departmental head to act. It is believed, however, that where their issuance is made mandatory, the moral obligation is present, at least unless there is such legitimate reason. But the nature of this obligation is more a question of constitutional ethics than of constitutional law.[42]

VII

An interesting point was considered in the case of Campbell v. United States.[43] In this case the law had provided for a drawback on imported articles manufactured in this country from imported raw material on which duty had been paid, in accordance with regulations to be prescribed by the Secretary of the Treasury. The Secretary of the Treasury issued his regulations under this act, and certain exporters of linseed cake manufactured from imported linseed on which duties had been paid applied for a drawback by making an entry in all respects in conformity with the regulations of the Secretary. But the collector, acting under instructions from the Secretary, refused to perform any act prescribed by the regulations except to receive the entry. Before the Supreme Court the government counsel claimed

---

[42] That is, unless the court will issue the writ of mandamus to compel the official to exercise his discretion in some manner (Cf. Willoughby, Principles of the Constitutional Law of the United States, student's edition, pp. 540-541).

[43] 107 U. S. 407.

that this action on his part defeated the claim of the exporters. The Court held, however, that they were entitled to the drawback. It said:

It would be a curious thing to hold that Congress, after clearly defining the right of the importer to receive drawback upon subsequent exportation of the imported article on which he had paid duty, had empowered the Secretary by regulations, which might be proper to secure the government against fraud, to defeat totally the right which Congress had granted. If the regulations of themselves worked such a result, no court would hesitate to hold them invalid as being altogether unreasonable.

But the regulations in this case are not unreasonable. Nor do they interpose any obstacle to the full assertion and adjustment of plaintiff's right. It is the order of the Secretary of the Treasury forbidding the collector to proceed under these regulations or in any other mode, which is the real obstacle. Is that order a defense to this action? Can the Secretary, by this order, do what he could not do by regulations, repeal or annul the law? . . .

The Court of Claims makes the mistake of supposing that the claim is founded on the regulations of the Secretary of the Treasury. This view cannot be sustained. It is the *law* which gives the right, and the fact that the customs officers refuse to obey these regulations cannot defeat a right which the act of Congress gives.

This case is thus authority for the statement that the official who issues regulations carrying out the establishment of a private right by a statute cannot properly refuse to enforce his own regulations. For him to do so would be to defeat the aim of the statute, and to frustrate a right granted by the statute under which he acted.

VIII

The problem of due process of law not only deals with the extent to which the legislature may go in delegating ordinance making powers to the Executive; but it is also concerned with the statutory requirements as to procedure and judicial review. Provided, however, that the statute fulfills in these two respects all the requirements of due process, the sole question which remains is one of jurisdiction: has the Executive acted beyond his statutory powers? [44]

---

[44] And the main questions which arise in this connection are the following: (1) Has the Executive complied with all the requirements for this class of cases in respect to the procedure by which he arrives at his determination in issuing the ordinance? (2) Does

It is a logical corollary of the nature of the delegated power of ordinance that it must be limited strictly to the terms of the delegation.   The resulting regulation cannot conflict with, or go beyond the sphere indicated by, the statute of grant.   In either case it would be an ultra vires act, which it would be the duty of the courts to refuse to enforce in cases where it might be involved.   The Supreme Court of the United States has been properly strict in its application of this principle, as a few illustrative cases will show.

In Morrill v. Jones [45] Congress had provided that " Animals, alive, specially imported, for breeding purposes, from beyond the seas, shall be admitted free (of duty), upon proof thereof satisfactory to the Secretary of the Treasury, and under such regulations as he may prescribe." [46]   Article 383 of the Treasury Customs Regulations provided that the collector must " be satisfied that the animals are of superior stock, adapted to improving the breed in the United States." Jones imported stock " specially . . . for breeding purposes," but the collector, acting under the above-mentioned regulation, refused to allow them to go duty free.   In upholding the right of Jones, under the statute, to import the stock in question, without paying duty, the Court said:

> The Secretary of the Treasury cannot, by his regulations, alter or amend a revenue law. All he can do is to regulate the mode of proceeding to carry into effect what Congress has enacted. In the present case, we are entirely satisfied the regulation acted upon by the collector was in excess of the power of the Secretary. The statute clearly includes animals of all classes. The regulation seeks to confine its operation to animals of " superior stock." This is manifestly an attempt to put into the body of the statute a limitation which Congress did not think it necessary to prescribe. . . . In our opinion, the object of the Secretary could only be accomplished by an amendment of the law. That is not the office of a treasury regulation.

Merritt v. Welsh,[47] like the case just considered, involved

---

the ordinance itself come within the limits of the terms of the delegation or is it in part or wholly ultra vires?   (3) Has there been " an arbitrary exercise of discretion through bias, fraud, or discrimination "?

[45] 106 U. S. 466.

[46] Rev. Stat. 2505.

[47] 104 U. S. 694. Cf. United States v. Two Hundred Barrels, etc.,

a regulation issued under a revenue law. Congress had provided duties on sugar according to the Dutch standard in color. The collector of the port of New York charged Welsh, the original plaintiff, according to a higher standard than his sugar tested out under the Dutch standard in color, claiming that it was artifically colored in the manufacture. He acted under general instructions from the Treasury Department, issued July 19 and September 2, 1879, which raised the class of sugars in question above their "apparent color," as imported, in accordance with tests as to the percentage of crystalline sugar they contained. But the Supreme Court, when the case came before it, refused to enforce these treasury instructions on the ground that they substituted another test in the place of the one clearly provided by the statute. It said:

Perhaps Congress may have acted under a mistaken idea, that color would always indicate quality. Perhaps, up to the time that the law was passed, as the processes of manufacture had been conducted, color was an approximate or general indication of quality. Suppose this to be so, does it derogate from the fact, that color was the standard which Congress, with the lights which it had, saw fit to adopt? Does it not tend to fortify that fact? If it be found by experience that the standard is a fallacious one, can the Executive Department supply the defects of legislation? Congress alone has the authority to levy duties. Its will alone is to be sought. . . . If experience shows that Congress acted under a mistaken impression, that does not authorize the Treasury Department or the courts to take the part of legislative guardians and, by construction, to make new laws which they imagine Congress would have made had it been properly informed, but which Congress itself, on being properly informed, has not, as yet, seen fit to make.

It is argued, that, although the Dutch standard of color is named in the statute, yet the intent of the law was to adopt it as a standard of quality; and if, in consequence of changes in the mode of manufacturing, it ceases to be such, the reason of the law ought to prevail, and quality ought to be still the test. And that quality was the object sought is inferred from the language of sections 2914 and 2915 of the Revised Statutes.

This reasoning would be very good if the law prescribing the standard were not explicit in its terms. Whatever may have been in the minds of individual members of Congress, the legislative intent is to be sought, first, from the words they have used. If

---

95 U. S. 571; United States v. Symonds, 120 U. S. 46.   Contrast United States v. Bailey, 9 Pet. 238; Caha v. United States, 152 U. S. 211.

they are clear, we need go no further. . . . There is no obscurity or ambiguity here.

The Court did not consider that there was anything in the provisos of the statute modifying or qualifying the plainly provided standard. These provisos authorized the Secretary of the Treasury to " select and furnish " the standard to collectors of ports of entry and by regulations to require the proper officers to take samples from packages " in such manner as to ascertain the true quality of such sugar." But this power of regulation clearly did not give the Secretary the power to change the standard explicitly laid down by Congress itself.

In the former of these cases the regulation had added to the provision of the law; in the latter they had substituted some other provision for that of the law. But since in both cases the provisions of the law were complete in themselves, and it was intended by Congress that the administrative rules merely prescribe the manner of their execution, the Court rightly held that the rules in question were invalid. Executing ordinances must under no circumstances add to or supercede the substantive rights and duties as defined in the statute.

IX

Valid ordinances protect federal officers who act under them against any state authority which may attempt to fine the federal officers for such action, or otherwise to interfere with their faithful discharge of the duties prescribed in the ordinances. This is so because of federal supremacy; which in this respect means that a federal officer acting under valid federal authorization cannot be interfered with by the states. The point was decided in Boske v. Comingore.[48] In that case Comingore, a collector of internal revenue, refused to file certain copies of records with certain state authorities, because he was prohibited so to do by regulations promulgated under statutory authority by

---

[48] 177 U. S. 459.

the Commissioner of Internal Revenue with the approval of the Secretary of the Treasury. Thereupon the collector was fined and caused to be imprisoned for contempt by a notary. He sued out a writ of habeas corpus and was discharged from custody by the United States district court of the Kentucky district. Appeal was taken to the Supreme Court, which affirmed the decision of the lower court. "Manifestly," said Mr. Justice Harlan in his opinion for the Court, "he could not have filed the copies called for without violating regulations formally promulgated by the Commissioner of Internal Revenue with the approval of the Secretary of the Treasury. If these regulations were such as the Secretary could legally prescribe, then, it must be conceded, the state authorities were without jurisdiction to compel the collector to violate them." This, it was held, was the case; and the order of release was affirmed.[49]

---

[49] Other cases of which space forbids extended discussion are: United States v. Eliason, 16 Pet. 289; United States v. Williams, 194 U. S. 279; United States v. Midwest Oil Co., 236 U. S. 459; Mitchell v. Harmony, 13 How. 115; United States v. Antikamnia Chemical Co., 231 U. S. 654; United States v. United Verde Copper Co., 196 U. S. 207; United States v. George, 228 U. S. 14; Illinois Central R. R. Co. v. McKendree, 203 U. S. 514; Merritt v. Cameron, 137 U. S. 542; Williamson v. United States, 207 U. S. 425; Deslions v. La Compagnie Générale Transatlantique, 210 U. S. 95; Grisar v. United States, 6 Wall. 363; Albridge v. Williams, 3 How. 1, 29. See also Opin. of the Attys. Gen. 2: 263, 320, 586; 5: 630; 6: 75, 220, 157; 7: 534; 9: 463, 517; 10: 469; 13: 416; 15: 94. Still another topic is whether the President may revoke or alter or completely revise his ordinances in the absence of express statutory authorization. Revocation might so affect statutory rights as to be invalid. But why should alteration or revision be invalid, if the new ordinances are not retroactively applied? See Lieber, Remarks on the Army Regulations, p. 39. Professor Powell uses the simile of the mosaic, which suggests the position of the President as one of *functus officio.*

CHAPTER VIII

THE RELATION OF THE PRESIDENT TO THE ORDINANCE MAKING POWERS OF HEADS OF DEPARTMENTS AND FEDERAL ADMINISTRATIVE COMMISSIONS

The President speaks and acts through the heads of the several departments in relation to the subjects which appertain to their respective duties. . . . We consider the act of the War Department in requiring this reservation to be made, as being in legal contemplation the act of the President.

—Wilcox v. Jackson.[1]

The President . . . is plainly bound in duty to render unquestioning obedience to Congress. And if it be his duty to obey, still more is obedience the bounden duty of his subordinates.

—WOODROW WILSON.[2]

On viewing the course which the proceedings of the War Department have not infrequently taken, I find that I owe it to my own responsibility, as well as to other considerations, to make some remarks on the relations in which the head of the department stands to the President, and to lay down some rules for conducting the business of the department which are dictated by the nature of those relations.

In general, the Secretary of War, like the heads of the other departments, as well by express statute as by the structure of the Constitution, acts under the authority and subject to the decisions and instructions of the President, with the exception of cases where the law may vest special and independent powers in the head of the department. . . .

The following course will be observed in future:

To be previously communicated to the President:

1. Orders from the Department of War establishing general or permanent regulations. . . .

—PRESIDENT MADISON to his Secretary of War.[3]

The head of each Department is authorized to prescribe regulations, not inconsistent with law, for the government of his Department, the conduct of its officers and clerks, the distribution and performance of its business, and the custody, use, and preservation of the records, papers, and property appertaining to it.

—Rev. Stat.[4]

Can it be said that to invest the secretary of the treasury with authority to prescribe regulations not inconsistent with law for the

---

[1] 13 Pet. 498.
[2] Congressional Government, pp. 273-274.
[3] Writings of James Madison, vol. iii, pp. 417-419.
[4] Sec. 161.

conduct of the business of his department, and to provide for the custody, use and preservation of the records, papers and property appertaining to it, was not a means appropriate and plainly adapted to the successful administration of the affairs of that department? Manifestly not. . . .

In determining whether the regulations promulgated by him are consistent with law, we must apply the rule of decision which controls when an act of Congress is assailed as not being within the powers conferred upon it by the Constitution; that is to say, a regulation adopted under section 161 of the Revised Statutes should not be disregarded or annulled unless, in the judgment of the court, it is plainly and palpably inconsistent with law.

—MR. JUSTICE HARLAN.[5]

I

The President may act through the head of the proper department in issuing most ordinances which he may be authorized by statute to issue; and in such case the act of the head of the department is the equivalent in law of the act of the President. The broad principle is suggested by the cases of Wilcox v. Jackson and Wolsey v. Chapman. In the former, the Court held that an order of the War Department requiring a certain reservation was equivalent to an order by the President, within the meaning of the act authorizing the President to make the said reservation. "The President," said the Court, "speaks and acts through the heads of the several departments in relation to subjects which appertain to their respective duties. Both military posts and Indian affairs, including agencies, belong to the War Department. Hence, we consider the act of the War Department in requiring this reservation to be made, as being in legal contemplation the act of the President; and consequently, that the reservation thus made was in legal effect a reservation made by order of the President, within the terms of the act of Congress."

In Wolsey v. Chapman [6] the contention was made that certain lands involved in the case were not 'reserved' lands within the meaning of an act of Congress. Mr. Chief Justice Waite, who delivered the opinion of the Court, after referring to Wilcox v. Jackson, said:

---

[5] Boske v. Comingore, 177 U. S. 459.
[6] 101 U. S. 755.

That case is conclusive of this, unless the word " proclamation "
as used in the present statute, has a signification so different from
" order " in the other as to raise a material distinction between the
two cases. We see no such intention on the part of Congress. A
proclamation by the President, reserving lands from sale, is his
official public announcement of an order to that effect. No particular form of such an announcement is necessary. It is sufficient
if it has such publicity as accomplishes the end to be attained. If
the President himself had signed the order in this case, and sent it
to the registers and receivers who were to act under it, as notice to
them of what they were to do in respect to the sales of the public
lands, we cannot doubt that the lands would have been reserved by
proclamation within the meaning of the statute. Such being the
case, it follows, necessarily, from the decision in *Wilcox v. Jackson*
that such an order sent out from the appropriate Executive Department in the regular course of business is the legal equivalent of the
President's own order to the same effect. It was, therefore, as we
think, such a proclamation by the President reserving the lands from
sale as was contemplated by the act.

In view of executive practice [7] it seems entirely legitimate
to extend the doctrine of these two cases to Presidential ordinance making as well as Presidential action in making land
reservations. It may be noted, however, that the cases did
not consider the possibility that Congress might require in
explicit terms that an order be signed personally by the
President or by the head of a department. In such case the
congressional prescription would probably have to be complied with, else there would be what the French term ' vice
of form.' This, however, is a mere matter of form. The
more significant problem is the matter of discretion; and that
may in practice be devolved by the President upon his subordinates. There is no way in which this could be prevented.
Were it not for the possibility of devolution in all ordinary
cases we should have to evolve supermen for our Presidents.

The rule as thus stated is not, however, without important
exceptions. The exceptions may be said to come within the
general statement that where the matter is such as to require
the personal attention of the President,[8] the ordinance must

---

[7] See Fairlie, " Administrative Legislation," in Michigan Law Review, January, 1920. Professor Fairlie mentions the extent to which
re-delegation was carried during the late World War, and raises the
question how many degrees of re-delegation are permissible.

[8] Willoughby, The Constitutional Law of the United States (student's edition), p. 481.

show that it has received his sanction. It was held by the Court in Runkle v. United States[9] that Runkle was entitled to pay which came due after the date of an executive order approving the decision of a court martial sentence, on the ground that the order was not valid. It was a mere departmental order which did not indicate that it represented the personal decision of the President. And since the action of the President, in approving court martial sentences, is judicial and not administrative, said the Court, therefore, it requires his personal attention; and any order of the war department purporting to be approval of such a sentence must indicate in some way that the matter was submitted to the Chief Executive, and decided by him. This is a power which he cannot delegate to his subordinates. The Court did not say that the signature of the Chief Executive was necessary; but declared that at least the order must be " authenticated in a way to show otherwise than argumentatively that it is the result of the judgment of the President himself."

Though this case involved the exercise of judicial rather than ordinance making power, it appears that some ordinances are of such political significance as to have to be issued by the President himself, or at least by the proper department in a document stating that the ordinance is that of the head of the state. As to the question what ordinances are of such a political character, it is the opinion of the writer that they include no material ordinances, no enforcement ordinances, even those applicable to private persons, and only such concretizing ordinances and sub-legislative powers as directly affect major personal and property interests. The latter class would seem to include great political acts like suspending the writ of habeas corpus.[10]

II

Thus except in special cases the President may delegate [11] his ordinance making powers to the heads of the appropriate departments, whose acts in such cases are in law his own.

---

[9] 122 U. S. 543.
[10] Ex parte Field, 5 Blatchford 63.   [11] See Appendix.

But what shall we say of powers of ordinance making delegated by Congress to the heads of departments without any mention of the President? Is he legally as well as politically responsible for the performance of such duties by his subordinates? And, what is of more practical importance, can he constitutionally control the exercise of the discretion thus reposed in them by the legislative department?

On the one side of the issue we have the opinion of Attorney General Cushing to the following effect: [12]

Take now the converse form of legislation, that common or most ordinary style, in which an executive act is, by law, required to be performed by a given Head of Department. I think here the general rule to be as already stated, that the Head of Department is subject to the direction of the President. I hold that no Head of Department can lawfully perform an *official* act against the will of the President; and that will is by the Constitution to govern the performance of all such acts.

And again, the attorney general says:

Now, all these multiform acts are under the constitutional direction of the President. In legal theory, they are his acts. But a large proportion of them are performed by his general direction without any special direction.

On the other hand we have the following facts: the executive departments are creatures, not of the Constitution directly,[13] but of Congressional statutes;[14] while the functions, powers, and duties of the heads of such departments are defined by Congress, in broad general terms or minutely, as to it seems best. In view of these facts might it not be argued, that, while practically the President can control the heads of departments through his power of removal, yet in law they are subject to Congress and not to him?

Now it will be admitted, as indeed the Supreme Court has indicated, that obedience should be rendered by such officers to the mandates of the statutes rather than to the orders of

---

[12] 7 Opin. of the Attys. Gen. 453 (1855).

[13] Neither departments of administration nor departmental heads are specifically provided for in the Constitution. That they will be set up is implied from incidental references to the latter in that document.

[14] Under the 'necessary and proper' clause of the federal Constitution.

the Chief Executive where the two are in conflict. Laws are in our system of superior obligation to executive directions; and all executive officers from the President down are morally bound to obey the law where it is specific and mandatory. The Supreme Court has said: [15]

> There are certain political duties imposed upon many offices in the executive department, the discharge of which is under the direction of the President. But it would be an alarming doctrine that Congress cannot impose upon any executive officer any duty they may think proper, which is not repugnant to any rights secured and protected by the constitution; and in such cases, the duty and responsibility grow out of and are subject to the control of the law, and not to the direction of the President. And this is emphatically the case, where the duty enjoined is of a mere ministerial character.

And again in the same opinion:

> It was urged at the bar, that the postmaster general was alone subject to the direction and control of the President, with respect to the execution of the duty imposed upon him by this law; and this right of the President is claimed, as growing out of the obligation imposed upon him by the constitution, to take care that the laws be faithfully executed. This is a doctrine that cannot receive the sanction of this court. It would be vesting in the President a dispensing power, which has no countenance for its support in any part of the constitution; and is asserting a principle, which, if carried out in its results, to all cases falling within it would be clothing the President with a power to entirely control the legislation of Congress, and paralyze the administration of justice.

In like tenor was the opinion expressed in Congressional Government [16] by the late President Wilson:

> No one, I take it for granted, is disposed to disallow the principle that the representatives of the people are the proper ultimate authority in all matters of government, and that administration is merely the clerical part of government. Legislation is the originating force. It determines what shall be done; and the President, if he cannot or will not stay legislation by the use of his extraordinary power as a branch of the legislature, is plainly bound in duty to render unquestioning obedience to Congress. And if it be his duty to obey, still more is obedience the bounden duty of his subordinates. The power of making laws is in its very nature and essence the power of directing, and that power is given to Congress. The principle is without drawback, and is inseparably of a piece with all Anglo-Saxon usage.

But not only is it the moral duty of President and heads of departments to obey the laws. For the latter, though, not

---

[15] Kendall v. United States, 12 Pet. 524.
[16] Pages 273-274.

to be sure, for the former, it is a legal duty which is enforceable in the courts by mandamus, provided the act to be performed is ministerial in character. The duty was actually enforced against the postmaster general in Kendall v. United States.[17]

How then shall we reconcile the opinion of Cushing, and the fact that through the power of removal the President has in practice a power of control, with the decision in the Kendall case? In the first place, that decision renders too broad the declaration of the attorney general that " no Head of Department can lawfully perform an *official* act against the will of the President." For the fact that the President ordered the postmaster general not to perform the ministerial act in question would not affect the power of the court to compel by mandamus the performance of such act if it were positively commanded by statute.

The real distinction is between a mandatory duty to perform a non-discretionary act and the permissive power to perform a discretionary act.[18] The latter of course includes the discretionary formulation of a uniform rule creating rights and duties. The former is a duty over the performance of which the President has no control, because, while he can remove an officer who performs or threatens to perform it, the actual performance will, in a proper case, be compelled by the courts. But discretion by its very nature involves, as we have seen, a choice of alternatives. If and when Congress sees fit to delegate to the head of a department a discretionary power, this means that that body leaves to such officer a choice; and since there is no judicial means of compelling the exercise of such a choice, it means further that Congress not only delegates a choice as to the content of the rule, but also makes it at the most a moral duty to exercise the choice at all.[19] For where there is no means of enforcement there

---

[17] 12 Pet. 524; cf. United States v. Black, 128 U. S. 40; see also Marbury v. Madison, 1 Cr. 137.

[18] Including the ordinance making power.

[19] On this particular point compare the words used by the Court in United States v. Black, 128 U. S. 40, and in Dunlap v. United States, 173 U. S. 65.

is no legal duty. And, by the same token, whether the power
of removal be derived from the Constitution in such a manner
as to be beyond the control of Congress or not, so long as the
supreme law or the statutory law allows to the Chief Magistrate a power of removal,[20] it allows to him, within certain
limits, not only a practical, but also a legal, power of ' administrative control ' over acts of department heads which involve
a choice.[21]   Those limits are set by the extent to which the
courts can, in the several forms of action at law or in equity,
control abuse of power, or fraud, or excess of jurisdiction, or
' vice of form,' in the exercise of discretion, or by mandamus
compel its exercise in some manner.   Within those limits
the fact that the law allows the President a method of control
must be deemed to constitute a recognition of his legal right
to control.   In this manner it comes about that not only may
the President, in most cases, allow the heads of departments
to issue his ordinances for him, but conversely he may control
the performance by them of their own ordinance making
powers.   Congress may specify that he or the head of the
proper department must perform the act.   But, after all, that
requirement, while it may be necessary to follow it to make
the act valid, is reducible to a matter of form.   In all cases
the act is the act of the President in contemplation of law;
while it is jointly the act of the President and the head of the

[20] For evidence that in 1789 it was held by Madison and others,
and finally accepted by Congress, that the vesting in the President of
' the executive power ' carries with it the power of removal, see
Thach, The Creation of the Presidency, chap. vi.

[21] This does not involve that ' correlative right of appeal ' to the
President which ordinarily flows from the ' power of direction '
vested in a superior officer.   The reason for this is that the act of
the subordinate is ordinarily the act of the President, in the eyes of
the law.   What is here involved is a power rather of ' administrative
control ' which flows directly from the President's power of removal,
which is, in turn, a result of his ' executive power.'   To put the
matter somewhat differently: the ' executive power ' vested in the
President means essentially a power of administrative control, and
this implies a power of removal, as a necessary ' administrative
sanction.'   Such an administrative sanction is all the more needed
because there is in such cases no ' judicial sanction ' (see White v.
Berry, 171 U. S. 366.   On the matter of appeals to the President,
see 10 Opin. of Attys. Gen. 527, and 15 Opin. of Attys. Gen. 94).

department if the latter formally participates. Any legal consequences fall upon the President [22] in all cases, and upon the subordinate in the latter class of cases.

In the writings of President Benjamin Harrison [23] we have at once evidence and a clear statement of this ' administrative control ':

The responsibility under the Constitution for the Executive administration of the Government in all its branches is devolved upon the President.

And again: [24]

In all important matters the President is consulted by all the Secretaries. He is responsible for all executive action, and almost everything that is out of the routine receives some attention from him. . . . Routine matters proceed without the knowledge or interference of the President; but, if any matter of major importance arises the Secretary presents it for the consideration and advice of the President. . . . There should be no question of making a ' mere clerk ' of the Cabinet officer; there is a yielding of views, now on one side, now on the other; but it must, of course, follow that when the President has views that he feels he cannot yield, those views must prevail, for the responsibility is his, both in a Constitutional and popular sense.

There are thus specific constitutional and practical reasons why the ordinance making powers of the heads of departments are to be treated as in large measure but part of the ordinance making powers of the President. There is no sharp distinction between them in government in operation or in most cases in the eyes of the law. In a sense all federal ordinances are potential Presidential ordinances. This is true, despite the fact that an otherwise valid ordinance issued by the head of the department authorized by law to issue it would be valid, even if he issued it in defiance of the President's actual

---

[22] Of course, this legal responsibility can be enforced, while the President is in office, only by impeachment for misconduct in this connection. No court, not even the Senate while trying an impeachment, can enforce a writ against the person of the President during his tenure of office. The President is, in a word, immune from personal service. (See Burgess, Political Science and Comparative Constitutional Law, vol. ii, p. 245.) Might he properly be impeached for department ordinances of which he had no actual knowledge?

[23] This Country of Ours, p. 70.

[24] Ibid., pp. 105-107.

wishes, and the further fact that the President could perhaps not act independently of the official to whom the power is delegated.

However, it is sometimes held that, while the principle above stated applies to the relationship of the Chief Magistrate to services like the State, War and Navy Departments, where the main [25] duties of the service are to administer functions granted to the President directly by the Constitution itself,[26] nevertheless other organizations—especially the Treasury Department [27]—are responsible to Congress rather than to the President. It is said to be significant that in 1789 the statutes organizing the Foreign Affairs and War Departments made the heads of those Departments responsible to the President, but required the head of the Department of the Treasury to report to Congress.[28] Now it will readily be admitted that the State and War and Navy Departments are and must be in a peculiar sense under Presidential control. But we also maintain that both in practice and in contemplation of law the Treasury is less so only in so far as its duties are made mandatory, specific, and ministerial. Practice was settled once and for all when President Jackson successfully used his power of removal to control the discretionary action of the Secretary of the Treasury in the so-called removal of bank deposits instance.[29] And it holds for all the departments, that where the law gives the subordinate a choice of alternatives, and at the same time gives the chief a weapon by which to control the subordinate in the exercise of that choice, it means for such control to be exercised. The

---

[25] The Department of State has certain 'home functions' not connected with the conduct of foreign affairs. That was why its name was changed. To these 'home functions' the statement in the text would not apply any more than to the functions of the Treasury Department.

[26] For example, to make treaties by and with the advice and consent of the Senate; to act as commander-in-chief of the army and navy (see the Constitution of the United States, Art. 2).

[27] This Department is especially mentioned because in Anglo-Saxon usage the control of the purse is peculiarly a prerogative of the legislature.

[28] See 1 Stat. L. 28-29, 49-50, 65-67.

[29] See MacDonald, Jacksonian Democracy, chap. xiii.

fact that in one case the statute expressly gives such control, while in the other it omits so to do, does not alter this essential principle of interpretation.[30] That this result was not at first clearly contemplated is probably true, but this does not alter the relationship of control necessarily created when Congress recognized the power of removal as an incident of

---

[30] Our theory is not inconsistent with the law. Rev. Stat. 193 enacts that "The head of each Department shall make an annual report to Congress. . . ." This is a proper requirement for the legislative department to make. Rev. Stat. 202 reads: "The Secretary of State shall perform such duties as shall from time to time be enjoined on or entrusted to him by the President relative to correspondences, commissions, or instructions to or with public ministers or consuls from the United States, or to negotiations with public ministers from foreign states or princes, or to memorials or other applications from foreign public ministers or other foreigners, or to such other matters respecting foreign affairs as the President of the United States shall assign to the Department, and he shall conduct the business of the Department in such manner as the President shall direct." Rev. Stat. 216 reads: "The Secretary of War shall perform such duties as shall from time to time be enjoined on or intrusted to him by the President relative to military commissions, the military forces, the warlike stores of the United States, or to other matters respecting military affairs; and he shall conduct the business of the Department in such manner as the President shall direct." Rev. Stat. 417 reads: "The Secretary of the Navy shall execute such orders as he shall receive from the President relative to the procurement of naval stores and materials, and the construction, armament, equipment, and employment of vessels of war, as well as all other matters connected with the naval establishment." Rev. Stat. 248, on the other hand, provides: "The Secretary of the Treasury shall, from time to time, digest and prepare plans for the improvement and management of the revenue and for the support of the public credit; shall superintend the collection of the revenue . . . shall make report, and give information to either branch of the legislature in person or in writing, as may be required, respecting all matters referred to him by the Senate or House of Representatives, or which shall appertain to his office; and generally shall perform all such services relative to the finances as he shall be directed to perform." Cf. also Rev. Stat. 396, prescribing the duties of the Postmaster General. From these quotations it is seen that the President is by statute expressly given both a power of administrative control and a *Verwaltungsverordnungsrecht* with respect to the Secretaries of State, War, and the Navy, but not with respect to the Secretary of the Treasury and the Postmaster-General. From this it follows that the President cannot issue material ordinances to the latter two officers except in so far as he can do so under his executive power and faithful execution duty (for which see chapter ix). But it does not follow that he cannot control the exercise of their discretion, for that control is implied in his power of removal (for which relative to the Secretary of the Treasury see 1 Stat. L. 67).

executive power.[31]   Or, to reason the matter in a slightly different way, we can say that 'the executive power' means primarily 'administrative control,' from which a power of removal is implied as a necessary 'sanction.'

So far we have spoken only of heads of departments.   Do the same principles apply to the special administrative boards and commissions set up by Congress in comparatively recent times?   It must be admitted that they were kept separate from the regular departments with a view to 'taking them out of politics.'   They are regarded as quasi-judicial bodies, standing midway between the political heads of departments and the semi-judicial comptroller of the treasury.[32]   Public opinion would probably not tolerate arbitrary or partisan removal by the President of members of the Interstate Commerce Commission and the other like boards.   Whether this is better than to leave the administrative control of such commissioners fully in Presidential hands is a question of policy.   Perhaps the success of these administrative tribunals in the federal government justifies their present detached position.   Perhaps it might be wise to separate out from the political departments other ordinance making functions connected with economic regulation.   Yet state experience has shown that, as such independent boards are multiplied, the public is unable to watch them, and inefficiency or corruption is the result.   And opinion in certain quarters leans strongly toward the idea that even where there are only a few federal boards, as at present, popular control is defeated by the fact that the members are appointed and not elected, and that they are not even subject to that ultimate popular check that would come through a direct and complete responsibility to the President, who is an elective officer.[33]

---

[31] On the vesting of 'the executive power' in the President, see chap ix below.   It is from this power that the power of removal and the administrative control flow.

[32] See Hotchkiss, The Judicial Work of the Comptroller of the Treasury, in Cornell Studies in History and Political Science, vol. iii.

[33] Labor and agricultural interests are apt to feel that such an appointive board with a detached position usually takes the viewpoint of the commercial and industrial interests.   Hence the demand for having 'dirt farmers' on such boards.

All this refers, however, to the present practice, and to the attitude of the country to the boards in question. In law, Congress has made the individual members of the Interstate Commerce Commission subject to removal by the President for causes stated in the law.[34] The existence of such causes is in the final determination of the President, no doubt; and it may be that he has also full power still to remove at his pleasure.[35] In that event, but only in that event, their ordinances are potentially controllable by the President. The question remains whether Congress may free such administrative tribunals, specially set up to concretize its legislative abstractions, from executive control. The power of appointment must be where the Constitution located it.[36] Can Congress constitutionally limit the President's power of removal?[37] Yet even if it cannot, by removal the President can only control individual commissioners. He can exercise legal control over acts of the body as a whole only through pressure brought to bear upon the several members individually.

III

No attempt can here be made to enumerate the many delegations of ordinance making powers which have been made to heads of departments. There are temporary delegations scattered through the statutes-at-large as well as certain delega-

---

[34] 24 Stat. L. 383 created the Interstate Commerce Commission, provided for the appointment of its members by the President and Senate, fixed their terms at six years (but not all terms to expire at once), and provided that " Any Commissioner may be removed by the President for inefficiency, neglect of duty, or malfeasance in office."

[35] Ex parte Hennen, 13 Pet. 230; Parsons v. United States, 167 U. S. 324; Shurtleff v. United States, 189 U. S. 311.

[36] In the President, by and with the advice and consent of the Senate; or, at the discretion of Congress for inferior officers in the President alone, the heads of departments, or the courts of law. It is unlikely, if permissible, that any but the first of these methods—or perhaps also the second—would be used in the case of administrative commissions. In the first, the Senate has a check through confirmation of new appointments.

[37] See Powell, "The President's Veto of the Budget Bill," in National Municipal Review, vol. ix, p. 538.

tions of permanent law embodied in the Revised Statutes. Not even all of the latter can be here cited; but from them a few examples may be given at random. First of all comes the general delegation contained in Rev. Stat. 161, which is cited at the head of this chapter. This is a broad grant of *Verwalt-ungsverordnungsrecht,* which is unfortunately curtailed by the fact that Congress itself, both in budgetary legislation and in the laws organizing the departments and prescribing their duties, has gone into such minute detail. Other examples may be added:

1. The Secretary of the Treasury shall make and issue from time to time such instructions and regulations to the several collectors, receivers, depositaries, officers, and others who may receive Treasury notes, United States notes or other securities of the United States, or who may be in any way engaged or employed in the preparation and issue of the same, as he shall deem best calculated to promote the public convenience and security, and to protect the United States, as well as individuals, from fraud and loss; he shall prescribe forms of entries, oaths, bonds, and other papers, and rules and regulations, not inconsistent with law, to be used under and in execution and enforcement of the various provisions of the internal-revenue laws, or in carrying out the provisions of law relating to raising revenue from imports, or to duties on imports, or to warehousing; he shall give such directions to collectors and prescribe such rules and forms to be observed by them as may be necessary for the proper execution of the law. . . .[38]

2. The Secretary of the Treasury may prescribe rules and regulations governing the recognition of agents, attorneys, or other persons representing claimants before his Department, and may require of such persons, agents and attorneys, before being recognized as representatives of claimants, that they shall show that they are of good character and in good repute, possessed of the necessary qualifications to enable them to render such claimants valuable service, and otherwise competent to advise and assist such claimants in the presentation of their cases. And such Secretary may after due notice and opportunity for hearing suspend, and disbar from further practice before his Department any such person, agent, or attorney shown to be incompetent, disreputable, or who refuses to comply with the said rules and regulations, or who shall with intent to defraud, in any manner willfully and knowingly deceive, mislead, or threaten any claimant or prospective claimant, by word, circular, letter, or by advertisement.[39]

3. The Solicitor of the Treasury shall establish such regulations, not inconsistent with law, with the approbation of the Secretary of the Treasury, for the observance of collectors of the customs, and, with the approbation of the Attorney-General, for the observance of

---

[38] Rev. Stat. 251.
[39] 23 Stat. L. 258; cf. 23 Stat. L. 101.

district attorneys and marshals respecting suits in which the United States are parties, as may be deemed necessary for the just responsibility of those officers, and the prompt collection of all revenues and debts due and accruing to the United States. But this section does not apply to suits for taxes, forfeitures, or penalties arising under the internal-revenue laws.[40]

4. The Secretary of War shall from time to time define and prescribe the kinds as well as the amount of supplies to be purchased by the Subsistence and Quartermaster Departments of the Army, and the duties and powers thereof respecting such purchases; and shall prescribe general regulations for the transportation of the articles of supply from the places of purchase to the several armies, garrisons, posts, and recruiting places, for the safe-keeping of such articles, and for the distribution of an adequate and timely supply of the same to the regimental quartermasters, and to such other officers as may by virtue of such regulations be entrusted with the same; and shall fix and make reasonable allowances for the store-rent and storage necessary for the safe-keeping of all military stores and supplies.[41]

5. There shall be appointed by the President, by and with the advice and consent of the Senate, a purchasing agent for the Post Office Department, who shall hold office for four years unless sooner removed by the President, and who shall receive an annual salary of four thousand dollars, give bond to the United States in such sum as the Postmaster-General may determine, and report direct to the Postmaster-General; and who shall, under such regulations, not inconsistent with existing law, as the Postmaster-General shall prescribe, and subject to his direction and control, have supervision of the purchase of all supplies for the postal service.

The purchasing agent, in making purchases . . . (requirements).[42]

6. The Commissioner of Patents, subject to the approval of the Secretary of the Interior, may from time to time establish regulations, not inconsistent with law, for the conduct of proceedings in the Patent-Office.[43]

7. The Secretary of the Interior shall make and publish such rules and regulations as he may deem necessary and proper for the use and management of the parks, monuments, and reservations under the jurisdiction of the National Park Service, and any violations of any of the rules and regulations authorized by this Act shall be punished as provided for in section fifty of the Act entitled "An Act to codify and amend the penal laws of the United States," . . . as amended . . . (36 Stat. L. 857). . . . He may also, upon terms and conditions to be fixed by him, sell or dispose of timber in those cases where in his judgment the cutting of such timber is required in order to control the attacks of insects or diseases or otherwise conserve the scenery or the natural or historical objects in any such park, monument, or reservation. He may also provide in his discretion for the destruction of such animals and of such plant life as may be detrimental to the use of any said parks,

---

[40] Rev. Stat. 377; cf. Rev. Stat. 379.
[41] Rev. Stat. 219.
[42] 33 Stat. L. 440.
[43] Rev. Stat. 483.

monuments, or reservations. He may also grant privileges, leases, and permits for the use of land for the accommodation of visitors in the various parks, monuments, or other reservations herein provided for, but for periods not exceeding twenty years; and no natural curiosities, wonders, or objects of interest shall be leased, rented, or granted to anyone on such terms as to interfere with the free access to them by the public; Provided however, That the Secretary of the Interior may, under such regulations and on such terms as he may prescribe, grant the privilege to graze live stock within any national park, monument, or reservation herein referred to when in his judgment such use is not detrimental to the primary purpose for which such park, monument, or reservation was created, except that this provision shall not apply to the Yellowstone National Park.[44]

---

[44] 39 Stat. L. 535.

CHAPTER IX

Constitutional Aspects of the Constitutional Ordinance Making Powers of the President

All legislative powers herein granted shall be vested in a Congress of the United States.

The Congress shall have power . . . To make all laws which shall be necessary and proper for carrying into execution the foregoing powers, and all other powers vested by this Constitution in the government of the United States, or in any department or officer thereof.

The executive power shall be vested in a President of the United States of America.

Before he enter on the execution of his office, he shall take the following oath or affirmation:—" I do solemnly swear (or affirm) that I will faithfully execute the office of President of the United States, and will to the best of my ability, preserve, protect and defend the Constitution of the United States."

The President shall be commander-in-chief of the army and navy of the United States, and of the militia of the several States, when called into the actual service of the United States; he may require the opinion, in writing, of the principal officer in each of the executive departments, upon any subject relating to the duties of their respective offices, and he shall have power to grant reprieves and pardons for offences against the United States, except in cases of impeachment.

He shall have power, by and with the advice and consent of the Senate, to make treaties, provided two-thirds of the Senators present concur.

He shall take care that the laws be faithfully executed.

—Constitution of the United States.

I

We have seen that the President of the United States has no powers except those delegated to him in the Constitution; and that that instrument does not delegate to him any ordinance making powers as such. The question arises, however, whether he possesses any constitutional powers of an ordinance making nature; and this requires an examination of the Constitution with a view to discovering whether any of the powers there granted to him confer, either expressly or impliedly, the right to create material law or material ordinances. In this examination we are limited by a fundamental principle with which our conclusions may not conflict.[1] The Constitu-

[1] See above, chap. v.

tion embodies the separation of powers as the cornerstone of the national government. It vests in Congress " all legislative powers herein granted," and then proceeds to enumerate seventeen specific powers of Congress to which is added the power " to make all laws which shall be necessary and proper for carrying into execution the foregoing powers, and all other powers vested in the government of the United States, or in any department or officer thereof." Applying to these provisions the maxim of constitutional construction *expressio unius est exclusio alterius,* we are forced to the admission that in general the President is prima facie excluded from the exercise of any independent legislative authority, even such as, were it not for the last part of the ' necessary and proper ' clause, he might be held to possess in order to enable him to carry out the powers which are by the Constitution vested in him. For it is expressly stated in that clause that Congress is to make laws for carrying into execution not only its own delegated powers but also those of the other departments and officers. This has not been interpreted in such a way as to make it necessary for Congress to legislate with regard to the constitutional powers of the Chief Magistrate before he can exercise them; but it clearly keeps him from legislating on the excuse that he is merely providing for the execution of his own powers.[2]

---

[2] One sometimes sees statements to the effect that each department has the powers of regulation which are necessary to carry out its powers (see Lieber, Remarks on the Army Regulations, p. 18). It is sometimes stated that each department has the powers which are necessarily incidental to the exercise of the powers vested in it, or necessary to protect it from encroachment by the other departments, even if such powers do not fall within the logical definition of the primary function of the department concerned (cf. Willoughby, Constitutional Law of the United States, vol. ii, sec. 743). Now it is quite true that our interpretation of the separation of powers must be realistic and in accord with common sense; and there are undoubtedly exceptions to be made to the absolute rule as stated in the text. But it seems dangerous to build these exceptions into a generalization, especially when that generalization conflicts (as do those mentioned above) with the undoubted principle that to Congress is delegated in express terms the power to provide for carrying into execution the functions of the judicial and executive departments as well as its own. This danger may be avoided by bringing

The first question for consideration is negatively what powers the President is by the separation of powers forbidden to exercise. This involves giving an interpretation of the meaning of the word "legislative" as it is employed in the Constitution; and in this interpretation we shall find the historical and contemporaneous signification important if not controlling.[3] What did the phrase "legislative powers" connote in the minds of the men who framed and adopted the Constitution?[4]

We know that the framers were familiar with the writings of three men who were in their day leading authorities on law and political theory.[5] Hence we may with propriety accept definitions of law and legislation which those three men held in common as being by every presumption the definitions of those terms as used in the Constitution. The men are Blackstone, Montesquieu, and Locke. The first defines municipal law as "a rule of civil conduct prescribed by the supreme power in a state, commanding what is right and prohibiting what is wrong." By the term rule he means "something permanent, uniform, and universal," as well as imperative.[6] Montesquieu, in his "Spirit of the Laws,"[7] speaking of the legislative power, says: "By virtue of the first, the prince or magistrate enacts temporary or perpetual laws, and amends or abolishes those that have been already enacted." In other passages he uses such terms with refer-

such exceptions, where possible, under some express power of the Executive. The authority to issue regulations which prescribe office hours or other very minor details of administration,—even where they affect the public—flows from the fact that the Executive is an independent department. Nothing is gained, however, by trying to express such an obvious exception or limitation in general terms, which are likely to be misleading.

[3] See above, chap iv.

[4] The fact that the framers did not define the terms "legislative powers" and "laws" as used in art. I, secs. 1 and 8, indicates that they used them in the currently accepted sense.

[5] On evidence of their use of the theories of these three men see above, chap. v, n. 4.

[6] Blackstone, Commentaries on the Laws of England, (Cooley's edition), Introduction, p. 38 ff.

[7] Pritchard's revision of Nugent's translation, Bohn's Standard Library, vol. i, passim.

ence to the legislative power as " general determinations "
and the " general will of the state." Locke, in his Second
Treatise of Government,[8] speaks of " Antecedent, standing,
positive laws," and of the right of the legislative power as the
right " to make laws for all the parts, and every member of
the society prescribing rules to their actions, and giving power
of execution where they are transgressed."

We thus find these writers defining laws as general rules of
conduct which the state will enforce. Their definition closely
corresponds with the technical definition of law which is accepted by jurists at the present time. The only difference
between their definitions and the one we have inherited is
that they do not include rules of conduct intended to govern
the action of organs and officers of government. They are
speaking of rules affecting private persons, not of administrative regulations. In Anglo-American usage, however, the
latter are often considered legislative. In France the power
of the President to create offices by decree is inferred from the
power of appointment;[9] while in German political theory
the power of organizing and regulating the administrative
services is deemed to belong properly to the chief executive
through administrative ordinances.[10] In England the prerogative power of the Crown with reference to the army and the
navy enables it to raise and to govern the same, at least unless

---

[8] Morley's Universal Library edition, p. 267 ff. Though Rousseau
had less influence upon the framers than the three quoted in the
text (see on this Merriam, American Political Theories, pp. 91-92),
nevertheless it may not be out of place, as evidence of the general
agreement of eighteenth century definitions of law, to mention that
Rousseau says that all laws are general, and gives the following
explanation: " Quand je dis que l'objet des lois est toujours général,
j'entends que la Loi considère les sujets en corps et les actions
comme abstraites; jamais un homme comme individu, ni une action
particulier . . . Ce qu'ordonne même le souverain sur un objet par-
ticulière n'est pas non plus une loi, mais un décret; ni un acte de
souveraineté, mais de magistrature " (Vaughn's edition of Rousseau's
Political Writings, vol. ii. chap. vi, pp. 49-50).

[9] Sait, Government and Politics of France, pp. 71-73.

[10] Laband, Staatsrecht des deutschen Reiches, vol. ii, p. 67 ff.; also
his Deutsches Reichsstaatsrecht, sec. 16, n.; Jellinek, Gesetz und Verordnung, p. 386 ff.; Meyer-Anschütz, Lehrbuch des deutschen Staatsrechtes, pp. 571-573; Lowell, Governments and Parties in Continental
Europe, vol. i, pp. 345-346.

parliament has legislated on these matters;[11] while apparently the Crown can also create offices [12] and regulate executive activities.[13] But, even so, parliament has for generations regulated all these matters in more or less detail, leaving little for prerogative regulation; and it is the general understanding that such matters are more properly regulated by that body. At any rate, this is the American theory. Since our Constitution speaks of appointment to offices "which shall be established by law," no power to create offices has ever been inferred from the appointing power of our President; and by practical construction it has been definitely settled that the power lies with Congress alone. This would seem to follow not only from the clause quoted above but also from the power of that body "to make all laws which shall be necessary and proper for carrying into execution the foregoing powers, and all other powers vested . . . in the government of the United States, or in any department or officer thereof." When the matter of organizing the executive departments was taken up in the first Congress, which included members of the Philadelphia Convention of 1787, it was assumed, apparently without question, that Congress was the organ to perform this function. Mr. Boudinot, who appears to have first introduced the subject on the floor of the House, is reported as saying: "The great executive departments which were in existence under the late confederation, are now at an end, at least so far as not to be able to conduct the business of the United States. If we take up the present constitution, we shall find it contemplates departments of an executive nature in aid of the President; it then remains for us to carry this intention into effect." [14] From that time to this Congress and not the President has created executive departments and offices and defined their powers and duties.

The statements of the above-mentioned writers may be

---

[11] See Cooley's Blackstone, vol. i, Book 1, p. 262; also the Federalist, No. 69.
[12] Cooley's Blackstone, vol. i, Book 1, p. 271.
[13] Lowell, Government of England, vol. i, pp. 19-20.
[14] Annals of Congress, vol. i, pp. 383-384.

further supplemented by a consideration of certain principles of the English constitution which the Englishmen who settled the new world undoubtedly brought with them. The first principle is that laid down in 1610 by Coke in the famous Case of Proclamations,[15] to the effect that the king could not create an offense where there was not one before. This became effective after the abolition, in 1641, of the Star Chamber which had enforced the illegal proclamations of the Crown; and in 1787-1788 it had long been an established principle. It was a part of Anglo-Saxon usage, therefore, that penal sanctions should be provided by the legislative organ alone, and never by the Executive. The second principle is that the king may not only not repeal nor alter the statutes passed by the legislature, but may not even add to them or issue ordinances supplementing their terms, unless he is authorized by statute so to do. This, likewise, was perhaps an inheritance of the colonists, although it may not have been practiced by colonial governors in all cases, especially when the colonies were, at first, regarded rather as private enterprises than as political dependencies.[16] But there is not the slightest hint in the early state constitutions or in Revolutionary political ideas of a general executive power of issuing supplementary ordinances.

Now if the term legislative power means only general regulations, is there any constitutional principle which would prevent the President from issuing special orders of an obligatory character? It could hardly be supposed that the framers of the Constitution intended to give the President an arbitrary power over the lives and property of citizens at the same time that they gave him no control over them by way of general regulations. This might be inferred; but it is not necessary to resort to such an inference, since the point is covered by the due process clause of the fifth amendment. It has been held that not even Congress, the legislative organ of the federal government, can so legislate as to take life, liberty,

---

[15] 12 Co. Rep. 74.
[16] Cf. Greene, The Provincial Governor, pp. 30 ff., 159-161.

or property without due process of law. In a dictum in the case of Hurtado v. California [17] it is indicated by the Court, as it undoubtedly would be held in a proper case, that special and arbitrary acts of a legislative body would be in violation of due process. A fortiori, such acts of the Executive would involve a lack of due process. In United States v. Lee [18] it was held that, where trial of title was not involved, the order of the President to federal officials to seize and hold a given piece of private property was not due process of law and was no justification for such a confiscatory act.

We thus see that the denial of ' legislative ' powers to the President means a denial of power to prescribe rules of either private or governmental conduct; or to prescribe a penal sanction for the same; or to supplement such rules, even when they are expressed in general terms, by the issuance of completing or enforcing ordinances; or to do any of these things by particular any more than by uniform orders. Not even can he do these things on the excuse that they are necessary to make effective his constitutional powers, or incidental to the performance thereof, or essential for the maintenance of his independence of the other two coordinate departments of government. This extreme statement of the case follows from the phraseology of the ' necessary and proper ' clause of the Constitution.[19]

II

Does this mean that the President has absolutely no legislative powers? Not at all. We have seen that it does not prevent Congress from delegating to him *une législation sécondaire et dérivée*.[20] Has he any independent legislative powers? There are two possibilities. The first is that the Constitution may grant him some power which was not considered by the framers as being strictly legislative, but which conforms to our technical definition. This case presents no

---

[17] 110 U. S. 516.
[18] 106 U. S. 196.
[19] Tucker, Constitution of the United States, vol. ii, pp. 693-694.
[20] See above, chap. vi.

constitutional difficulties. The second possibility is that the Constitution itself may have made exceptions to the strict logical theory on grounds of expediency, and have given to the President powers which are in both the constitutional and technical sense legislative.[21] It becomes necessary, therefore, to examine Article II and other relevant portions of the Constitution to discover if there are any powers given the Chief Magistrate which are, or involve, the independent issuance of material laws or material ordinances. The functions of the President fall within the following distinct classes:

1. Those extra-legal powers which are entirely political or social, and which are of juristic significance only when the question arises whether they are permissible or not.[22] Such are the practical powers which the President may have as leader of his party and of the nation.[23] These arise out of the influence that flows from the power and prestige of his office, and may be exerted to cause Congress to pass laws, to induce the settlement of industrial disputes,[24] to urge con-

---

[21] It must of course be understood that there is a prima facie case against the existence of any such powers, in view of the general principle of the separation of powers. To overcome this prima facie case we must in each instance show that the grant is, or involves in its very nature, legislative powers. It is not enough to show that a legislative power is a convenient aid to its exercise. But once it is demonstrated that the grant essentially is, or involves, legislative powers, constitutional difficulties are resolved. For it is a principle of construction that a general provision gives way before a specific exception. The distinction which we would draw is that between the exercise of legislative power as a mere aid to the execution of the powers given, and the exercise of legislative power as so much a part and parcel of the powers themselves, that they cannot be dissociated from them. The former is not permissible. The latter is permissible, though there is a presumption against its existence; and in the exercise of such power the President is undoubtedly subject to such regulations as Congress may have made upon the subject under the 'necessary and proper' clause.

[22] Every objective act of any person, whether of the state or a private person, is either legal or illegal. The distinction between legally-relevant and legally-irrelevant acts of the state, drawn in Nakano, The Ordinance Power of the Japanese Emperor, p. 38, seems erroneous to the present writer.

[23] Wilson, Constitutional Government in the United States, chap. iii.

[24] Presidents have effectively used the prestige of their office and their influence with public opinion to force settlements and com-

tributions of charity upon the people,[25] or even to institute such social reforms as the curbing of 'race suicide.'[26] With these we are not concerned.[27]

2. Those powers which he exercises under authorizations from Congress and his constitutional duty to take care that the laws be faithfully executed. The content of these powers is naturally determined by the statutes. They do not concern us here, having been discussed in Chapter VI.

3. One power which he exercises by virtue of constitutional grant, but which does not result in the creation of legal rights and duties, is his power of informing Congress on the state of the Union and making recommendations to them.[28]

4. Those powers, granted by or implied from the Constitution, which conform to our definition of 'executive orders' or 'official orders'—acts which create rights and duties with reference to one person or organ and not uniformly. These are the powers of appointment, in conjunction with the Senate;[29] filling vacancies during recess of the Senate; re-

---

promises in industrial disputes where their legal power to act was practically nil.

[25] 40 Stat. L., part 2, 1774.

[26] This was done by President Roosevelt.

[27] It is in point to remark that many of the most important powers of the President fall, at least in part, within this category. Thus, when the text books refer to his 'control of foreign relations' they refer to what is in reality a combination of individual express and implied constitutional powers relating to foreign affairs and the extra-legal influence that flows from them, taken together. The generalization of the text books includes both the legal powers and the extra-legal influence which the President possesses in this field. The same may be said of such expressions as 'determination of foreign policy'; 'the power, not to declare war, but to make war inevitable'; 'the power to exert a *positive* influence over the contents of laws by the threat of veto and the use of patronage'; etc. This treatise is concerned solely with the President's strictly legal powers.

[28] This power in no way is, nor involves, ordinance making. In recommending legislation to Congress, the President does not even have the right of formal initiative; his messages contain mere advice. In drafting them he exercises 'discretion' but not discretion as to the creation of legal rights and duties, whether of a uniform or particular character.

[29] The President may also appoint without the advice of the Senate persons to act as his personal agents in the conduct of foreign relations, but such agents are not 'officers' of the United States

moving from office;[30] pardoning;[31] convening Congress or one of its houses in special session; adjourning Congress in case of disagreement between the houses as to the time of adjournment;[32] requiring in individual cases opinions in writing of particular heads of departments;[33] issuing 'official orders' such as the one involved in the Neagle case.[34]

5. One power, that of passing upon bills sent up from Congress, which he has as a co-partner with Congress in the process of legislation.[35]

(see Wriston, " Presidential Special Agents in Diplomacy," in American Political Science Review, August, 1916). There can be no ' officer ' without an ' office ' created by Congress for him to hold (see Constitution of the United States, art. ii, sec. 2). The act of filling vacancies, as given in the Constitution, is merely a limited and restricted power of appointment. In this connection we may repeat that the power of appointment does not carry with it the power to create the office. We may note that the act of nominating involves the legal consequence of placing the name of a given person before the Senate for action. It is analogous to the right of initiative in legislation; but at the most it is not legislative. The act of commissioning is the final act by which the President completes an appointment. As such it is a step in the power of appointment.

[30] This is implied from the executive power vested in the President (see Thach, The Creation of the Presidency, chap. vi, on the Removal Debate of 1789).

[31] See U. S. v. Klein, 13 Wall. 148; Willoughby, Constitutional Law of the United States, vol. ii, secs. 686 ff.

[32] The powers mentioned involve discretion as to certain legal results in regard to the internal workings of the government; but both the convening and the adjourning of the assembly are *particular* acts, not acts involving the bringing into operation of a uniform rule. They both come, therefore, within the definition of acts of official discretion as distinguished from acts of legislative discretion. They are ' official ' rather than ' executive ' because they apply to a *governmental* body rather than to a *private* person or corporation. The first has of course been exercised, but the second is the only power of the President that has never been exercised (see Taft, The Presidency, pp. 40-42).

[33] When the President requires the opinion in writing of a head of department, in regard to a particular matter, he is issuing an order which it is the sworn duty of the officer to obey and for the disobedience of which the officer may be dismissed by the President; but such an order is obviously not a rule of administrative conduct. It is an administrative order of particular application. This power need not have been specified in the Constitution, according to Hamilton, The Federalist, No. 74 (73), Ford's edition, for it is included in the ' faithful execution ' clause.

[34] In re Neagle, 135 U. S. 1. It is hard to say whether this was a specific order or an order to the deputy marshal to pursue a ' course of conduct.'

[35] The nature of this power will be considered later in contrasting it with the treaty making power.

6. Those powers which partake of the character of ordinance making in the sense of creating material ordinances or material laws. These are the powers of acting as commander-in-chief of the army and navy; of making treaties with the consent of the Senate; of abrogating treaties by his own authority; of granting general pardons or amnesties; of recognizing foreign governments or states; of laying down uniform rules concerning the giving of opinions by the heads of departments; of issuing, under his 'executive' power and 'faithful execution' duty, administrative orders of uniform application or prescribing for one officer general duties; and of performing certain other special functions under his 'faithful execution' duty. These we must proceed to discuss; but examples of several sorts of constitutional ordinances of the President may first be given.

There were several proclamations of amnesty after the Civil War, issued by Presidents Lincoln and Johnson. All of these except the last made " prudential reservations and exceptions." They were dated December 8, 1863; March 26, 1864; May 29, 1865; September 7, 1867; July 4, 1868. The Proclamation of President Johnson dated Christmas day, 1868, made no exceptions whatever. It declared: [36]

Now, therefore, be it known that I, Andrew Johnson, President of the United States, by virtue of the power and authority in me vested by the Constitution and in the name of the sovereign people of the United States, do hereby proclaim and declare, unconditionally and without reservation, to all and to every person who, directly or indirectly, participated in the late insurrection or rebellion, a full pardon and amnesty for the offense of treason against the United States or of adhering to their enemies during the late civil war, with the restoration of all rights, privileges and immunities under the Constitution and the laws which have been made in pursuance thereof.

Ten years before the civil service reform act of 1883 [37] the President issued, in an Executive Order, a uniform rule regulating the conduct of administrative officials. No mention was made of any statutory authority, though it probably came

[36] Richardson, Messages and Papers of the Presidents, vol. ix, p. 3906.
[37] 22 Stat. L., 403-407.

under earlier legislation on the subject. It is cited here in order to raise the question as to whether the President could issue such a regulation under his executive power alone. It was dated January 17, 1873, and signed by Hamilton Fish, Secretary of State, " by order of the President." It declared: [38]

> In view of the premises, therefore, the President has deemed it proper thus and hereby to give public notice that from and after the 4th day of March, A. D. 1873 (except as herein specified), persons holding any Federal civil office by appointment under the Constitution and laws of the United States will be expected, while holding such office, not to accept or hold any office under any State or Territorial Government, or under the charter or ordinances of any municipal corporation; and further, that the acceptance or continued holding of any such State, Territorial, or municipal office, whether elective or by appointment, by any person holding civil office as aforesaid under the Government of the United States, will be deemed a vacation of the Federal office held by such person, and will be taken to be and will be treated as a resignation by such Federal officer of his commission or appointment in the service of the United States. . . .
>
> Heads of Departments and other officers of the Government who have the appointment of subordinate officers are required to take notice of this order, and to see to the enforcement of its provisions and terms within the sphere of their respective Departments or offices as relates to the several persons holding appointments under them, respectively.

In answer to queries as to the meaning of the above an interpretative Executive Order was issued under date January 28, 1873.[39]

Take now an example of orders issued to the members of the army: [40]

(General Orders No. 114.)

WAR DEPARTMENT, ADJUTANT GENERAL'S OFFICE.

Washington, August 21, 1862.

I. No officer of the Regular Army or of volunteers will hereafter visit the city of Washington without special permission. Leaves of absence will not be considered as including the city of Washington, unless so stated, and leaves for

[38] Richardson, Messages and Papers of the Presidents, vol. ix, pp. 4172-4173.
[39] Ibid., vol. ix, pp. 4173-4174.
[40] Quoted in Lieber, Remarks on the Army Regulations, p. 120.

that purpose can only be given by the authority of the War Department, through the Adjutant General.

II. Officers on leave of absense will not leave the limits of their military department without special permission.

By order of the Secretary of War:

E. D. TOWNSEND,

Assistant Adjutant General.[41]

The above General Order was rescinded by General Orders No. 31, 1866.[42]

Again, we may quote from Mr. Lincoln's proclamation of the blockade,[43] issued only four days after his call for 75,000 of the militia. In this document the President said he had " deemed it advisable to set on foot a blockade of the ports within the States aforesaid, in pursuance of the laws of the United States and of the law of nations in such case provided. For this purpose, competent force will be posted so as to prevent entrance and exit of vessels from the ports aforesaid (that is, the ports of South Carolina, Georgia, Alabama, Florida, Mississippi, Louisiana, and Texas). If, therefore, with a view to violate such a blockade, a vessel shall approach, or shall attempt to leave either of the said ports, she will be duly warned by the commander of one of the blockading vessels, who will endorse on her register the fact and date of such warning; and if the same vessel shall again attempt to enter or leave the blockaded port, she will be captured and sent to the nearest convenient port, for such proceedings against her and her cargo as prize as may be deemed advisable." He continued:

And I hereby proclaim and declare that if any person, under the pretended authority of the said States, or under any other pretence, shall molest a vessel of the United States, or the persons or cargo on board of her, such person will be held amenable to the laws of the United States, for the prevention and punishment of piracy.

---

[41] See, for examples of army ordinances under delegated power, Richardson, Messages and Papers of the Presidents, vol. xiii, pp. 5602; vol. xiv, p. 6034.

[42] Lieber, Remarks on the Army Regulations, p. 120. Chap. iv of Lieber, Remarks on the Army Regulations, deals with the different editions thereof.

[43] 12 Stat. L., 1259.

The last paragraph of the quotation was aimed at the threatened grant of " pretended letters of marque " by the South which was mentioned in the preamble of the proclamation.

On April 27th the President extended the blockade to the ports of Virginia and North Carolina.[44]

One of the most famous Presidential ordinances of our history was the Emancipation Proclamation of January 1, 1863. This ordinance was constitutional in source of authority, emergency in purpose, legislative in application, and nonsupplementary in scope. In part it read: [45]

> Now, therefore, I, Abraham Lincoln, President of the United States, by virtue of the power in me vested as commander-in-chief of the army and navy of the United States, in time of actual armed rebellion against the authority and government of the United States, and as a fit and necessary war measure for suppressing said rebellion, do, on this 1st day of January A. D. 1863, and in accordance with my purpose so to do, publicly proclaimed for the full period of one hundred days from the day first above mentioned, order and designate as the States and parts of States wherein the people thereof, respectively, are this day in rebellion against the United States the following, to wit: . . . .
>
> And by virtue of the power and for the purpose aforesaid, I do order and declare that all persons held as slaves within said designated States and parts of States are, and henceforward shall be, free, and that the Executive Government of the United States, including the military and naval authorities thereof, will recognize and maintain the freedom of said persons. . . .
>
> And upon this act, sincerely believed to be an act of justice, warranted by the Constitution upon military necessity, I invoke the considerate judgment of mankind and the gracious favor of Almighty God.

III

We have observed that the power " to require the opinion, in writing, of the principal officer in each of the executive departments, upon any subject relating to the duties of their

---

[44] Ibid., 1259.

[45] Ibid., 1269. This, and the proclamation of the blockade, are here cited because they were probably constitutional, in the light of the broader view of the Constitution born in the crisis of 1861. About many of the war acts of Lincoln we may say that they were either under delegated power (see 12 Stat. L., 1262, 755, 13 Stat. L., 734-735, 12 Stat. L., 1266) or were admittedly illegal (see 12 Stat. L., 1260), or were unconstitutional in fact if not in the view of the President (see 13 Stat. L., 730). Congress later made blanket retroactive delegations, however.

respective offices," is on its face a power to issue 'official orders.'

But perhaps the President might under this clause issue a general order requiring all heads of departments to furnish him with written opinions on all questions (let us say) of a certain character or importance within their respective departments, or requiring a given head to furnish opinions on all questions of a specified class. In such a case the order in question would be a material ordinance; for it would be a uniform or general rule of governmental (as distinguished from social) conduct which the superior officer could enforce by the administrative sanction of dismissal.[46] This is, however, a very specialized power, and one which has lost even the significance which it might have had if the legal and political solidarity of President and cabinet had not developed to make it unnecessary. It is not worth while, therefore, to give it further attention, particularly since it would probably come under the power to see that the laws be faithfully executed, even if the Constitution had not specifically mentioned it.[47]

What is the essential nature of the power of recognition? It is not an expressed power, but is implied from the powers of receiving ambassadors, of appointing them (with the consent of the Senate), and of entering into negotiations leading to a treaty.[48] The function belongs to the President and to him alone.[49] It certainly involves discretion. In fact it is a 'political power,' the decision of giving or withholding recognition being vested in the absolute and final discretion of the Chief Executive. The wisdom of such decision the courts will not review; but they accept as conclusive the action of the President, where it is involved in cases which they are called upon to decide.[50] Furthermore, we have here a case of

[46] See above, chap. ii.

[47] See the opinion which Hamilton expressed in No. 74 (73) of the Federalist (Ford's edition). His opinion dealt, however, with particular orders, not general ones.

[48] Mathews, The Conduct of American Foreign Relations, chap. vii.

[49] Willoughby, Constitutional Law of the United States, vol. ii, secs. 194, 580.

[50] Ex parte Baiz, 135 U. S. 403; Foster v. Neilson, 2 Pet. 253.

discretion as to the creation of legal rights and duties; for the act of recognition of a government or of a state involves automatically certain rights and duties not only as between the two states involved but also as between the nationals thereof.[51] Finally, it involves the discretionary creation of rights and duties of uniform rather than individual application, and uniform application to private persons in each state. The act of recognition thus fulfills the definition of an act of co-legislation in the material sense. It does not create a 'rule' of law, but it involves discretion as to the circumstances in which uniform rights and duties are to be brought into play. In this it is analogous to the ordinance involved in the leading case of Field v. Clark.[52]

The power of issuing pardons and reprieves is certainly a discretionary power which results in the creation of legal rights and duties. It grants to the pardoned the right to restoration to his former legal status, and it imposes upon the state the duty to respect that status.[53] Yet once again, where an individual is pardoned, we have an act of executive discretion, not an act of legislation or ordinance making. It is only in the case of a Presidential proclamation of amnesty that we have an example of an ordinance. Such a proclamation the President has the right to issue under his pardoning power;[54] but this is so specialized a power and one so seldom called into play that it will not be necessary to go into the details of its working. Suffice it to say that we agree with M. Jèze that a pardon is not, but that an amnesty is, a legislative act.[55] The distinction is between an act of particular

---

[51] Cf. Kenneth v. Chambers, 14 How. 47. See note on "Effect of Decrees of Unrecognized Foreign Governments," in Michigan Law Review, vol. xxiii, p. 802.

[52] 143 U. S. 649.

[53] On the nature of a pardon see Willoughby, Constitutional Law of the United States, sec. 686 ff.

[54] See, for example, the amnesty proclamation of President Washington issued after the Whisky Rebellion in Western Pennsylvania (Richardson, Messages and Papers of the Presidents, vol. i, p. 181. See also Willoughby, Constitutional Law of the United States, vol. ii, sec. 687).

[55] Les principes généraux du droit administratif (deuxième édition, 1914), pp. 9 ff., 142, 217.

discretion and a discretionary act which applies uniformly to all persons within a given class. The one is without, the other within, the operation of the régime of law.

IV

We come now to the veto and treaty-making powers of the President, which we may consider together. In the first place, we note that both statutes and treaties are material law. The Constitution declares that not only the instrument itself, but the laws and treaties made in pursuance thereof, are the supreme law of the land. The courts have construed this to mean that, in so far as treaties do not require legislation to bring them into effect but are self-executing, to that extent they are law which can be directly enforced in the courts.[56] As between conflicting statute and treaty, therefore, the courts have declared that the latest in time is law.[57] In the second place, it is clear that since the President is given participation in the bringing into operation of both statutes and treaties, he is in both cases given participation in law making. There is, indeed, this distinction between the two cases: that in statute law making the President participates only to the extent of acceptance or rejection of a measure the contents of which he cannot directly share in determining; while in treaty making not only does he by negotiation take the initiative in determining the content of the act, but his will finally determines whether or not the act shall go into operation. At every stage his is the active will, except that the Senate may either refuse assent outright or propose amendments or reservations which he must accept or let the treaty drop. But the President participates in the making of both statutes and

---

[56] Willoughby, Constitutional Law of the United States, secs. 208, 212, 214. "Treaties formed by the Executive of the United States are to be the law of the land. To cloak the executive with leg. authority is setting aside our modern and much-boasted distribution of power into legislative, judicial, and exec.—discoveries unknown to Locke and Montesquieu, and all the ancient writers. It certainly contradicts all the modern theory of government, and in practice must be tyranny" (Journal of William Maclay, p. 75).

[57] But see Willoughby, Constitutional Law of the United States, sec. 208 (cf. sec. 207).

treaties, except where in respect to the former his veto is overridden. We are thus faced with the question whether such participation constitutes the function of ordinance making.

With respect to statutes the answer to this query is obvious. For a statute is passed by the regular legislative assembly, and is thus a law in the formal as well as the material sense of the term. It is in contrast with just such an act that we may define a formal ordinance as an act of government which, in its content, partakes of the nature of a legislative or ordinance making act, while, in its source, it is issued by some governmental authority (usually an executive or administrative officer or organ) without the assent of the regular legislative assembly. A statute of Congress which is creative of legal rights and duties is at once material and formal law. The fact that the President signs such an act means no more than that he is the partner of, or, if one pleases, the constitutional check upon, the legislature in its function of legislating. In contrast, a proclamation of the President in which Congress does not participate may be material, but is never formal, law.

On the other hand, treaties which are creative of legal rights and duties that are directly enforceable in the courts, are ordinances for the reason that the assent of the regular legislative assembly is not required for their enactment. Treaties are by the Constitution (as interpreted by the courts) declared to be material law; but they are in no wise formal law. In their effect they are on a parity with statutes; in their source they are to be sharply distinguished from statutes. But it is also to be noted that treaties are ordinances of the President by and with the advice and consent of the Senate, not ordinances of the President acting alone. For this reason, as well as because of the fact that the constitutional law of treaty making and treaty enforcement has been worked out in detail by volumes devoted entirely to that subject,[58] this treatise

---

[58] See Crandall, Treaties, Their Making and Enforcement, and Butler, The Treaty-Making Power (2 vols.), as well as the discus-

need not consider the character of a treaty, except to note that it is material law and formal ordinance. It is sufficient here to note that, while the character of treaties as internationally binding contracts is the concern of international law or relations, and not of the internal law of the states that are parties thereto, nevertheless the peculiar [59] character of treaties in the United States as material law makes them fall within the category of ordinance. This has not been recognized by commentators on our constitutional system for the reason (which has caused many other errors and much loose thinking) that such writers have not attempted scientific classification in jurisprudence, but have been content to use the term ordinance (if at all) without accurately defining its meaning. Our juristic categories are mere historical categories, which is tantamount to saying that they are not scientific. It is of course necessary to keep always in mind the historical meaning of terms, because of the theory of our law that terms mean what they did at the time of their enactment.[60] That theory is to be sure the product of an era when men thought in static terms, and not in terms of evolution. It has the advantage of furnishing stability, and the danger of furnishing a straight-jacket. Since it is at the very foundation of our constitutional interpretation, we have in this treatise largely based our reasoning upon it. But without neglecting historical meanings when dealing with constitutional construction, we may introduce scientific categories for the sake of accuracy in analysis.

This ordinance making power of the President and the Senate which is involved in the treaty making power is overwhelmingly important for the following reasons: First, treaties are law and enforceable as such in our courts: they may override statutes of Congress with which they conflict, the rule being that, as between statute and treaty which are

sions in general treatises like Willoughby, Constitutional Law of the United States (see index), and in various articles.

[59] Chief Justice Marshall in Foster v. Neilson, 2 Pet. 253.

[60] But see Willoughby, Constitutional Law of the United States, sec. 26.

in conflict, the latter in time prevails.[61] Secondly, there are no limits to the treaty making power flowing from the distribution of powers between the national government and the States, treaties being able to cover subjects reserved, as against Congessional legislation, to the several States.[62] Thirdly, in general, the treaty making power, while exercised under the Constitution and subject to its provisions, is not by that document limited in any way, provided only it is exercised with reference to matters that, in international practice, properly come within the scope of international agreement.[63] Fourthly, treaties are the only important and frequent constitutional ordinances of the Chief Magistrate which are of general application within the continental United States.[64] Fifthly, the President alone without the consent of the Senate may abrogate treaties, as President Taft did with reference to a treaty with Russia.[65]

V

There are three clauses of Article II of the Constitution which should be, and often are, read together. These are the opening sentence of the Article, which vests the executive power in the President; the 'faithful execution' clause; and the clause prescribing the Presidential oath of office. The question arises whether the vesting of the executive power in the Chief Executive is a grant of general executive power,[66] or a mere declaratory expression which summarizes the specific grants which follow; and, if it is a grant per se, whether any ordinance making powers may be implied from it.

---

[61] Ibid., vol. i, 207-208.

[62] The People v. Gerke, 5 Cal. 381; Missouri v. Holland, 252 U. S. 416 (1920); Willoughby, Constitutional Law of the United States, vol. i, sec. 190, 210 ff.

[63] Ibid.; see also Geofroy v. Riggs, 133 U. S. 258.

[64] All other sorts are applicable only in the American theater of war or in conquered enemy territory or in dependencies in the absence of Congressional action, or are applicable to administrative officers only and not private persons, or to very special classes of private persons (amnesties). Recognition does not create, but only brings into operation, rights and duties for all nationals involved.

[65] Taft, The Presidency, pp. 112-114.

[66] Berdahl, War Powers of the Executive in the United States, chap. i.

With respect to the first part of the inquiry the evidence is somewhat conflicting, but tends to confirm the view that we have here a positive grant of general power of an executive nature. Against this view we have the fact that state courts have as a rule construed similar [67] general clauses, when followed by specific grants to the governors, as being only definitions of the powers which follow and not separate grants.[68] In some cases, however, state constitutions denominate the governor only the 'chief' executive, and in all of them the popular election of several other executive officials makes him such in practice; while the President is clearly 'the' Executive.

Again, we have the recorded opinion of James Wilson as stated in the Philadelphia Convention that " He did not consider the Prerogatives of the British Monarch as a proper guide in defining the Executive powers. Some of the prerogatives were of a Legislative nature. Among others that of war & peace &c." And more conclusive is the fact that both he and Madison expressed rather narrow views of the essential elements of executive power. Wilson is reported as saying

[67] However, a distinction may be drawn between the 'supreme' or 'chief' executive power (especially the latter) vested in some governors and 'the' executive power vested in the President.

[68] See Field v. People, 3 Ill. 79. The Constitution of Illinois contained the following clause: "The executive power of the state shall be vested in a Governor." The court refused to imply a power of removal from this clause (cf. Goodnow, Principles of the Administrative Law of the United States, pp. 94-95). President Roosevelt expressed, on the other hand, the revolutionary and utterly unjustifiable view that the President can do whatever the Constitution and laws do not forbid him to do (Notes for a Possible Autobiography, pp. 388-389). This doctrine is not at issue here; for it is the exact opposite of the true principle (Taft, The Presidency, pp. 125-132). For striking evidence of the unlegal character of Mr. Roosevelt's mind see Burgess, Recent Changes in American Constitutional Theory, p. 36 ff. Mr. Taft severely criticizes Mr. Roosevelt's theory; but the present writer understands him to say merely that the President must find his authority to act in every case in a given clause. The claim that the express (but general) clause on 'the executive power' is a delegation and not merely declaratory is not necessarily inconsistent with this viewpoint. Anyway, Mr. Taft in the same volume refers to the power of removal as being considered in 1789 an incident of executive power, and, more important still, gives a very liberal interpretation to the 'faithful execution' clause.

that "The only powers he conceived strictly executive were those of executing the laws, and appointing officers, not (appertaining to and) appointed by the Legislature." King records that Madison "agrees with Wilson in his definition of executive powers—executive powers ex vi termini, do not include the Rights of war & peace &c. but the powers shd. be confined and defined." [69] But this does not disprove our point, if the interpretation of the faithful execution clause be made broad enough.

On the other side of the issue we start with the opinions of Madison and others expressed in the first Congress that the power of removal flows from the executive power of the President.[70] The reasoning then employed is admirably summed up in a note on Ellsworth's speech which occurs in the Journal of William Maclay; [71]

> I buy a square acre of land. I buy the trees, water, and everything belonging to it. The executive power belongs to the President. The removing officers is a tree on this acre. The power of removing is, therefore his. It is in him. It is nowhere else. Thus we are under the necessity of ascertaining by implication where the power is.

But if the power of removal is a tree on the acre of executive power, why may there not be also other trees quite as important?

Take another instance of contemporaneous evidence: in the famous Pacificus-Helvidius debate which Madison [72] and Hamilton [73] waged in the papers over President Washington's proclamation of neutrality there is an explicit claim set forth by Hamilton that the clause in question is a general grant. We may quote from his letter to the Gazette of the United States for June 29, 1793:

> The second article of the Constitution of the United States, section first, establishes this general proposition, that " the EXECUTIVE POWER shall be vested in a President of the United States of America."

---

[69] Farrand, Récords of the Federal Convention, vol. i, pp. 65-66, 70.

[70] See the admirable discussion of this debate in Thach, The Creation of the Presidency, chap. vi. See also Story on the Constitution, sec. 1537 ff.; Goodnow, Comparative Administrative Law, vol. i, p. 64.

[71] Page 114; see also pp. 103-104, 109, 111, 112, 115.

[72] Writings of James Madison, (Hunt, editor), vol. vi, p. 138 ff.

[73] Works of Alexander Hamilton, (J. C. Hamilton, editor), vol. vii, p. 76 ff.

The same article, in a succeeding section, proceeds to delineate particular cases of executive power. . . .

It would not consist with the rules of sound construction to consider this enumeration of particular authorities as derogating from the more comprehensive grant in the general clause, further than as it may be coupled with express restrictions or limitations; as in regard to the co-operation of the Senate in the appointment of officers, and the making of treaties; which are plainly qualifications of the general executive powers of appointing officers and making treaties. The difficulty of a complete enumeration of all the cases of executive authority, would naturally dictate the use of general terms, and would render it improbable that a specification of certain particulars was designed as a substitute for those terms, when antecedently used. The different mode of expression employed in the constitution, in regard to the two powers, the legislative and the executive, serves to confirm this inference. In the article which gives the legislative power of the government, the expressions are, "All legislative powers herein granted shall be vested in a congress of the United States." In that which grants the executive power, the expressions are, " THE EXECUTIVE POWER shall be vested in a President of the United States."

The enumeration ought therefore to be considered, as intended merely to specify the principal articles implied in the definition of executive power; leaving the rest to flow from the general grant of that power, interpreted in conformity with other parts of the Constitution, and with the principles of free government.

The general doctrine of our Constitution then is, that the EXECUTIVE POWER of the nation is vested in the President; subject only to the *exceptions* and *qualifications*, which are expressed in the instrument.

Other authorities, of later times but carrying great weight, have expressed views that tend in the same direction. Thus Story in his treatise on the Constitution, speaking of the fact that the President has given exequaturs to consuls, says this power may be fairly inferred from the other parts of the Constitution, " and indeed seems a general incident to the executive authority." [74] Likewise, in the case of Kansas v. Colorado [75] the Supreme Court, contrasting the opening sentences of Articles I and III, pointed out that the former vested in Congress all legislative powers therein granted, whereas the latter vested in the federal courts ' the ' judicial power of the United States. A similar contrast had already been drawn by Hamilton between Articles I and II.[76]

---

[74] Sec. 1565.
[75] 206 U. S. 46, 81-83. See Corwin, The President's Control of Foreign Relations, pp. 30-32.
[76] See quotation above.

Then finally, we have the views of at least two Presidents. Thus Benjamin Harrison, in his book entitled This Country of Ours, referring to the question of having cabinet members independent of the President, declared: [77]

The adoption of this view would give us eight Chief Executives . . . and would leave the President, in whom the Constitution says " the Executive power shall be vested," no function save that of appointing these eight Presidents. It would be a farming out of his Constitutional powers.

And again:

The responsibility under the Constitution for the Executive administration of the Government in all its branches is devolved upon the President.

Grover Cleveland in his Presidential Problems expressed the following opinion: [78]

The Constitution declares; " The executive power shall be vested in a President of the United States of America," and this is followed by a recital of the specific and distinctly declared duties with which he is charged, and the powers with which he is invested. The members of the Convention were not willing, however, that the executive power which they had vested in the President should be cramped and embarrassed by any implication that a specific statement of certain granted powers and duties excluded all other executive functions; nor were they apparently willing that the claim of such exclusion should have countenance in the strict meaning which might be given to the words " executive power." Therefore we find that the Constitution supplements a recital of the specific powers and duties of the President with this impressive and conclusive additional requirement: " He shall take care that the laws be faithfully executed." This I conceive to be equivalent to a grant of all the power necessary to the performance of his duty in the faithful execution of the laws. . . . The " Committee on Style " . . . reported in favor of an oath in these terms: " I will faithfully execute the office of President of the United States, and will to the best of my ability preserve, protect, and defend the Constitution of the United States ";

---

[77] Page 70: cf. chap. vi.

[78] Page 14 ff. With reference to the oath, we hold that it cannot be considered as a substantive grant of power, but that it may be used in a manner analogous to a Preamble, to throw light on the meaning of the grants that are made. In this sense Mr. Cleveland was justified in referring to it. Mr. Cleveland seems to rely upon the faithful execution clause as removing any ambiguity that might be derived from the fact that the general clause on executive power is followed by specifications. We agree to the extent of saying that, while the two clauses may not be identical in meaning, they do reinforce each other in proving that the President is given control over the federal administration.

and this form was adopted by the Convention without discussion, and continues to this day as the form of obligation which binds the conscience of every incumbent of our Chief Magistracy.

It is therefore apparent that as the Constitution, in addition to its specification of especial duties and powers devolving upon the President, provides that " he shall take care that the laws be faithfully executed," and as this was evidently intended as a general devolution of power and imposition of obligation in respect to any condition that might arise relating to the execution of the laws, so it is likewise apparent that the convention was not content to rest the sworn obligation of the President solely upon his covenant to " faithfully execute the office of President of the United States," but added thereto the mandate that he should preserve, protect, and defend the Constitution, to the best of his judgment and power, or, as it was afterward expressed, to the best of his ability. Thus is our President solemnly required not only to exercise every power attached to his office, to the end that the laws may be faithfully executed, and not only to render obedience to the demands of the fundamental law and executive duty, but to exert all his official strength and authority for the preservation, protection, and defense of the Constitution.

It is a cardinal rule of construction that effect must be given to all parts of the Constitution.[79] Hence, if the clause in question is not considered as being a grant, what was the need of including it? We cannot conclude that it was a mere ornamental decoration declaratory of the enactment of the separation of powers. On the other hand, we may say that if the clause on executive power is a separate grant, which involves some or all of the specific grants and also other executive powers in addition, of what use are the specific grants if they are included in the general grant? The answer to this is, that these specific grants, in at least some cases, place limitations upon the executive power, as when they require Senatorial concurrence in their exercise.[80]

From what we know of the ideas of the framers it appears that they considered the ' faithful execution ' duty the chief

---

[79] Note the reasoning—based upon this cardinal principle—by which the courts infer, from the fact that a grand jury indictment is mentioned in the federal bill of rights, that such an indictment is not required under due process. See Hurtado v. California, 110 U. S. 516.

[80] It might indeed be said that the general clause is a grant but does not include the others; in other words, is a grant entirely in addition to the others. But the answer to this is that, in point of fact, it clearly includes at least the faithful execution clause.

function of a distinctly executive nature; [81] that they added for political reasons [82] other powers which they considered either as executive in nature, or as powers which, while not strictly Executive, were yet for practical reasons proper ones for the executive to exercise; and that they added the statement about executive power to make it clear that they intended to enact the separation of powers, [83] and perhaps also to leave no doubt that, if other clearly executive powers might be needed which did not come within the specific enumerations, they might be exercised by the President. [84] Especially was it meant to include what we should today term 'administrative control.' We have seen in a previous chapter that, from this view of the grant, Congress in 1789 implied the power of removal as a necessary means of enforcing such administrative control. [85] But does the executive power involve a formal power of directing, by uniform or general ordinances, the manner in which subordinates shall perform their duties? [86]

In view of the separation of powers as made in the Constitution, it cannot be held that from his executive and faith-

---

[81] See the opinions of Wilson and Madison quoted above from Farrand, Records of the Federal Convention, vol. i, pp. 65-66, 70.

[82] It is true, in general, that the statesmen of the era of adoption gave more attention to the 'political' powers of the President than to his 'administrative control' (Goodnow, Principles of the Administrative Law of the United States, p. 73 ff.). As Madison afterwards wrote to Jefferson, "The questions concerning the degree of power turned chiefly on the appointment to offices, and the controul on the Legislature" (Farrand, Records of the Federal Convention, vol. iii, p. 133). The particular 'political reasons' that may have induced them to give several independent powers to the President were the reaction from weak executives under the Revolutionary Constitutions and the realization that the weakness of the Confederation lay in its lack of enforcing power. Shays' Rebellion had taken place in Massachusetts in 1786-1787. See Story on the Constitution, secs. 1413, 1416, p. 161 ff.; The Federalist, No. 70.

[83] Goodnow, Principles of the Administrative Law of the United States, p. 32.

[84] Whether this was their purpose or not, the clause is open to such broad construction (Thach, The Creation of the Presidency, pp. 138-139).

[85] Chap. viii.

[86] Story on the Constitution, sec. 459; Willoughby, Constitutional Law of the United States, secs. 19-22.

ful execution powers the President derives a power to issue ordinances affecting the rights of private individuals, or even the power to organize the administrative services and fix their functions.[87]   On the other hand, it might be understood as giving the Chief Executive the power to issue ordinances which, while not fixing the main functions of federal officers,[88] nevertheless embody minor regulations as to how, when, and where they are to perform the functions set forth in the statutes.[89]   The distinction is clear enough in principle, though the sharp line of cleavage may not be easy to trace in concrete cases.   But certainly the issuance of administrative orders and ordinances is the most systematic as well as the most effective method by which the President may perform the constitutional duty of seeing to the execution of the laws.[90]   Here is a point where legislative functions (as understood in our jurisprudence) and executive functions merge into one another; and if the power be kept within the proper limits it does not violate the Constitution.   To deny this power to the President would be either to assert that the 'faithful execution' and 'executive power' clauses are almost meaningless, or else to affirm that the powers conferred by them can be used only in individual or particular cases.[91]

Briefly, the limits of the power are these: such *Verwaltungs-verordnungen* are illegal when they command any infringe-

---

[87] See above, this chapter.

[88] This follows from the 'necessary and proper' clause.

[89] Cf. In re Neagle, 135 U. S. 1.

[90] In many states this power has little meaning, apparently, in itself, and the governor is powerless, except where he has by express grants the powers of appointment and removal.   Yet this is not proper.   In the case of the federal government, there is reason to believe that this clause was understood in a very broad sense by the framers.   It will be remembered that Madison took such a view of the clause, or of what was no doubt its equivalent, in discussing his motion on the Executive which we have referred to above.   The power "to carry into effect the national laws" became in the final draft the power "to take care that" they be faithfully executed.   Both seem to correspond to similar, though variously worded, clauses in the state constitutions of the time.

[91] There is no reason to hold that a power to order A to perform an act *once* is permissible, while the power to order A, B, C, D, E, etc., to perform it, or to order A to perform it *continuously*, is illegal.

ment of the interests of private persons which is unauthorized by law, or any action which is contrary to law. As between executive orders and statutes, the heads of departments and all officers of the government are bound to follow the latter until they have been declared invalid by the courts.[92] Nor may the executive orders of this character regulate the functions of officers in a manner which seems to usurp the power of Congress to enact the laws necessary and proper to carry into execution the powers vested by the Constitution in that body and in other departments and officers of the government. This gives Congress the power to create departments and to prescribe their major duties, and the President has no concurrent power in the premises. Everything that he does must be ancillary to the statutory rules of Congress and conducive to their better execution. This includes only rules of personnel administration dealing with the relations of officers as such to their work and their outside activities in general, and rules that make specific the ways and means, the times and places, of performing the administrative functions set forth in the acts of the legislature.

In conclusion, it may be added that unless Congress sees fit to provide penalties for the violation of such administrative ordinances, or processes for their enforcement, they have no sanction attached to them, except that involved in the power of removal. This is what is termed above an ' administrative sanction ' as contrasted with a penal or a judicial sanction. It is perhaps, not a sanction at all in the strict sense, for the reason that the President need not apply it in an individual case unless he sees fit.[93]

---

[92] James Hart, " The Ordinance Making Powers of the President," in North American Review, July, 1923.

[93] A court of law is bound to enforce a penal statute; but the President makes his rule and enforces it also, and can in any given case dispense with enforcement. Thus an executive order requiring civil service employees to refrain from certain political activities is a mere nullity unless the President actually carries out his threat of dismissal for disobedience.

VI

Some conception of the meaning of this power may be deduced from the reasoning in the famous case of In re Neagle.[94] The circumstances leading to the case were as follows:

There was evidence to the effect that, because of a certain judicial decision and because his court had imprisoned them for contempt of court, Justice Field was in danger of violence at the hands of one Terry and his wife. The circuit duties of the justice led him to California, where Terry lived, and the Attorney-General, knowing of the situation, instructed Neagle, a deputy marshal, to protect Field. While at breakfast, Field was attacked by Terry, who struck him two blows on the face. Just as Terry was about to draw a knife, Neagle, to save Field's life, shot Terry. Neagle was indicted in the state courts of California for murder, brought his case before the Circuit Court by suing out a writ of habeas corpus, and was ordered to be discharged by that court. The case was then appealed by the sheriff to the Supreme Court of the United States.

Because the case came up on appeal, and not on writ of error, the Court went into facts as well as the law; and on that score it concluded that the circumstances fully justified Neagle. But section 753 of the revised statutes provided for the only cases when the writ of habeas corpus should extend to a prisoner in jail; and the only two which could possibly apply to this case were when he was held in custody in violation of the Constitution or a law of the United States, or for an act done or omitted in pursuance of a law of the United States. The question on which the decision hinged, therefore, was whether Neagle was held in violation of the Constitution or a law, or for an act done or omitted in pursuance of a law of the United States.

We may analyse the reasoning of the decision with a view to criticising it in the light of the dissenting opinion. This reasoning involves the following propositions:

94 135 U. S. 1.

1.   Mr. Justice Field was engaged in his official duties while traveling to the performance of his duties as much as when sitting on the bench.

2.   It was the duty of the President to protect him in the exercise of such duties.

3.   It was within the power of Congress to provide for the removal from the state's custody (by the writ of habeas corpus) of an officer acting under the orders of the President in protecting the justice.

4.   The actual provision of the law of Congress concerning the writ was broad enough to include this case.

(1)   The dissenting opinion refused to see " anything of an official character in the transaction." It distinguished between Field as a private individual and Mr. Justice Field as a federal judge. But while he does not appear to have been at that time actually in discharge of duties, it would seem that, if the President could protect him while on the bench, he should have the power to protect him while going to the discharge of his official duties, if it were known that his life was threatened for acts done while in discharge thereof. Any official of a government deserves protection from that government against those who attack him for governmental acts, if not for private acts.

(2)   " The authority," said Mr. Justice Lamar, in his dissent, " is sought to be traced here through the self-preservative power of the federal judiciary implied from the Constitution; and then through the obligation of the executive to protect the judges, implied from the Constitution, whereas there is no such implication in either case, for the simple reason that by the Constitution itself the whole of these functions is committed to Congress."

The majority view was quite different. After citing cases illustrating " the principle of the supremacy of the government of the United States, in the exercise of all the powers conferred upon it by the Constitution," the Court went on to show that the judiciary could not furnish the protection to which the justice was entitled, and that the legislative branch

could only furnish it by passing laws, which the argument to
be refuted assumed it had not done.   It then said:

If we turn to the executive department of the government, we
find a very different condition of affairs.   The Constitution, section 3,
Article 2, declares that the President "shall take care that the laws
be faithfully executed," and he is provided with the means of ful-
filling this obligation by his authority to commission all the officers
of the United States, and, by and with the advice and consent of the
Senate, to appoint the most important of them and to fill vacancies.
He is declared to be the commander-in-chief of the army and navy of
the United States.   The duties which are thus imposed upon him he
is further enabled to perform by the recognition in the Constitution,
and the creation by acts of Congress, of executive departments, which
have varied in number from four or five to seven or eight, the heads
of which are familiarly called cabinet ministers.   These aid him in
the performance of the great duties of his office, and represent him
in a thousand acts to which it can hardly be supposed his personal
attention is called, and thus he is enabled to fulfil the duty of his
great department, expressed in the phrase that "he shall take care
that the laws be faithfully executed."
Is this duty limited to the enforcement of acts of Congress or
treaties of the United States according to their *express terms*, or
does it include the rights, duties and obligations growing out of the
Constitution itself, our international relations, and all the protection implied by the nature of the government under the Constitution?
. . .
We cannot doubt the power of the President to take measures for
the protection of a judge of one of the courts of the United States,
who, while in the discharge of the duties of his office, is threatened
with a personal attack which may probably result in his death, and
we think it clear that where this protection is to be afforded through
the civil power, the Department of Justice is the proper one to set in
motion the necessary measures of protection.   The correspondence
already recited in this opinion between the marshal of the Northern
District of California, and the Attorney General, and the district
attorneys of the United States for that district, although prescribing
no very specific mode of affording this protection by the Attorney
General, is sufficient, we think, to warrant the marshal in taking the
steps which he did take, in making the provisions which he did make,
for the protection and defence of Mr. Justice Field.

To this, however, the dissenting justices made the following
objection: " Waiving the question of the essentiality of any
such protection to the existence of the government, the manifest answer is, that the protection needed and to be given
must proceed not from the President, but primarily from
Congress. Again, while it is the President's duty to take care
that the laws be faithfully executed, it is not his duty to
make laws or a law of the United States. The laws he is to
see executed are manifestly those contained in the Constitu-

tion, and those enacted by Congress, whose duty it is to make all laws necessary and proper for carrying into execution the powers of those tribunals. In fact, for the President to have undertaken to make any law of the United States pertinent to this matter would have been to invade the domain of power expressly committed by the Constitution exclusively to Congress. That body was perfectly able to pass such laws as it should deem expedient in reference to such matters . . . and there was not the slightest legal necessity out of which to imply any such power in the President." And again: " The gravamen of this case is in the assertion that Neagel slew Terry in pursuance *of a law* of the United States. . . . Anything purporting to be a law not enacted by Congress would not be ' in pursuance of ' any provision of the Constitution."

(3) As for the third proposition, the best argument for it, and a conclusive one, is stated by the Court. " To the objection made in the argument," it is said, " that the prisoner is discharged by this writ from the power of the state court to try him for the whole offence, the reply is, that if the prisoner is held in the state court to answer for an act which he was authorized to do by the law of the United States, which it was his duty to do as a marshal of the United States, and if in doing that act he did no more than what was necessary and proper for him to do, he *cannot* be guilty of a crime under the law of the State of California."

(4) There was no specific ' law ' of Congress which authorized the deputy marshal to protect the justice while traveling to discharge his official duties. The Court, however, said: " In the view we take of the Constitution of the United States, any obligation fairly and properly inferrable from that instrument, or any duty of the marshal to be derived from the general scope of his duties under the laws of the United States, is a ' law ' within the meaning of this phrase." Specifically, this meant that the term ' law ' as used in the statute dealing with the writ of habeas corpus did not, in the opinion of the Court, mean merely ' statute ' of Congress, but that " this view of the statute is an unwarranted restriction

of the meaning of a law designed to extend in a liberal manner the benefit of the writ of habeas corpus to persons imprisoned for the performance of their duty. And we are satisfied that if it was the duty of Neagle, under the circumstances, a duty which could only arise under the laws of the United States, to defend Mr. Justice Field from a murderous attack upon him, he brings himself within the meaning of the section we have recited. This view of the subject is confirmed by the alternative provision, that he must be in custody ' for an act done or omitted in pursuance of a law of the United States or of an order, process, or decree of a court or judge thereof, or is in custody in violation of the Constitution or of a law or treaty of the United States.' " In other words, ' law ' as here used included Presidential orders issued under a constitutional obligation.

The court relied also on the argument that the deputy marshal was given by statute " the same powers, in executing the laws of the United States, as the sheriffs and their deputies in such state may have, by law, in executing the laws thereof " ; that the sheriffs in California were authorized to preserve the peace and prevent and suppress affrays; and that, therefore, the deputy had these powers in preserving the peace of the United States violated by Terry in attacking a federal judge in the discharge of his duties. This line of reasoning seems to be brought in to supplement the first argument by introducing statutory authority for the action of the deputy. But the fallacy involved in it is pointed out with exactness in the dissenting opinion of Mr. Justice Lamar, in which Mr. Chief Justice Fuller concurred. This dissent says:

The fallacy in the use made of section 788, in the argument just outlined, is this:

That section gives to the officers named the same measure of powers when in the discharge of their duties as those possessed by the sheriffs, it is true; but it does not alter the duties themselves. It does not empower them to enlarge the scope of their labors and responsibilities but only adds to their efficiency within that scope. They are still, by the very terms of the statute itself, limited to the execution of " the laws of the United States ": and are not in any way by adoption, mediate or immediate, from the code or the common law, authorized to execute the laws of California. The statute, therefore, leaves the matter just where it found it.

By way of summary we may say that the argument that Neagle was given powers analogous to those of the California sheriffs in executing federal laws, while true, is so far beside the point that its clear refutation by the dissenting opinion should prevent its being considered the ratio decidendi of the Court's decision. Of the four links in the main chain of reasoning we accept at least three. That is to say: Mr. Justice Field was in performance of his duties, though not at the moment of the incident sitting on the bench; the President under his power to see that the laws are faithfully executed can issue particular (or, for that matter, general) orders to deputy marshals to protect federal judges who are in danger; and this order imposes an obligation upon the deputy, in the discharge of which, on the theory of federal supremacy, he may by Congress be protected by the grant of a hearing in federal courts. Whether the wording of the statute concerning the issuance of the writ of habeas corpus could be interpreted as including cases where there was no statutory duty, but only an ordinance or executive act prescribing such duty, is a mere matter of interpretation which does not concern us. The point is, that the Supreme Court recognized such a Presidential order as a valid discretionary administrative regulation from which flow certain legal results. Specifically it offers a basis for removing a case from state to federal courts when the official under indictment acts under such regulation.

The trouble with the dissenting opinion is that it is premised upon too rigid and impractical an interpretation of the separation of powers. It carries the maxim *expressio unius est exclusio alterius* to an extreme that shows a lack of realistic insight into the nature of the governmental process. The Presidential order, if general, would be legislative in the same sense that every *Verwaltungsverordnung* is such. Yet the denial that the President can give such orders to his subordinates means precisely that the President is required by the Constitution in its faithful execution clause to do that which by that same Constitution in the separation of powers he is denied the means of accomplishing. It is a rule of construction that every clause of the instrument has real meaning; and an equally valid rule that the particular forms an exception to the general instead of being destroyed by it. The general principle that the President cannot legislate is modified to the extent that he can issue administrative ordinances, not to be sure to create substantial duties of officers, but nevertheless to fill up the interstices of their regular statutory duties.

VII

The duty of the President to see that the laws are faithfully executed is not exhausted by controlling the law enforcing powers of his subordinates and by issuing to them administrative regulations or ordinances. Treaties as well as statutes are laws in the sense of the Constitution; and at times the President finds himself under the obligation of exercising legislative powers in American protectorates under his duty of faithfully executing treaties. Mr. Taft has written as follows:

The widest power and the broadest duty which the President has is conferred and imposed by a clause in section three of article two, providing that "he shall take care that the laws be faithfully executed." This same duty is enforced by (the oath of office). . . .[95]
The laws that the President must take care shall be faithfully executed are not confined to acts of Congress.[96]

Mr. Taft goes on to state that treaties as well as statutes are included in the term ' law ' as it occurs in this clause, and gives an illustration taken from his own experience as Secretary of War under President Roosevelt. The treaty in question was the Platt amendment of the treaty between the United States and Cuba, which provided:

The government of Cuba consents that the United States may exercise the right to intervene for the preservation of Cuban independence and the maintenance of a government adequate for the protection of life, property, and individual liberty.

[95] Our Chief Magistrate and his Powers, p. 78.
[96] Ibid., p. 85 ff.

When the outbreak of a revolution in Cuba made intervention imperative, Secretary Taft advised the President "that this treaty pro tanto extended the jurisdiction of the United States to maintain law and order over Cuba in case of threatened insurrection and of danger of life, property, and individual liberty, and that under his duty to take care that the laws be executed this was a 'law' and his power to see that it was executed was clear."

A law of Congress in the specific case was not needed, and was not sought. Let us see what this intervention involved. Mr. Taft tells us: [97]

I was obliged to ask for the army and navy and by authority of President Roosevelt to institute a provisional government, which lasted nearly two years. It restored order and provided a fair election law, conducted an election, and turned that government over to the officers elected under the Constitution of Cuba. . . . Congress appropriated the money needed to meet the extraordinary expenditures required, and recognized the provisional government in Cuba in such a way as to make the course taken a precedent.

The potentialities of this power to govern, by legislating for, as well as administering the government of, another country with whom the United States is at peace, provided we have an authorizing treaty with such country, will readily be perceived to be enormous. The illustration shows how in unexpected ways the executive powers of the President may, in exceptional cases, become legislative powers, and that too, without violating the letter or the spirit of the constitutional separation of powers.

Another incident of even greater significance is given by the same ex-Secretary of War, whose views are of especial legal significance because of the fact that he is the present Chief Justice of the United States. He asserts that the laws which the President is to see executed are not confined to statutes and treaties. His illustration is best given in his own words: [98]

By an act approved April 28, 1904, the President was directed to take possession of and occupy, on behalf of the United States, the

---

[97] Ibid., p. 88.
[98] The Presidency, pp. 83-85.

Canal Zone, the dominion over which had been acquired under the Hay-Varilla Treaty just then ratified. The seventh section of that act provided that all the military, civil, and judicial powers, as well as the power to make all rules and regulations necessary for the government of the Canal Zone, should be vested in such a person and should be exercised in such a manner as the President should direct, until the expiration of the Fifty-eighth Congress. The Fifty-eighth Congress expired without making provision for future government of the Zone.

I was secretary of war from 1904 to 1908, and in charge of the canal work, and the question arose as to what was to be done in this legislative lapse after the death of the Fifty-eighth Congress. I had no hesitation in advising the President, and I may add that he had no hesitation in accepting the advice, that under his duty to take care that the laws be faithfully executed, when express authority from Congress to continue a going government essential to the construction of the canal failed, he was justified in maintaining the existing government and continuing the *status quo*. Congress made no further provision for the government of the Zone for seven years, and by its acquiescence in our course vindicated our view of the President's duty.

It seems clear that the ' law ' in this case was the authority to build the canal, for which a government was necessary. From the duty to execute this law properly flowed the power to legislate for the Canal Zone, a power which was not authorized until later, and then by silent acquiescence and grant of supplies. It may be said that this acquiescence constituted retroactive delegation of power by Congress. Rather is it a case of independent power to legislate as an incident of executive power. For it seems clear that the power to maintain the status quo involved the continuation of the power to make rules and regulations.

We may close this section with another instance of executive rule making. Lieber, in his Remarks on the Army Regulations, mentions a set of regulations issued without statutory authorization to govern the operations of the revenue cutter service.[99] The striking points about this instance are that penalties for violation of the rules are attached, that it is an exceptionally broad exercise of independent or non-delegated regulative power, and that for these reasons Lieber and Fairlie after him express doubts as to the constitutionality

---

[99] Lieber, Remarks on the Army Regulations, p. 139 ff. (Appendix D). This work of Lieber's, though published in 1898, has a large amount of material on our subject, but in a rather unorganized form.

of these rules. Here is raised a question of the scope of the executive power of issuing *Verwaltungsverordnungen*—a question that has not been authoritatively settled.

VIII

When we turn to the power of the President as commander-in-chief of the army and navy we find a power which by its very terms involves regulation and ordinance making. But to understand the nature of this power as intended by the framers of the Constitution we must consider it in connection with certain powers which were elsewhere delegated to Congress.

The Constitution makes the President " Commander in Chief of the Army and Navy of the United States, and of the Militia of the several States when called into the actual Service of the United States." But it also gives to Congress the following powers: " To declare War, grant Letters of Marque and Reprisal, and make Rules concerning Captures on Land and Water "; " To raise and support Armies "; " To provide and maintain a Navy "; " To make Rules for the Government and Regulation of the land and naval Forces "; " To provide for calling forth the Militia " for named purposes; " To provide for organizing, arming, and disciplining, the Militia, and for governing such Part of them as may be employed in the Service of the United States, reserving to the States respectively, the Appointment of the Officers, and the Authority of training the Militia according to the discipline prescribed by Congress "; and " To make all Laws which shall be necessary and proper for carrying into Execution the foregoing Powers, and all other Powers vested by this Constitution in the Government of the United States, or in any Department or Officer thereof."

From the above enumeration certain principles are at once clear. In the first place, the only reasonable interpretation of these clauses is one which would deny the implication, from the power of the President as commander-in-chief, of any power (independent of statutory authority) of declaring war, granting letters of marque and reprisal, making rules concerning prizes, raising armies (as by enlisting men), using general funds in the treasury to support the army, enlisting sailors, building naval vessels or providing the upkeep of the same, calling forth the militia, making regulations for organizing or arming the militia, appointing officers of the militia, or training the same when not in the federal service.[100] Discretion with reference to certain aspects of many of these matters in actual practice has been delegated to the President by Congress.[101] But he obviously has no independent power to do those things because they have been conferred explicitly upon the legislature, and do not form a necessary part of the function of commanding an army and a navy.

The situation is somewhat more difficult in regard to the power of making rules for the government and regulation of the land and naval forces, and the power of providing for the government of the militia when in the federal service. For while these powers are granted to Congress, the President's power of commanding the army and navy and militia (when in federal service) is obviously so closely connected with this power of Congress that at first blush they seem hopelessly to overlap each other. The problem, therefore, is to reconcile the power of regulation which is granted to Congress with the power to command which is granted to the President. It is to be noted in the first place that the former power is one to "make Rules for the Government and Regulation" of the forces; which apparently does not include the primary function of military command, namely the conduct of actual operations and maneuvers of the army and navy in time of peace and war, the decision of military policies in the conduct of campaigns,[102] and the control over enemy territory in the

---

[100] *Expressio unius est exclusio alterius.*

[101] See Stat. L., passim, for examples of such delegations.

[102] " Through, or under, his orders, therefore, all military operations in times of peace, as well as of war, are conducted. He has within his control the disposition of troops, the direction of vessels of war and the planning and execution of campaigns. With Congress, however, lies the authority to lay down the rules governing the organization and maintenance of the military forces, the deter-

actual occupation of our armies.[103] These would seem to be given to the President upon any interpretation of the power to command, while they are not so clearly included in the power given to Congress. It was probably the intention of the framers to give the control of these matters exclusively to the President;[104] though of course the Anglo-American theory of the Executive, backed up by the grant to Congress of the powers to govern and regulate the forces and to pass in its discretion laws to carry out the powers vested in the President as well as its own powers,[105] makes it clear that if the President fails, by exercise of his veto power, to prevent Congress from encroaching upon even his independent and exclusive powers, he has no redress, but must enforce the will of the legislature. Any other theory would give to the executive the powers of dispensation and suspension which the English Bill of Rights finally took from the English Crown.[106]

From this it is clear that when Congress has not by law tied his hands (which it probably has no moral right to do) the President has at least the powers of command, in the strictly military sense; and that these powers involve ordinance making. But it is not practically possible to draw a sharp and clear-cut distinction between the powers of military command and the power to regulate the forces and to govern them.[107] And so the question arises whether and how far the Executive can pass regulations concerning the general

---

mination of their number, the fixing of the manner in which they shall be armed and equipped, the establishment of forts, hospitals, arsenals, etc., and, of course, the voting of appropriations for all military purposes " (Willoughby, Constitutional Law of the United States, sec. 713; cf. Ex parte Milligan, 4 Wall. 2).

[103] This is discussed a little later in this chapter.

[104] This is the view of Lieber, Remarks on the Army Regulations, p. 18; cf. also Farrand, vol. i, p. 292; vol. ii, pp. 157, 158; vol. iii, p. 218.

[105] Of course it is not to be implied from the necessary and proper clause that Congress has any moral right to exercise this power in such a manner as to curtail or destroy any constitutional power of the Executive.

[106] Cf. Wilson, Congressional Government, pp. 273-275.

[107] See Lieber, Remarks on the Army Regulations, pp. 11-16.

conduct of men and officers, regulations that are literally of the same sort as the ones which Congress may pass. It is of course perfectly clear that, in respect to such a concurrent power, the regulations of Congress take precedence over those of the chief in command, where they are in conflict. Perhaps it was intended that Congress should pass at least the main rules on the subject, leaving it to the Executive in his own discretion to supplement them by minor regulations which should not conflict with the laws.[108] Such at any rate has been the practice,[109] except that Congress has, in many instances at least, taken care to sanction or to authorize Presidential regulations, thus making it doubtful whether they might in the absence of such sanction or authorization be issued upon the independent authority of the President.[110] And it is incontrovertible that where Congress puts the stamp of its approval upon regulations already issued, they become adopted by law, henceforth having the validity of law, and cannot, unless Congress expressly so provides, be altered by ordinance.[111] Likewise, when Congress authorizes the making of army ordinances within certain limitations, the Executive is bound by such limitations even if it be granted that he would otherwise have a broader independent power to issue ordinances on the same subject.[112] But not all Presidential regulations have been under delegations from Congress.

From the above interpretation of the relevant constitutional provisions we gather certain principles, which may be summarized as follows:

1. Congress has the *exclusive* power to raise armies and establish navies, and also the power to regulate their general administration in as much detail as it sees fit.

---

[108] Cf. ibid., pp. 56, 11 ff., and Winthrop, Abridgment of Military Law, p. 8.

[109] Cf. the " Military Laws of the United States," with the Army and Navy " Regulations " and " General Orders."

[110] But see Lieber, Remarks on the Army Regulations, p. 49.

[111] Ibid., pp. 6, 56. But note that supplementary ordinances issued under delegations may be altered at will unless the statute prohibits, though they are binding upon the issuing authority until so altered (ibid., pp. 7, 39).

[112] Willoughby, Constitutional Law of the United States, sec. 713.

2.   The President as commander-in-chief has the *exclusive* power to command the army and the navy in the *military* sense, which includes: (a) ordering them to any part of the world in peace as well as war, (b) directing their operations in times of hostility, and (c) through them governing enemy territory conquered in time of war.[113]   He also has a *concurrent* power as commander-in-chief to issue at least minor administrative regulations with or without delegations from Congress, and though such regulations may not be in conflict with provisions of law, they may deal with phases of the same subjects not covered by the law.[114]   Let us examine in somewhat more detail each of these Presidential powers.

Judge-Advocate General G. Norman Lieber, in his work entitled Remarks on the Army Regulations and Executive Regulations in General (1898), divided army regulations into three classes: (1) " those which have been approved and adopted by Congress.   These cannot be modified or amended until the Congressional sanction has been removed."   (2) " Those made pursuant to, or in execution of, a statute. These may be modified or amended, but individual exceptions to them cannot be made."   (3) " Those made by the President as commander-in-chief, and not falling under " either (1) or (2).   " These may be modified, and exceptions to them may be made." [115]   Winthrop, in his work on Military Law, gives the following rules concerning regulations:[116]

1.   They must not contravene the law.
2.   They must not regulate.
3.   They must confine themselves to their subject.
4.   They must be uniform.
5.   They *should* be equitable.

---

[113] As commander-in-chief the President may enter into armistices with the enemy (see Willoughby, op. cit., sec. 202).   Under the same power came his authority to make the agreement with Britain to limit the number of armed vessels upon the Great Lakes.   This agreement can hardly be called municipal law, however.

[114] Lieber, op. cit., p. 16.

[115] Pages 6 ff., 91.

[116] Quoted in Lieber, op. cit., pp. 100-101.

On numerous occasions the Supreme Court has referred to the army and navy regulations as "having the force of law." [117]

In regard to the President's exclusive military powers, we need say little about his general power of command, which is plenary, except to note its character as ordinance making; [118] and may turn to a consideration of the basis of the power of the President to establish military government in enemy territory conquered in time of war. It is a recognized principle that he may establish military and civil government in such territory, and may empower such government to levy import duties for its own support and for the support of the army of occupation. This power, furthermore, continues not only from the moment of occupation to the signing of the treaty of peace, but also in full measure until notice of the ceding of such territory reaches the government of occupation; and even then, by the general administration of law and order, if not by legislation except in case of 'necessity,' until Congress itself legislates for the territories.

We must first examine the reasoning by which we can reconcile such a power of legislation or ordinance making, which is not supplementary but rather "gives manifestation to some original idea," with the fundamental constitutional doctrine that the legislative powers delegated to the federal government are vested in Congress. Then we may consider what has been executive practice in this matter, and what authority for this interpretation there is in the decided cases.

We have seen that, where the Constitution itself specifically

---

[117] See United States v. Freeman, 3 How. 567; Gratiot v. United States, 4 How. 118; United States v. Eliason, 16 Pet. 301; Kurtz v. Moffit, 115 U. S. 503.

[118] Thus it is under this power that the President directs by General Orders the movements of troops and many other matters connected with military campaigns, etc. See Taft, Our Chief Magistrate and His Powers, p. 94: "He (the President) can order the army and navy anywhere he will, if the appropriations furnish the means of transportation." May he order them to invade another country, or would that be tantamount to a declaration of war and hence violate the prohibition implied in the power of Congress to declare war?

gives to the Executive powers which are or involve ordinance making, the prima facie presumption which the separation of powers doctrine sets up against executive legislation is overcome. The more specific grant must of course take its place as an exception to the general doctrine. The only problem is whether a given power can legitimately be interpreted as being or involving ordinance making. But in the case before us there can be little doubt. We shall presently see that it has in practice been interpreted as involving such a function; and the same conclusion is equally sound in strict theory. It is a recognized principle of international law that the conquering state has the right to govern enemy territory conquered and occupied in war.[119] It is equally clear that since the control of war and peace is exclusively placed in the federal government, the power under discussion is properly considered a resulting federal power.[120] Now in the practice of nations, as known at the time the Constitution was adopted, it was, as it has always been, the generals in the field, acting under authority from the government at home, who have set up such governments as we are discussing. Hence, when the federal Constitution grants the President the position of commander-in-chief it is the irresistible conclusion that it means for him, or his subordinates acting in his name, to conduct military government.[121] It is not in strictness a right which he derives directly from international law; but a right which international law and practice aid in reading into the constitutional power of the commander-in-chief.

In our constitutional history there have been three instances when the President has set up governments in occupied territory, and legislated for them, or authorized such governments to do so. The first was in the occupation of California in the War with Mexico; the second was in the occupation of

---

[119] Hall, International Law, chap. iv.

[120] Cf. Willoughby, Constitutional Law of the United States, secs. 189-190.

[121] That is, we are dealing with a military matter, which may or may not be regulated by the legislature in general terms. Hence, its control, subject to statutory rules, is in the hands of the commander-in-chief.

Southern Territory during the War for Southern Independence; [122] and the third was in the occupation of Spanish possessions during the War with Spain. Out of these cases arose controversies that involved decisions by the Supreme Court which have affirmed this power of the President, and which make it clear that it is a legislative power. It is not our purpose to study in any exhaustive way the law of military occupation, but some of the more important cases will be cited to illustrate the principle which we maintain, that here is a constitutional power involving non-supplementary ordinance making. It is, to be sure, not a general power of legislation; nor the power to legislate for persons within the United States or its territories,—except that in the interim before Congress acts in regard to newly acquired territory the Court has hinted the Executive may perhaps in case of necessity legislate. But it does apply to private persons within the occupied territory, even though they are citizens of the United States; and indeed in a matter like customs duties it is a power that affects the rights of all persons who trade with such territory. It is a special power, but none the less an important power of ordinance. The fact that it has never been studied from this angle is one more proof of the inadequacy of our traditional juristic vocabulary, of the unscientific character of our legal terminology.

In Cross v. Harrison [123] it was held that the military and civil government, established under order of the President in California, after the conquest of that territory and its occupation by the armed forces of the United States in the War with Mexico, had constitutionally exacted the following duties of importers of goods from foreign countries: (1) between the date of the treaty of peace ceding California to the United States and the date at which the governor received official notice of the said treaty, duties collected according to the war tariff fixed under Presidential authority; (2) between the

---

[122] See Willoughby, op. cit., sec. 721.
[123] 16 How. 164. Cf. The Grapeshot, 9 Wall. 129; United States v. Rice, 4 Wheat. 246; New Orleans v. Steamship Co., 20 Wall. 387.

date of such official notice and the date at which the collector appointed by the President in accordance with Congressional legislation assumed the duties of his office, duties collected at the same rate as those collected under laws of Congress at regular ports of collection of the United States under the revenue laws.

In this decision there was necessarily involved a recognition of the constitutionality of legislation by the President as commander-in-chief, or in his name by the government set up under Presidential authority, in such conquered enemy territory. There was further involved the recognition of the right of such government to continue, with administrative and legislative powers, until it received official notice of the cession of such territory to the United States, and thereafter with at least administrative powers until Congress saw fit to legislate with reference to the government thereof.

The constitutional basis of the power of the President to govern such territory during the war is clearly his power as commander-in-chief. Professor Willoughby declares that after peace and cession of the territory the right of the President to continue such government flows from " his general obligation to see that the authority and peace of the United States are everywhere maintained throughout its territorial limits." [124]   Perhaps it is sufficiently explained as being reasonably implied in the nature of the power of military government of enemy territory itself. It does not necessarily follow from the making of peace and cession of such territory to the United States that the authority of the Executive is not to continue until succeeded by another.

The fact brought out by the Court that the treaty of peace recognized the war-time military government does not alter the fact that, aside from treaty, the conquering state has the right in international law, and the President has the independent right in constitutional law, to set up such a government.

---

[124] Willoughby, op. cit., (student's edition), p. 139 (cf. p. 505). Cf. also his statement in his larger work (which is the one quoted herein except where express mention of the other is made) at sec. 722.

In Cross v. Harrison Congress had indeed sanctioned the acts of the military government in California before the case was decided; and so the argument might be advanced that this was a case of retroactive delegation, in consonance with a well-known principle of agency, and not a case of the exercise of independent constitutional power.[125] But Congress did not take this view, for it declared that the acts of the government were valid. And at any rate the principle which the case is usually held to support is undoubted, even if not strictly the ratio decidendi of this particular decision.

It may be, however, that the authority of such a government, after the cession of the territory at least, is by the tacit consent of Congress, which has the right itself to act.[126]

Dooley v. United States [127] was a suit to recover duties paid under protest upon imports from New York at the port of San Juan, Porto Rico, under the terms of proclamations of General Miles and the President of the United States. These duties were collected partly before and partly after the treaty ceding Porto Rico to the United States, but in every instance before Congress, by the Foraker Act, had legislated for the newly acquired possession. The revenue thus collected was used by the military authorities for the benefit of the provisional government.[128]

The Court held that the duties collected after occupation and before the date of the treaty were legally collected, under the international right of the United States as a conquering nation. It was declared to make no difference that the goods imported came from the United States, because that country and Porto Rico were at that time still in the relation of foreign countries. In the opinion of the Court a passage from Halleck is quoted which contains the following words: " We, therefore, do not look to the constitution or political institutions of the conqueror, for the authority to establish a government for the territory of the enemy in his possession,

---

[125] *Omnis ratihabitio retrotrahitur et mandato equiparatur.*
[126] Willoughby, op. cit., sec. 722.
[127] 182 U. S. 222.
[128] Summarized from the statement of the case in the opinion.

during its military occupation, nor for the rules by which the powers of such government are regulated and limited." From the point of view of international law, which is what Halleck was discussing, this is entirely correct; but the question before the Court was one of constitutional law. The fact that action is justifiable in international law does not ipso facto justify it in municipal law. Whatever power any branch of government acting under a limited constitution exercises must, from the point of view of that constitution, find its authority in the instrument itself. It will readily be admitted on all sides that the international right of the conquering state (which is in international practice carried out through its military commanders) will influence the interpretation of the powers of the President as commander-in-chief.[129] It also seems clear that except where our constitutional system and our laws contain limits of an expressed or implied character upon such a power, the scope and extent which it is to have are properly to be determined by reference to the principles of international law.[130] But the source of the power must, in the eyes of a court of the United States, be solely and exclusively in the supreme law of the land.

The Court further held in the Dooley case that the duties had been illegally collected which had been exacted upon goods imported from the United States into Porto Rico between the dates of the treaty of cession and the Foraker Act. For, after the treaty Porto Rico was no longer foreign territory; and while the right to administer the government continued until Congress acted, it was declared that this right did not include the right to legislate, at least to the extent of levying duties upon goods imported into such island from the United States. Said the Court:

> The spirit as well as the letter of the tariff laws admits of duties being levied by a military commander only upon importations from foreign countries; and, while his power is necessarily despotic, this must be understood rather in an administrative than in a legislative

---

[129] That this has actually been the case is to be gathered from the way the power is stated by the various authorities.

[130] Willoughby, op. cit., secs. 720, 722.

sense. While in legislating for a conquered country he may disregard the laws of that country, he is not wholly above the laws of his own. . . . His power to administer would be absolute, but his power to legislate would not be without certain restrictions,—in other words, they would not extend beyond the necessities of the case.

Suffice it to say, for our purposes, that the power of the President is more limited after the cession than it was before that event and during the war. Before cession the limits are largely, if not wholly, to be found in the laws of war,[131] which give him a power as broad as the necessity requires, with certain general limitations;[132] and in the absence of statutory limitation he is the sole judge of the extent of his powers. After cession the government he has set up may be continued until Congress acts; but there are the constitutional limitations with reference to government in territory under American sovereignty;[133] and existing acts of Congress are more apt to apply.[134] In general, the power to legislate is probably limited to what the exigencies of the situation demand.[135]

Into the limitations of this power we need not go any further than to say that the Supreme Court has pointed out several limitations in the decided cases.[136] It may not, however, be out of place to mention the decision in the case of Fleming v. Page.[137] In that case the question was whether duties could be collected upon goods imported from Tampico, Mexico, under the tariff act of 1846, during the time when that place was held in the Mexican War by the forces of the United States acting under the authority of the President as commander-in-chief. The Court, speaking through Chief Justice Taney, held that such duties could be collected, since Tampico was a foreign port within the meaning of the tariff act. Tampico, said the Chief Justice, was temporarily in the

---

[131] Ibid.

[132] Hall, International Law, chap. iv.

[133] Willoughby, op. cit., sec. 722.

[134] They were applied in the Dooley case. See the opinion.

[135] Cf. Willoughby, op. cit., sec. 722.

[136] For examples, see Raymond v. Thomas, 91 U. S. 712; Jecker v. Montgomery, 13 Wall. 498.

[137] 9 How. 603.

possession of the United States, and, as against the rest of the world, a part thereof during such possession; but it was not a part of the Union in the meaning of the tariff act, because the authority of the President to conquer enemy territory during the war did not include the power to acquire permanent sovereignty over the same, and conquest did not of itself extend the boundaries of the Union. That can only be done by the legislative or treaty making powers. It is true that this principle is broader than the facts of the case warranted. For the President had not attempted to turn military occupation into acquisition. Strict adherence to the facts, therefore, leads us to say that the Court held, first that the revenue laws applied only to goods from foreign territories, and secondly that occupation did not per se result in changing the status of previously foreign territory; and that it indicated that in a proper case it might hold that the President could not, if he tried, turn occupation into acquisition.

PART IV

POLITICAL INTERPRETATION

CHAPTER X

POLITICAL IMPLICATIONS AND POTENTIALITIES OF THE ORDINANCE MAKING POWERS OF THE PRESIDENT

The subject, as it is needless to debate here, has its own difficulties, which are not peculiar to any stage or form of government. The executive power in the state must have certain powers to act in cases for which legislation has not provided, and modern legislation has not got beyond the expedient of investing the executive with authority to meet such critical occasions.

—STUBBS.[1]

Although the general scheme of administrative organization should be provided by legislative act, provision should be made for enabling the governor to meet emergencies by conferring on him the power to redistribute functions among administrative agencies in the interest of economy and efficiency, on the analogy of the power conferred on the President by the Overman Act. In the interests of efficiency and flexibility, the duties and functions of the administrative officers and employees should be determined to a large extent by executive orders and regulations rather than by detailed provisions of legislative acts. The director of each department should be empowered to prescribe regulations, not inconsistent with law, for the government of his department, the conduct of its employees, and the distribution and performance of its business.

—MATHEWS.[2]

Der formelle Sinn der Verordnung ergibt sich aus dem Satz der konstitutionellen Doktrin, dasz die Volksvertretung einen Anteil an der Regelung der Rechtsordnung, aber nicht an der Leitung der Verwaltung, eine Mitwirkung an dem Erlasz der Gesetze, aber nicht an dem Erlasz der Verordnungen hat.

—LABAND.[3]

Un Etat qui s'imposerait de vivre exclusivement sur ses lois, en ce sens que son activité serait indéfinement enchaînée à des décisions ou mesures prises préalablement par voie législative, un tel Etat se

---

[1] Constitutional History of England, vol. ii, p. 619; cf. Carr, Delegated Legislation, p. 21 ff.

[2] "State Administrative Reorganization," in American Political Science Review, August, 1922.

[3] Deutsches Reichsstaatsrecht, sec. 16 (Das Öffentliche Recht der Gegenwart, Band 1).

mettrait pratiquement dans l'impossibilité de subsister: et de fait, aucun Etat de cette sorte n'existe nulle part. . . . Dans la plupart des cas en effet, les lois se bornent à poser des règles générales et abstraites, c'est-à-dire à fixer de façon préventive un certain ordre juridique pour l'avenir. Or, il est manifeste que la loi ne saurait tout prévoir. . . . La procédure législative, avec ses longueurs, ne se prête guère à l'adoption de mesures qui demandent à être prises rapidement, afin de faire face immédiatement aux circonstances passagères; en outre, les assemblées législatives ne possèdent ni les moyens d'information, ni les capacités techniques, indispensables pour déterminer convenablement ces mesures, c'est là une mission que l'autorité administrative est seule capable de bien remplir. . . . La Constitution . . . n'a pas admis les assemblées à siéger en permanence, et pourtant, dans les intervalles des sessions, il faut bien que l'Etat garde le possibilité de prendre, par le voie administrative, les mesures de circonstance dont le besoin se fait constamment sentir. D'autre part, il est non moins manifeste que ces mesures, précisément parce qu'elles dépendent des événements journaliers et varient suivant les faits qui les provoquent, devront pouvoir être décidées par l'autorité administrative à qui elles incombent, d'après les besoins du moment, donc librement, avec un pouvoir d'appréciation actuelle. . . . Mais alors, il n'est guère exacte de ramener l'administration à une idée d'exécution passive des lois. . . . Exécuter la loi, au sens donné par Rousseau au mot exécution, ou tenir de la loi un pouvoir d'action et de volonté, ce sont là deux notions différentes.

            —CARRÉ DE MALBERG.[4]

Half the statutes on our books are in the alternative, depending on the discretion of some person or persons to whom is confided the duty of determining whether the proper occasion exists for executing them. But it cannot be said that the exercise of such discretion is the making of the law.

            —Moers v. City of Reading.[5]

Si le législateur établit des règles abstraites et statue pour l'ensemble d'un vaste territoire, il est de toute évidence qu'il ne peut tout prévoir, ni les obstacles pouvant résulter des circonstances de temps ou des circonstances de lieu, ni les conditions contingentes et transitoires d'application. Tout n'est donc pas dit dans la loi et quand il s'agira de la mettre à exécution, c'est-à-dire, d'imposer les directions qu'elle ordonne, il faudra souvent donner aux principes très compréhensifs qu'elle contient, les developpements nécessaires et la mettre en état de produire son maximum d'utilité, en un mot, la compléter.

            —RAIGA.[6]

The ordinance making power is a problem for the political scientist as well as a subject of study for the jurist, the historian, and the students of comparative government, of ad-

---

[4] Théorie générale de l'Etat, tome 1, p. 467. The reference should be read in full.

[5] 21 Penn. St. 188, 202.

[6] Le Pouvoir réglementaire du Président de la République (1900), pp. 6-7.

ministrative organization and technique, and of constitutional law.[7] What is its relation to the theory of democracy as understood in America? To the principle of modern governments that legislation be by or with the consent of the popular assembly? To the increasing growth of the regulative functions of government in the present generation? To the question of the proper relation which should subsist between the legislative and executive branches of government? What are the social and economic causes of the development of the ordinance making power in the United States? What are the implications of the power and its potentialities of future development? These and similar questions can be answered only by the political scientist.

The problem is not, however, the same for all classes of ordinances.[8] In particular it is quite different in respect to the power of issuing independent ordinances from what it is in regard to the power of co-legislation. Again, it is not the same for the type of ordinance which embodies material law as it is for that type which contains material ordinances and co-ordinances. Naturally, it also makes a great deal of difference whether the power is connected with emergencies or whether it is connected with the administration of laws of social and industrial regulation in ordinary times and circumstances. Finally, it is just as clear that with reference to all these classes it must be decided whether the power is to be given directly by the fundamental law or left to delegation by the legislature in permanent or temporary statutes as it may see fit. If any one type of ordinance be taken, it must be considered in relation to the other three bases of classification.

If now we start with the problem of the emergency ordinance, some general conclusions may be ventured. In the

---

[7] See the divisions of this treatise: Part I. Juristic Analysis; Part II. Constitutional Development; Part III. Constitutional Construction; Part IV. Political Interpretation; Part V. (Appendix) Technical Analysis. If space allowed, there might be added Parts on the Historical Setting and Comparative Analysis.

[8] See the four major bases of classification of ordinances set forth in chap. iii.

first place, it is a lesson which seems to be enforced by our experience in the three great crises discussed in a previous chapter, that an emergency power of ordinance must upon occasion be exercised in some fashion by the Executive—or at least by a legislative committee acting upon executive request.[9] If such power is not given, or is given in too limited terms, it will be illegally exercised to the extent that this proves necessary.[10] In such case resort must had to the act of indemnity. In countries like the United States, where such an emergency arises only about once in fifty years, it may be better not to give the President very extensive powers either by constitutional or statutory grant. For our legalistic tradition is strong enough to compel a usurping Executive to appeal to the Congress for retroactive delegation of power; our dislike of executive power is so great that a President will not dare attempt to turn such usurpation into a coup d'état.[11] Unfortunately, perhaps, these safeguards are not as sure as they once were; for in recent decades there has been a weakening of respect in the American mind for law as such.

---

[9] This is of course not an American method. But see Constitution of Czechoslovakia, art. 54, translated in McBain and Rogers, The New Constitutions of Europe (1922), pp. 310, 321-323.

[10] The following quotations, from the interpreter of the constitutional aspects of the Civil War Period, Professor Dunning, are in point: "This frank substitution of a 'popular demand' for a legal mandate, as a basis for executive action, is characteristic of the times. The President's course was approved and applauded. . . . The general concurrence in the avowed ignoring of the organic law emphasizes the completeness of the revolution which was in progress. The idea of a government limited by the written instructions of a past generation had already begun to grow dim in the smoke of battle" (Essays on the Civil War and Reconstruction, p. 18). "In the interval between April 12 and July 4, 1861, a new principle thus appeared in the constitutional system of the United States, namely, that of a temporary dictatorship. All the powers of government were virtually concentrated in a single department, and that the department whose energies were directed by the will of a single man" (p. 21). "To maintain that the framers of the Constitution contemplated vesting in any man or body of men the discretionary right to set aside any of its provisions, seems too much like judging the past in the light of the present. To believe that the nation could have been preserved without the exercise of such a discretionary power, invokes too severe a strain upon the reasoning faculties of the careful student of the times" (pp. 48-49).

[11] See my discussion of this point in "The Emergency Ordinance: A Note on Executive Power," in Columbia Law Review, June, 1923.

Power to act in an emergency should be broad in scope, should in some cases be power to give manifestation to some original idea, if it is given in anticipation of possible future emergencies.   In such case to limit the discretion of the Executive is to destroy the effectiveness of the power.[12]   Of course, if the delegation is made only after the particular emergency has arisen, the delegating authority may perhaps specify more details.   Yet even then this course is dangerous. Delegation is needed in part for the reason that the legislature cannot anticipate developments of the situation.   For it to try to do so means that it endangers quick and efficient handling of matters as they arise.   This is so with respect to ordinances embodying material ordinances as well as those embodying material laws, both sorts being needed in emergencies.[13]

[12] Where constitutions specifically provide for emergency ordinances, there are usually the provisos that such ordinances may be issued only when the legislature is not in session and must be submitted to the next session of that body (see Meyer-Anschütz, Lehrbuch des deutschen Staatsrechtes, p. 577; art. 63 of the Prussian Constitution of 1850; the present Constitution of the German Republic, art. 48, translated in McBain and Rogers, The New Constitutions of Europe, pp. 185-186).   Only the second proviso is mentioned in this case.   Both were contained in the provision of Denmark of 1866 (Black, The Relation of Executive Power to Legislation, p. 127).   The same is true of the Japanese Constitution (art. viii; for a discussion of this power see Nakano, The Ordinance Power of the Japanese Emperor, chap. xiii), and of the Russian Constitution of the old régime (art. 45).   Neither limitation was, however, imposed in Württemberg (Lowell, Governments and Parties in Continental Europe, vol. i, p. 341).   In the Prussian provision (art. 63) the *purposes* of emergency ordinances are set forth as follows: "only in case the maintenance of public safety or the relief of an extraordinary state of distress urgently requires it."   The *existence* of this urgency is, of course, left to the discretion of the Executive.   Cf. the wording of the Japanese and other provisions. The Japanese Emperor issues emergency ordinances "in the place of law."

[13] See the Overman Act, discussed in chap. iv.   Authorization of *Verwaltungsverordnungen* may become an emergency need in wartime, and that for several reasons: 1. It may be necessary to free the administrative services from some of the red tape necessitated by minute statutory regulation of their activities.   2. It may be needed to adjust an administrative system of the American type, where no bureaucracy has developed, to the sudden strain of war activities.   3. It may be requisite in order to allow flexibility in organization, so that the Executive can quickly make the changes

One final issue presents itself with respect to emergency ordinances. Should the power be given in the Constitution itself or be left to be delegated by the assembly? In this country the late war proved that we can depend upon Congress to give sufficient power for the Executive to conduct a war.[14] In many governments the head of the state is given in the written constitution a general power of issuing emergency ordinances.[15] Not so in the United States. Nor does there seem to be a real need for such a clause. It might, however, be wise for Congress to keep upon the statute books anticipatory delegations of emergency power in case of war or rebellion.[16] Such permanent enactments should cover recognized types of power which it might be needful for the President to exercise in a great crisis.[17] Other delegations might then be left until a particular case arose.

II

We may next consider the issuance by the Executive of formal ordinances which are also either ordinances or coordinances in the material sense of the terms.[18] In general, it seems that the German conception that this is a proper executive function,[19] that such ordinances are ordinances par

---

which experience shows to be needed; etc. Modern warfare is as much a matter of administration as of actual fighting.

[14] The attitude of that body was summed up in the declaration (amidst applause) of Langley: "So if the President needs the weapons of autocracy in this war with autocratic Germany, I am in favor of giving them to him" (Congressional Record, vol. lv, part 4, p. 4019; cf. pp. 3802, 4899, 3951 ff., 3901, 4403 ff.).

[15] See above, note 12.

[16] Such as 39 Stat. L., 166 ff. (National Defense Act of 1916); 39 Stat. L., 645.

[17] Such as, (1) the power to use the army and to call out the militia to put down rebellion or resist invasion (see the law which Lincoln cited as his authority for calling out the 75,000 militiamen in 1861, 1 Stat. L., 424, proclamation in 12 Stat. L., 1258; see Dunning, Essays on the Civil War and Reconstruction, chap. i); (2) the power to use the railroads or even to take them over in a war crisis (see the act passed in 1916 under which President Wilson took over the railroads, proclamation in 40 Stat. L., 1733); (3) the power to suspend the privilege of the writ of habeas corpus in case of war or rebellion; etc.

[18] See definitions in chap. ii.

[19] "Die Verwaltungsverordnungen sind ein Ausfluss des Verhält-

excellence,[20] is partly justified.[21]   The head of the state, or the responsible ministry in parliamentary governments, may be expected to know better than the legislature what are the needs of organization and the needs of regulation of the several services whose function it is to carry out the will of the state as expressed in material law.   Then, too, administration to be efficient must be flexible, and this is impossible if resort must be had to the legislature every time a slight change is to be made.[22]   We have seen that this fact is in part recognized by the delegation to departmental heads in the Revised Statutes of power to issue administrative regulations not inconsistent with law.[23]   But in practice Congress goes into such detail both in budgetary and other administrative control[24] that this delegation is more limited in scope than

---

nisses der über- und Unterordnung, welches unter den Verwaltungsorganen besteht, und daher auch ohne spezielle gesetzliche Ernächtigung zulässig " (Meyer-Anschütz, Lehrbuch des deutschen Staatsrechtes, pp. 571-572); "Ihre Schranke finden sich lediglich in den vorhandenen Gesetzen " (ibid., p. 572).

[20] Laband, Deutsches Reichsstaatsrecht, sec. 16.

[21] Cf. Mathews, " State Administrative Reorganization," in American Political Science Review, August, 1922.

[22] Much of the time of Congress and our state legislatures is consumed with patching up the administrative system now in this detail, now in that.   The average member is not competent to pass upon these matters.   What is more in point, the committees that specialize in these subjects have to rely upon the advice of administrative officers.   The result is simply a cumbersome and inefficient method of applying the knowledge which with the chief administrative officers is born of experience.

[23] Sec. 161.

[24] The present method of appropriating funds in Michigan offers a fruitful suggestion.   Thus Act No. 300, Public Acts, 1921, appropriated for the Department of Agriculture for the fiscal year 1921-1922 a sum of $463,409.00, allocated to the following subjects: (1) personal service; (2) supplies; (3) contractual service; (4) maintenance of equipment; (5) outlay for equipment; (6) payment of premiums of State Fair.   This law seems reasonably general, but it makes no provision for transfers from one title to another, probably because the titles are so broad.   Then there is added a clause which gives a needed administrative control over the expenditure of the appropriation: " Provided, That all amounts appropriated under this act shall be subject to the approval of the State Administrative Board " (sec. 5).   Under the act of 1921 creating this Board, it is given supervisory control over all state departments (Public Acts, 1921, No. 2, sec. 3).   Also, under the act of the same date creating the State Department of Agriculture (Act No. 13, Public Acts, 1921),

might appear from the general terms in which it is worded. In the emergency of war Congress had to pass an Overman Act to allow the President to redistribute functions and consolidate services as the needs of the crisis required. Professor Mathews has suggested that in the States the governors be given in a permanent form a similar emergency power, as well as broad discretion in administrative organization and regulation in ordinary times. It would seem that the President might also, subject to general laws of Congress and the limits of the budget, be granted by the permanent law (not by constitutional provision) some such authority. In practice he would of course depend upon the head of each department to work out, subject to his approval, the details of such administrative regulations. It is hardly wise—as it is probably not constitutional—for Congress to delegate to the Chief Magistrate such full discretion in the premises in this matter as is given to the Emperor of Japan by the Japanese Constitution.[25] Neither is the present situation necessary or desirable whereby the President and his cabinet members have insufficient power to issue ordinances in the material sense. It is true that they are not now entirely confined to co-ordinances;[26] but their power is all too meager as it is. It

---

the Commissioner of Agriculture is authorized to " appoint such assistants and employees as may be necessary to perform the duties hereby imposed, the number of such assistants and employees, and the compensation payable to all persons so appointed and employed, being subject to the approval of the State Administrative Board " (sec. 1). Sec. 5 provides that " All of the powers and duties imposed by this act on the State Department of Agriculture shall be exercised and performed under the supervisory control of the State Administrative Board." Under these several provisions of law there is a degree of flexibility plus administrative control. Incidentally, the State Administrative Board consists of the elective executive officers of the state (except the lieutenant governor), which does not insure harmony within the Board itself (Public Acts, 1921, No. 2, sec. 1).

[25] " The Emperor determines the organization of the different branches of the administration, and the salaries of all civil and military officers, and appoints and dismisses the same. Exceptions especially provided for in the present Constitution or in other laws, shall be in accordance with the respective provisions (bearing thereon)" (art. x; see also art. xii).

[26] This is because Rev. Stat., sec. 161 is a ' blanket ' clause, not a

can with safety be broader than the power of independent executive legislation.[27]   In this country we have carried to an extreme what Professor Freund so suggestively has termed 'legislative administration.' [28]

III

The third phase of the subject is related to the primary [29] establishment of rights and duties for citizens generally or citizens of a reasonably defined class,[30] in connection with the ordinary and normal functioning of the government.   In a word, aside from special emergencies and the organization and regulation of the administration, should the blocking out of broad policies affecting the private citizens be left to the Executive?   Our problem is whether Congress or the Executive should have this power, aptly described as the power to issue "original, primary and spontaneous commands defining the free sphere of conduct of individuals in their relations with the State or between themselves," as distinguished from the subordinate power to supplement such original and primary definitions by concretizing ordinances.[31]

---

delegation limited in scope to a given problem.   See the distinction as drawn in chaps. ii, iii, and vi.

[27] The creation of material law involves the substantive function to which the creation of material ordinances is adjective.   The one is a matter of social regulation, the other a matter of business.

[28] "American Administrative Law," in Political Science Quarterly, vol. ix, p. 403 ff.   Under the 'necessary and proper' clause the organization and regulation of the administrative departments are vested in Congress; although under the power of direction involved in the power of removal the control of such discretion as Congress may leave to the department heads rests with the President to the extent that he desires (or finds the time and has the knowledge) to exercise it.

[29] This means 'legislation' as distinguished from 'co-legislation,' which is the supplementary elaboration of legislative abstractions (see Nakano, The Ordinance Power of the Japanese Emperor, pp. 53-57).   The analysis there set forth is in agreement with the conclusion independently arrived at by the present writer; but he cannot include in the definition of 'law' an act of individual application, nor exclude from the term in its broadest meaning completing ordinances or co-laws (see chap. ii).

[30] Classification which is based upon a relevant criterion does not violate the principle of uniformity of application (see the opinion of Mr. Justice Field in Barbier v. Connolly, 113 U. S. 27).

[31] Nakano, The Ordinance Power of the Japanese Emperor, p. 58.

Out of mediaeval chaos there grew up in Europe the absolute monarchies of early modern times.[32] At the dawn of the modern national state the autocracy had few restraints upon its almost plenary power. In the Renaissance, therefore, the king was throughout Europe in theory the law-giver in the state.[33] Sovereignty of the state meant absolute internal control of the subjects by the ruler, as well as absolute external independence of that ruler, as the personification of the state, from control by any foreign power.[34] It was first in England that modern parliaments were placed upon a real footing in the commonwealth, and rose to demand a share in legislation. First summoned to vote supply, parliaments came to use this power as a weapon by which to force recognition of their right to assent to legislation.[35] Thus is the transition made from the principle quod principi placuit, legis habet vigorem[36] to the newer principle quod omnes tangit ab omnibus approbetur.[37] When the king in council had been the legislative

---

The author of this treatise has a power of illuminating analysis comparable to that shown by his fellow-countryman, Ito, in his Commentaries.

[32] Burns, Political Ideals, chap. vi (Renaissance Sovereignty).

[33] Bodin said: "As the prince is bound by no laws of his predecessor, much less is he bound by his own laws." And again: "This, then, I hold: A prince may abrogate, modify, or replace a law made by himself and without the consent of his subjects. [sic] " Also this: "I hold, therefore, that the sovereignty of the prince is in no degree diminished by calling together the assemblies or estates." He admits the "approval and promulgation" of laws is "commonly done in an assembly or senate," but denies that this affects his theory. Some of his statements are self-contradictory, but these need not concern us. It is only the main idea of autocracy with which we are here concerned (De Republica, passim; taken from Coker's Readings in Political Philosophy, p. 231 ff.; cf. the Prussian theory of monarchy discussed in chap. v; cf. the dictum: L'état, c'est moi). Even since the rise of the English Parliament the legislative power has been vested in the 'king in parliament' (cf. Hobbes, The Leviathan).

[34] Burns, Political Ideals, chapter vi.

[35] Anson, Law and Custom of the Constitution, Part 1, chap. vii.

[36] The Institutes, Book 1, title 2, De Iure Naturali et Gentium et Civile. The full text reads: Sed et quod principi placuit, legis habet vigorem, cum lege regia, quae de imperio eius lata est, populus ei et in eum omne suum imperium et potestatem concessit (cf. Maitland, Constitutional History of England, pp. 103-104, 198).

[37] But see Adams, Constitutional History of England, p. 186.

organ there had been no distinction between law and ordinance, unless it was that the former required the assent of the great council, the latter the consent of the ordinary council only.[38] But with the principles established that statutes must be enacted only with the consent of parliament,[39] that important and permanent changes in the law should be by statute,[40] and that the king in council could not alter the statute law,[41] there was a real basis for the distinction between the two forms or modes of making law.[42] From England the principles of popular representation and of participation of the representatives of the people in legislation spread to the rest of the constitutional governments of the world.[43] These principles have vogue today not only in governments founded upon the idea of popular sovereignty,[44] but also in governments where democracy is effective in practice though royal sovereignty has never been formally repudiated in theory,[45] as well as in those countries even where constitutional government has come by grant from the monarch who still retains his sovereignty but merely agrees to exercise it in a certain manner.[46]

Despite this transition from legislation by the king to legis-

---

[38] See ibid., pp. 205-207; 4 Coke's Institutes 25; Jellinek, Gesetz und Verordnung, p. 22; Maitland, Constitutional History of England, pp. 92, 186-187; Anson, Law and Custom of the Constitution, part 1, p. 212; Stubbs, Constitutional History of England, vol. ii, p. 615 ff.

[39] But see Adams, op. cit., pp. 205-207.

[40] See Maitland, op. cit., pp. 20-21, 92.

[41] Gneist, History of the English Constitution, vol. i, p. 422.

[42] Adams, op. cit., pp. 205-207. The King at first retained, but later lost, a concurrent but subordinate power of ordinance. But today parliament frequently finds it expedient to delegate regulative power to the Executive (Lowell, Government of England, vol. i, pp. 20, 363 ff.).

[43] Cf. Goodnow, Principles of Constitutional Government, p. 3.

[44] For example, the United States and Belgium.

[45] For example, England, where the King is legally sovereign, but exercises his functions 'in parliament,' 'in council,' and 'through his courts.'

[46] For example, Japan. However, the Japanese Emperor is given in the constitution extensive independent powers of legislation by ordinance. Even in Japan, however, legislation by laws is the rule, legislation by ordinance the exception (Nakano, The Ordinance Power of the Japanese Emperor, p. 60; see pp. 3-4 for the kinds of monarchical government as set forth in the text above).

lation by or with the consent of the assembly, it has been found practically necessary in democracies, and theoretically logical in autocracies, for the executive to be granted, or to retain, considerable powers of legislation.[47] Furthermore, such legislation in all countries involves the creation of laws or co-laws in the material sense and for ordinary times as well as other types of ordinances. The exceptions are the greatest in the case of the Emperor of Japan, but even there the ordinance making powers of the head of the state are exceptions to the general principle of Article V of the Constitution that " The Emperor exercises the legislative power with the consent of the Imperial Diet." [48] In most other countries, including Prussia under the Constitution of 1850, the king cannot except in special and strictly limited sorts of cases create material law.[49] This is especially true of the President of the United States, who has neither constitutional nor delegated powers of legislation as such. Yet at times, and especially in the late war, Congress has had to delegate to him almost full discretion within certain generally defined limits; [50] while some of the powers granted him in the supreme law are in effect of an independent and law-making character.[51] One need only mention his power to make treaties with the advice and consent of the Senate, but without the consent of the House of Representatives. In general, we may say that all such powers which the Chief Magistrate is given by the Constitution itself are such as are necessarily left to the Executive because of certain practical or political

---

[47] Nakano, chap. i, especially p. 12; cf. Boelling, Das Recht der Prüfung von Verordnungen nach dem Staatsrechte des Reiches und Preussens, sec. 2; see Anson, Law and Custom of the Constitution, part 1, chap. vi; Lowell, Government of England, vol. i, pp. 20, 363 ff.).

[48] See above, note 46.

[49] See Lowell, Governments and Parties in Continental Europe, vol. ii, pp. 138, 195, n. 2; vol. i, pp. 44-46, 165, 335, 345. This ' exceptional' power of course is very broad in some countries, as these references show. The main point is, however, that it is recognized as an exception to the rule that material law is to be created by or with the advice of the representative assembly.

[50] See chaps. iv and vi.

[51] See chap. ix.

reasons. They are all in some sense 'special'; even treaties and amnesties, which create primary rights and duties for private persons in continental United States.[52]

Now while it is admitted that a few 'special' exceptions must be made to the established principle, and that at least some regularly recurring types of action must be authorized in the constitution rather than by statute, nevertheless the general principle itself it is not worth while to question. Its acceptance, even with modifications, by constitutional autocracies seems to indicate that it is in conformity with the needs of modern social and economic conditions, and not merely the result of the political theory of popular sovereignty.[53]   Certainly it would be inconsistent with that theory to give a hereditary monarch the personal exercise of general legislative discretion; while it will generally be admitted that it is a clearer expression of that theory to give such discretion to a popular assembly than to give it to a popularly elected President. In the long run locally elected representatives are closer to the people than the Chief Executive. The latter may, for a time, be more representative in relation to the particular reforms to secure which he was elected to office. But when new issues arise, a President of strong personality is apt to use his own judgment, which may not be that of his people; while the legislators are now more responsive to popular wishes than he is. Legislation by the popular assembly seems, in fact, to be more suited to democracies, whether they are based upon a legal theory of popular or of royal sovereignty.

Of course, the principle of democracy may itself be challenged. That is, however, a mere academic question, at least

---

[52] Treaties, at least, may cover any proper subject of international agreement. But in practice they affect private rights at relatively few points, and usually for very limited classes of persons.

[53] Or is the acceptance due to the imitative instinct, and lack of political inventive genius? Even so, however, the statement in the text stands for all practical purposes. To question the principle as such is an academic rather than a practical contention. It is the prevailing formal principle of the day, though its substantive significance varies greatly in different countries.

with reference to the United States. For it is the accepted principle.[54] A word or two on the subject, however, will not be amiss. The American democrat believes in a sort of 'divine right of the people' which is as untenable as the dogma of the 'divine right of kings.' The problem is not separable from one's ethical ideal, to be sure; but it is not one of absolute right. Its solution is relative to the economic needs and political development of the given community.[55] Where it is workable with any degree of success democracy is justified, not by its fruits, but negatively because of the actual or potential tyranny [56] and the psychological oppressiveness [57] of other forms of government.[58]

It may be said, however, that even if 'government by mass opinion' satisfies our American sense of justice better than 'government by the opinion of the one or the few,' nevertheless we should displace 'government by opinion' by 'government by science.' Theoretically even Democracy should bend the knee to Science; [59] and undoubtedly in administration, in sub-legislation, and in co-legislation we should strive to introduce 'government by science.' These matters have to [60] be turned over to the One or the Few, and in them Science should as far as possible displace Discretion. But to

---

[54] "Under normal conditions, therefore, the problem of the statesman is to obtain as good government as is compatible with self-government" (Fenwick, "Democracy and Efficient Government," in American Political Science Review, November, 1920).

[55] Mill, Representative Government, chaps. i-iv.

[56] Human nature being what it is, men invested with power over the masses tend to abuse that power, to use it for their own personal benefit, and to forget the 'good of the people.'

[57] This 'subjective' objection is the main one at the basis of Mr. Dicey's and Mr. Bryce's objections to French *droit administratif* (see Dicey, Law of the Constitution, chap. xii; Bryce, Modern Democracies, vol. i, pp. 277-279; cf. Duguit, "The French Administrative Courts," in Political Science Quarterly, September, 1914).

[58] However, for Democracy as a positive ideal, see Burns, Political Ideals, chap. xii.

[59] Sir Henry Maine predicted in his Popular Government a future warfare between Science and Democracy.

[60] They are regulated by legislative assemblies in greater detail in Anglo-Saxon countries than elsewhere. This 'legislative administration' has proved so hopelessly bad that the phrase 'have to' is hardly too strong.

the larger social and industrial questions science can give no categorical answer.[61]   The only contrast is between two sorts of Opinion, lay and expert.   Hence, with respect to legislation, as distinguished from co-legislation, the concrete issue is, between 'government by mass opinion' and 'government by scientific opinion.'   Scientists are human, and scientific autocrats will, like other sorts, tend under such conditions to seek their own interests.[62]   Their discretion may be wiser, but it is also biased.   Hence, while the 'people' are not able intelligently to decide fundamentals any more than details, yet it is the safer way to leave these former questions to their representatives rather than to an Executive at whose disposal even the most abundant scientific equipment is placed.[63]

IV

We have to consider the causes and raison d'être of co-legislation.   "An important item," remarks Dean Pound, "is partition of the field of legal order between legislation and common law and also between judicial justice and administrative justice.   Social engineering may not expect to meet all its problems with the same machinery." [64]   No more appropriate text might be chosen for a discussion of the growth and future of administrative co-legislation in the United States with reference to its relation to legislation, the common law, administration, and judicial action.   Let us turn back for the moment to the nineteenth century, and particularly

---

[61] It can in these cases only furnish statistics and suggestive principles.   On definite programs, however, trained scientists disagree. This is in large part due to the fact that there is no agreement on the 'end' to be sought.

[62] This they might do even if science could determine the larger policies; but they would be less likely to do so, both because it takes a baser man to seek deliberately than sub-consciously his own interest, and because the people, unless very ignorant, would discover falsifications of science.

[63] For we have decided above that a body of locally elected Congressmen is more responsive in the long run to Public Opinion than is the President.

[64] "The Theory of Judicial Decisions," in Harvard Law Review, June, 1923.

to the period between 1815 and the Civil War. In that era we find in the federal government, as well as the several States, few statutes passed in practice and laissez faire the prevailing theory. In the States this was accomplished by and closely connected with ' judicial justice ' based upon an individualistic interpretation of the common law. The connecting link between the two theories was of course the Jeffersonian ideal of as little governmental interference as was compatible with the preservation of order [65] and the protection of certain rights that were assumed to be unalienable.[66] Under the spell of the theory of natural rights men even spoke as if there were a sphere of individual activity entirely outside the jurisdiction of government. Such a conception held the germ of anarchy, because it denied that it is the objective law which furnishes the authoritative definition of all subjective rights.[67] The only legitimate issue between Jefferson and the socialists is merely whether the state will leave to the individual a wide range [68] of choice in conduct or whether it will prescribe his conduct at every turn. In either event it is the state that defines his sphere. It so fell out that, in the last century, conditions in a developing country made it wise to leave to each man a range as wide and free as possible and limited only by the similar range of his neighbor; and that the delimitation of the boundaries of the ranges was largely left to the courts in the decision of cases under the common law. As for the federal government, it had no common law jurisdiction,[69] its legislative powers were limited, and it fell in with the current ideas on local

---

[65] Croly, The Promise of American Life, chap. ii.

[66] Cardozo, The Nature of the Judicial Process, pp. 77-78; Pound, " Juristic Science and the Law," in Harvard Law Review, vol. xxxi, pp. 1047, 1048.

[67] For the distinction between droit objectif (objectives Recht) and droit subjectif (subjectives Recht) see Duguit, Droit constitutionnel (deuxième édition), p. 1.

[68] See Vinogradoff, Common Sense in Law, p. 61 ff.

[69] See Willoughby, Constitutional Law of the United States (student's edition), p. 445. But see Goodnow, Social Reform and the Constitution, chap. iv.

self-government that Congress should be kept rather strictly within its enumerated powers.[70]

It was in part a result of this situation that administrative or executive functions were in large measure confined to the mere carrying out of the statutes and the performance of special duties like granting pardons and commanding the armed forces. There were, however, several important reasons why little discretion, and especially little rule-making discretion, was left to the Executive alike in state and nation. Thus, there was the tradition largely inherited from England that the Executive had no independent or constitutional authority—no authority aside from statutory delegations—of supplementing by ordinances the terms of statutory law dealing with private interests.[71] Added to this was the legislative method, also inherited from the mother country,[72] of enacting detailed statutes, with concrete and specific provisions, and with generalities often modified by limiting provisos.[73] All this was of course in striking contrast with the continental development of an independent power of co-legislation and the habit on the part of continental legislative assemblies of expressing in their laws only broad, general principles and leaving it to the executive to follow with completing ordinances.[74] The result was that in the English method it was the judiciary that interpreted and applied in particular cases such generalities as found their way into the statutes,[75] while in the continental method it was the executive that bridged the gap between the abstract rule and its individual application by the issuance of concretizing or enforcing ordinances. After all, however, the main reason the

---

[70] Croly, The Promise of American Life, chap. iii.
[71] Cf. Gneist, History of the English Constitution, vol. ii, pp. 22 ff., 349.
[72] See Lowell, Governments and Parties in Continental Europe, vol. i, pp. 44-46.
[73] Cf. chap. i.
[74] Lowell, Governments of France, Italy, and Germany, pp. 44-45, 139-140, 200.
[75] Freund, "The Substitution of Rule for Discretion in Public Law," in American Political Science Review, November, 1915.

time-honored English way was continued in state and federal legislation was because it harmonized with American needs.[76] With the theory abroad in the land that the legislature should legislate as little as possible, it was entirely possible for it to debate and prescribe every minute detail and try to anticipate every contingency. And with problems before them of relative simplicity and stability, the laymen who are chosen by popular elections could with less absurdity than today attempt to decide in detail for future events. Then, too, in a time before men in the United States began to think of the scientific approach to governmental problems,[77] it was not thought so ridiculous as it would be now for a popular assembly to determine the specifics of policy upon the basis of partisan or at any rate political considerations.[78] Finally, from the time of the Revolution until the War of Secession the American people retained more or less of that distrust of executive power which had been inspired by their unpleasant relations with colonial governors and with George III.[79] When discretion was necessarily placed in other organs than the legislature, the men of 1776 and the men of 1850 alike preferred to give it to the jury rather than to the governor or the President, the superintendent of schools or the secretary of the treasury.

Since the War of Secession, however, and especially in the

---

[76] Those were the needs of a new country that could best be developed by the granting of free play to individual initiative.

[77] Before 1880 men's minds were occupied with conquering a new continent and with certain overshadowing 'political' issues like the extension of the suffrage, the tariff (which was viewed as a sectional issue), internal improvements, states' rights vs. nationalism, slavery, nullification, secession, the preservation of the Union, and Southern Reconstruction. American science had not really developed, and the 'scientific approach' to government was unknown.

[78] We do not frame our tariff laws on the basis of science today, because the tariff is still a matter of 'policy' or 'discretion.' Yet the idea of an expert tariff commission shows a tendency to apply 'policies' in the light of scientific investigation and findings. But see Page, Making the Tariff.

[79] See Elliot's Debates, vol. v, p. 327. The reaction against a strong executive was followed by a period in which the danger of anarchy led conservatives to see the need of an executive at once strong and safe (The Federalist, No. 70). Yet the distrust of too strong an executive hung on through the nineteenth century. See Story on the Constitution, sec. 1413, 1417.

last twenty or thirty years, the conditions under which American political institutions function have been greatly changed.[80] The war itself ended forever States' rights as a fundamental principle of our system and weakened its importance as a rule of expediency. It thus laid the foundation for that gradual growth of federal activity which the economic conditions of the new era were demanding. What were these new conditions? In the present century the crowding of people into cities and the concurrent development of medical and other sciences have made evident the need for restraining individual action where it was left free fifty years ago; while the expansion of group activity in all fields of human relations has necessitated both statutory alterations of the common law and legislative enactments to deal with aspects of cooperative action which that law had never anticipated. As a consequence there has been a growing demand for legislation and for the expansion of the functions of the state.[81] With experimentation in legislation has come an inevitable growth of state administrative machinery.[82] Since the federal government has itself entered more and more fields of social and industrial legislation,[83] there has also been a corresponding expansion of federal administration.[84] Thus new governmental functions added to the burden alike of legislatures and of administration; and both well nigh broke down under the strain.

Contemporaneous with the increasing demand for laws, and

---

[80] See Croly, The Promise of American Life, chap. v.

[81] It is a matter of common knowledge that many persons appear to think that a problem can be solved by the magic words " be it enacted." Cf. Bryce, " Conditions and Methods of Legislation," in his University and Historical Studies, pp. 75-76, 89-90.

[82] White, " The Growth and Future of State Boards and Commissions," in Political Science Quarterly, vol. xviii, p. 631.

[83] This expansion has been a sort of ' police ' regulation legally justified under the postal, taxing, and commerce powers of Congress.

[84] Witness the creation of the departments of commerce and of labor, and the agitation for a department of public welfare; and especially the setting up of administrative commissions like the Interstate Commerce Commission, The Federal Trade Commission, The Federal Reserve Board, The Federal Farm Loan Board, and the Tariff Commission.

in part as a result of the burdens which this entailed, went the decline of legislatures in honesty and capacity and hence in popular esteem. "There is evidence," declared Viscount Bryce in his Modern Democracies,[85] "to indicate in nearly every country some decline from that admiration of and confidence in the system of representative government which in England possessed the generation who took their constitutional history from Hallam and Macaulay, and their political philosophy from John Stuart Mill and Walter Bagehot; and in the United States that earlier generation which between 1820 and 1850 looked on the Federal System and the legislatures working under it in the nation and the States as the almost perfect model of what constitutional government ought to be." In the States of the Union this distrust of legislatures has led to numerous constitutional amendments in which the people have restricted in one way or another legislative authority or have withdrawn subjects altogether from legislative control. Further, by the initiative and referendum they have attempted to make it possible to override their judgment, and to push through measures despite their opposition.[86] Primary laws and other similar types of legislation have also tried to ' restore government to the people.'

At best constitutional restrictions upon legislative authority have hampered state activity in social and business regulation, and have tended to make seats in the legislatures relatively less attractive; while direct primaries have not automatically restored popular nominations, and direct legislation has proved no substitute for legislative action but merely threats held over the heads of the houses. Moreover, these remedies have not been written into the federal Constitution, in part because this instrument is more difficult to amend than are the state constitutions. It is rather in another direction that the people of the several States and of the nation have hit upon a really fruitful means of adjusting

[85] Vol. ii, pp. 335-336; see also chaps. lviii, lix.
[86] Bryce, Modern Democracies, vol. ii, p. 342.

the representative system of the nineteenth century to the economic needs of the twentieth.

That direction is through the exaltation of the Executive, first as a sort of tribune of the people and leader of the legislature in the effectuation of popular mandates,[87] and then as an organ suited to work out by detailed regulations or individual decisions the specifics of policy which the legislature is not fitted to provide.[88]   The growth of gubernatorial leadership was paralleled in the federal system by Presidential guidance and control of Congress during the administrations of Roosevelt and Wilson.   In like manner 'government by commission' was resorted to in the States and in the nation.   In this development of administrative tribunals and of broad discretionary powers by the regular administrative departments, traditional distrust of executive power and bureaucratic control, as well as the traditional method of enacting statutes in minute detail, gave way before the pressure of circumstances.   Partly to save time, partly to shift responsibility,[89] partly because they were helpless before the numerous, complex, and rapidly changing problems with which government is nowadays faced as never before, the legislatures and Congress enacted in many instances general laws and left the ordinary administrative services or specially created boards and commissions the task of applying the generalizations by special orders or of filling up the details by uniform concretizing ordinances.[90]   With this the people were satisfied,

---

[87] Woodrow Wilson, Address before the Commercial Club of Portland, Oregon, May 18, 1911. Noted in Mathews, Principles of American State Administration, p. 72. See also Wilson, Constitutional Government in the United States, chap. iii. Cf. Garner, "Executive Participation in Legislation," in Proceedings of the American Political Science Association, vol. x, p. 183; Orth, "Presidential Leadership," in Yale Review, vol. x, pp. 449-466.

[88] The political aspects of the first tendency in a way conflicts with the technical aspects of the second. But, as we shall demonstrate, even in subordinate legislation technical advice must be only placed at the disposal of political decision, and must not try to control it.

[89] Cf. Ford, The Rise and Growth of American Politics, p. 284, dealing with the way Congress dodges politically dangerous issues. The same phenomenon is probably present in certain delegations.

[90] For one class of authorizations of 'regulations' to be issued by

because they had little confidence in the popular assemblies, and found in elected or appointed boards the promise of a more scientific approach than had been seen in the log-rolling and venality of law-makers. There took place in the States a rapid multiplication of boards and commissions, with little or no attempt to correlate these with each other or with the existing departments. In the national government there was first the Interstate Commerce Commission; and in quite recent years there have been added to it, not only the war boards called forth by the emergency and the expansion of federal control of 1917-1918,[91] but also the Federal Trade Commission, the Federal Reserve Board, the Federal Farm Loan Board, and the Tariff Commission. From time to time also the President himself and the heads of departments under his responsibility have been delegated in the statutes discretionary and even rule-making powers. This last has been done from the Presidency of Washington; [92] but it has probably been a more usual method in later years.

With this shift of emphasis to administrative justice came the realization that governmental administration is less efficient than the administration of private enterprises.[93] Without administrative reform, therefore, attempts at governmental control of the procesess of modern industrialism would prove utterly futile. Consequently there arose a demand first for the merit system,[94] then for budgetary procedure,[94] and then for administrative reorganization and integration into a hierarchical system culminating in the Chief Executive at the top. The results of this demand can be traced in the laws. The federal Civil Service Act was passed in 1883. In

---

administrative officers, see Westervelt's Pure Food and Drug Laws, Federal and State, pp. 13, 14, 15, 16, 1454, 1526. These regulations are, however, as a rule ' executing ' rather than ' completing ' ordinances. For the distinction see chap. iii.

[91] W. F. Willoughby, Government Organization in War Time and After, passim; Berdahl, War Powers of the Executive in the United States, especially part 3.

[92] See chap. iv.

[93] Report of the Efficiency and Economy Committee of Illinois (1915).

[94] See Foulke, Fighting the Spoilsmen.

1921 the federal Budget and Accounting Act was enacted. Along with these went numerous state laws instituting civil service reform and budgetary systems.[95]   Also about 1910 there began a movement for administrative reorganization which bore its first fruits in Illinois in 1917.[96]   At present this movement is spreading to other States with increasing momentum,[97] as such movements if successful are wont to do. Only recently a tentative plan for federal reorganization was drafted by a committee consisting of three Representatives, three Senators, and Mr. Walter F. Brown representing the President.[98]   In the federal government, unlike the States, the President has always been the real head of the administration.   In both the future must see the merit system of appointments effectively extended to promotions, demotions, discipline, and discharge.[99]

With the reconstruction of the administrative department we can look with greater complacency upon delegations to that department of rule-making discretion by the legislative branch.   The President and governor should be placed in a position of full responsibility for discretionary decisions; but the subordinate officials, upon whose study and practical experience the Chief Executive and department heads must base such decisions, must be placed upon a permanent and relatively effective basis.

We have not as yet solved the problem of legislative reconstruction.   This is still a problem of the future.[100]   Perhaps

[95] W. F. Willoughby, The Movement for Budgetary Reform in the States.

[96] Mathews, Principles of American State Administration, chap. lx; Buck, " State Budget Progress," in National Municipal Review, November, 1921.

[97] See Fairlie, " Illinois Administrative Code," in American Political Science Review, May, 1917; Mathews, " Administrative Reorganization in Illinois," in National Municipal Review, November, 1920.

[98] See, for example, American Political Science Review, vol. xv, pp. 380-384, 568-579; vol. xvi, pp. 579-581; National Municipal Review, vol. viii, pp. 615-620; vol. x, pp. 334-336, 393; Review of Reviews, vol. lxi, pp. 295-302; Fox, " Pennsylvania Reorganizes," in National Municipal Review, September, 1923.

[99] See Procter, Principles of Public Personnel Administration, passim.

[100] Lord Bryce spoke of popular assemblies as "essential" (Modern Democracies, vol. ii, p. 357).

in the States we shall reconstitute the representative system by removing constitutional restrictions and concentrating broad legislative powers in a unicameral commission of well paid citizens. This will not, however, be feasible in the federal government. At any rate the writer believes that in both state and nation one important element in the solution will be the development of the potentialities of administrative co-legislation. With this development the future of popular assemblies as the basis of constitutional and especially of democratic government is intimately related. This method, unaccustomed as we are to it, will doubtless play a conspicuous part in any scheme to save representative government from collapse. Through its agency we may be able to harmonize that type of government with the basic economic facts of the time. It thus appears that administrative reconstruction is the prelude to the development and placing upon a permanent footing of administrative legislation; while the latter is a necessary element in the adaptation of the representative system of the nineteenth century to the conditions and needs of the twentieth.

In the case of administrative tribunals, the discretion which in the past has been delegated to them has in large part been executive discretion or discretion in particular cases,[101] as distinguished from legislative discretion in the strict sense. This has been due to the need for individualization,[102] the variety of the conditions being one of the most perplexing aspects of modern industrial problems. It is because of this variety, in large degree though not exclusively, that general legislation has been impossible. On the other hand, in many matters of a less strictly industrial nature administrative or executive officials have been delegated rule-making discretion or discretion with reference to the circumstances under which rules

---

[101] For example, public utilities commissions prescribe, after hearings, rates for individual gas companies, or railroads, or interurban lines, etc. Sometimes the gas company of one city may be allowed one rate, and that of another city in the same jurisdiction another rate.

[102] Pound, Introduction to the Philosophy of Law, p. 135-137; see p. 129 ff.

are to come into operation,—in other words, ordinance making discretion in the strict sense.[103]   The extent to which this procedure was adopted in the wartime regulation of commerce and industry in the late German War suggests the probability that the future will see a growing use of it in connection with peace-time legislation of the same character.   Perhaps President Harding's insistence on flexible tariff rates to be changed by the Executive is an indication of what we may expect in other fields.[104]   Then shall we have changed from judicial justice supplemented upon occasion by legislative justice, first to administrative justice as a supplement to ever increasing attempts to secure justice through legislation, and then to administrative legislation as a recognized and regularized complement to legislation by popular assemblies under executive leadership.

V

The next step in the discussion of this significant development will be to sum up the advantages and then the disadvantages of supplementary legislation as opposed to legislation in detail by the popular chambers.   The most acute discussion of this question is that of Professor Freund in an article in the American Political Science Review,[105] which bears the title " The Substitution of Rule for Discretion in Public Law "; and most of the arguments given below are suggested by the views there expressed by this distinguished student of administrative law.   The advantages of administrative over legislative regulation may be summarized as follows:

1.   Neither legislatures nor their standing committees can become as intimately acquainted with industrial and social problems as can those who rub elbows with those problems in the actual administration of the laws.   This intimate knowledge, born of experience, gives the administration a " better sense of what is practically enforceable," and allows it, with-

---

[103] Especially but not solely in the case of ' executing ' ordinances.
[104] See his message to Congress of December 6, 1921.
[105] November, 1915.   Quotation marks in this section indicate a quotation from this article unless the contrary is indicated.

out too great flexibility, better to " plan a program of development." Legislatures are known to pass laws without reference to the practicability of their enforcement in order to curry favor with the voters or organized groups thereof.

2.   Because of the slowness of legislatures [106] and the fact that they are often not in session,[107] it results that : (a) their mistakes cannot be corrected as quickly as those of the administration, and (b) their laws cannot as readily be changed to meet changed conditions.   Professor Freund almost goes so far as to assert that it would not be an advantage that administrative action would give " flexibility and adaptability to circumstances." [108]   But while we agree that stability and

---

[106] This is true despite the methods of cloture introduced into modern legislatures. In the Senate of the United States cloture can even since 1917 hardly be said to exist.

[107] The executive and administrative functions are continuous functions. Not so with the legislative.

[108] " The grant of rule-making powers . . . is often advocated mainly for the greater flexibility of enactment or change. From this point of view much may also be said against the practice, since an unstable policy in requirements of any kind is undesirable, and it is doubtful whether powers are likely to be exercised in that spirit.   The real advantage, however, of such powers is that the bodies in which they are vested are likely to be better trained and informed and more professional in their attitude than legislative bodies, and that the powers being subordinate in character are more readily controllable by reference to general principles, whether laid down by statute or by common law.   The body will be sufficiently judicial in character to have respect for precedent, and its policy is therefore likely to be less variable than that of the legislature. These factors will tend to make rule-making more scientific than statute-making.   There has been too little experience with the working of rule-making bodies in this country to warrant conclusions of much value; the precise line of demarcation between matter to be determined by statute and matter to be left to regulation has not yet been satisfactorily settled, and procedural safeguards for the making of rules have hardly yet been developed. . . . If common-law methods can be made applicable to the development of statutory rules, so much the better.   There is much reason to believe that many phases of standardization (rates, methods of assessment, safety requirements, classification) can be much more readily secured through the constant thought and ruling of an administrative commission than through the necessarly sporadic acts of a legislative assembly. Legislative power can, in other words, be exercised more effectually and more in accordance with the spirit of the Constitution through delegation than directly.   This consideration should weigh against abstract theories regarding the non-delegability of legislative power " (Freund, Standards of American Legislation, pp. 301-302).

certainty are rather to be desired than change, nevertheless we recognize that change is at times necessary, especially in inaugurating a new scheme of regulation and in times of rapidly changing circumstances.

3. The legislature can only lay down a rigid rule, and there its activity stops; and if that rule is specific it is the duty of the Executive to try to enforce it as the law.[109] On the other hand, if discretion be left to the Executive, he can at first make flexible rules, increase their rigidity by degrees, and meanwhile win over the interests to be regulated by tact and diplomacy. In the words of Freund, the administrative branch can " mix suasion with command." [110]

4. In general, greater " permanence and continuity " and even scientific value result from " official action." Popular assemblies are notoriously fickle. Government by such assemblies is equivalent to government by opinion, or what is worse, government by political manipulation and bargaining. " Self-governmental organs lack the inherent checks which in professional organs evolve principle out of constantly recurring action," while administrative action " permits the

---

[109] This is true in theory but not workable in practice. The impression the present writer has got from the first-hand study of administration is that the rigid mandates of the law spell ' must if you can ' or even merely ' should ' to administrators. Flexibility in legal arrangements would thus bring them in line with the facts and develop a weakness of administration into an asset.

[110] " In fixing these standards two courses lie open to the department. First, it may employ an expert in cheese, an expert in cabbage, an expert in butter, an expert in potatoes, and so on, and leave to these experts the duty of determining the standards. Second, it may call together from all over the state people who are engaged in the business of producing and of buying and selling these products; and with the assistance of these people or groups interested it may determine standards which can be agreed upon as fairly reasonable. It is the latter course, the democratic rather than the bureaucratic, which the marketing department (of Wisconsin) has tried to follow" (Turner, " Democracy in Administration," in American Political Science Review, May, 1923). This ' democratic ' method, as the article points out, allays distrust and substitutes education for dictation. The method is possible in the case of legislative regulations unsupplemented by administrative completing ordinances; the legislative rules need only be general and not specific. But no system can be evolved unless the administration can issue completing ordinances of uniform application.

process of establishing rules to be surrounded by procedural guarantees and other inherent checks which will tend to produce a more impartial consideration than the legislature is apt to give, and which should in the course of time, if not immediately, substitute principle for mere discretion." This is so because official action, when it is " sufficiently detached from the strife of interest [111] and imbued with a sense of professionalism," " shares with judicial action the respect of precedent and the respect of expert opinion, habits of mind which distinguish both from the irresponsible action of popular bodies." Even when the issuance of supplementary ordinances is left to the President without procedural guarantees, the definiteness and completeness of his responsibility is likely to prevent many of the typical evils of legislative action. But if federal ordinance making is regularized and made permanent it is perfectly possible to place safeguards around Presidential legislation without dissipating Presidential responsibility.[112] Then will problems to which pure science can as yet give no specific answer be decided nevertheless in the scientific spirit and as far as possible upon the basis of scientific principle. Then will government by manipulation be displaced by gov-

---

[111] This does not, of course, mean the elimination of ' representation of interests ' in administrative co-legislation, provided such representatives act in a purely advisory capacity (see Garfield, " Recent Political Development: Progress or Change? " in American Political Science Review, February, 1924).

[112] The way in which this may be done is brought out by Mill in his Representative Government (chap. xiv) in discussing the relation between a political head and his professional advisers. His example is the Council of the Governor-General in India as it existed in his day. The Governor-General had the ultimate power of decision, but both he and his councillors recorded their opinions; and while he bore full responsibility, they participated in the majority of decisions and were responsible for their recorded advice. With us the President could still be held responsible in a general way, the head of the department concerned being immediately responsible. They might be required to seek professional or scientific advice, or cause semi-scientific investigations to be conducted. They could also be required to receive advice from representatives of the interests to be affected, who would be chosen by such interests. In both cases, it would probably be feasible to require the advisers to record their advice for the benefit of the public. Cf. President Garfield's article quoted in note 111.

ernment by professional sagacity mixed with scientific approach.

5. If the legislature has to do only with the fundamental principles of policy and not with details, the minds of the legislators and of the public can be directed to the broader aspects of the social and economic problems of the day, which are the only aspects upon which the people and their representatives are qualified to pass judgment.[113] The only ways in which this result can be produced, are by leaving a power of co-legislation to the Executive or by leaving to administrative boards or to Mr. Dicey's twelve shop-keepers the application to individual cases of statutory generalities. But the absence of principle in the verdicts of juries is a matter of common observation; and there can be little doubt that supplementary administrative rules are better.

These advantages of the delegation to the Executive of co-legislative powers are, however, in part offset by certain disadvantages, which may now be noted:

1. Preceded as it is by no public discussion,[114] administrative action is less easily controlled by the influences of public opinion than is action by a debating legislature. Now it may be true that the administration is right and public sentiment wrong; but in a popular government it is not proper for the administration in important matters of dis-

---

[113] It is of course true that neither the average legislator nor the average citizen is well 'qualified' to determine either the fundamentals of policy or details and specifics. Nevertheless, in a democracy they must decide, or at least be given every opportunity to decide, the former. This is justified, if for no other reason, because, while some individual or group might be better qualified for decision, he or they would in all probability be warped in their decisions by their own interests. There is too much of this personal element under our rough approximation to 'democracy.' But it is less likely to lead to oligarchy than the placing of policy-formation in the hands of a determinate group of men who are not made responsible to the electorate.

[114] This defect can be eliminated or minimized by providing notice to the parties to be affected, as in sec. 1 of the English Rules Publication Act, 1893 (see Carr, Delegated Legislation, Appendix I). But this method does not necessarily insure that the general interest of the public will be as adequately considered as where the legislature threshes out a problem in the public view.

cretion to ignore the ideas of the public, and those ideas can ordinarily be ascertained with a fair chance of certainty only if the matter is threshed out in the public forum.[115]

2.   Closely related to the first point is the fact that legislators are imbued with a "keener sense of what is politically expedient" than are administrative officials.   Well-intentioned reforms may be spoiled rather than promoted by the hasty adoption by the administration of rules which are theoretically excellent but in advance of the political culture of the community.   In matters of discretion, as distinguished alike from matters of routine and matters which can be settled by an appeal to science, political expediency must never be lost sight of.   To take it into account is ever the part of statesmanship equally in democracies and in other forms of government.[116]

3.   Because legislators are looked upon as the representatives of the people in a peculiar sense, and because even a popularly elected Executive, and a fortiori appointed officials, are regarded in the United States as having something of the taint of autocracy or bureaucracy about them, it follows that the enactments of the *Volksvertretung* have with us a " higher moral authority " than administrative orders.   When

---

[115] That is, unless the administration adopts a policy of 'democracy in administration.' Even then, however, there is less of popular control than of the representation of the particular interests which are to be affected.

[116] " The vigorous, resourceful, active young expert is in a hurry. He is impatient of delay. He wants to perform his state work efficiently and have some real results to display. He knows all about roads and he wants everyone to feel how much he knows. . . . The road the engineer builds may be scientifically one hundred per cent efficient. If the farmer thinks not, a storm of criticism falls upon the department which put it through " (Turner, " Democracy in Administration," in American Political Science Review, May, 1923). Political decisions must take account of all the factors involved; and what the people concerned think should be done is at least one element that must enter into the decision as to what should be done. Mere cold science is never the sole consideration in politics. That enthusiastic experts may forget this fact is in a way in conflict with the first advantage of administrative action mentioned above; namely, that administrators have a " better sense of what is practically enforceable."

political exhortors urge obedience to the law as law they are thinking of statutes rather than of ordinances.

4. Executive legislation has, of course, its own inherent dangers. Thus under the spoils system that existed in the heyday of the Jacksonian era, to have delegated legislative power to administrative officials would not have been to take it out of the hands of politicians but to give it to politicians one degree removed from popular control. Whether or not that would have been better than specific and detailed statutory regulations, at any rate some of the peculiar merits of a proper system of ordinance making would not have been given free play.[117] Even under a scheme in which the lower grades of offices are filled by permanent officials recruited, promoted, demoted, disciplined, and removed under the merit system, and in which the political chiefs must largely depend upon these officials in making their decisions, it may nevertheless fall out that perspective will be lost in routine and that for scientific methods will be substituted traditional procedure and inefficient red tape.

VI

It is true that in England there is beginning a reaction [118] against government by statutory rules and orders; [119] but it is the opinion of the writer that this is a necessary and—within proper limits and with adequate safeguards—a desirable development. The " case for delegation " is well put by Mr. Cecil T. Carr in his well-balanced little volume on Delegated Legislation.[120] In brief, he lists three [121] " justi-

---

[117] The fact-finding and investigatory functions, like the advisory function, are leading factors in the potential significance of co-legislation in reconciling representative government with industrialism, specialization of classes, and modern science (cf. Garfield, " Recent Political Development: Progress or Change? " in American Political Science Review, February, 1924).

[118] See Carr, Delegated Legislation, p. 55.

[119] This is the official English term used to designate at least certain classes of departmental ordinances (see ibid., pp. 45-47).

[120] Chap. iii.

[121] Mr. Carr mentions a fourth justification as the most important; namely, the occurrence of emergencies. But this is a specialized problem which we have treated separately. With his

fications" which would seem to be conclusive. The first is the administrative advantages of the procedure, some of which have been discussed in the previous section. The second is the lack of time of legislative bodies in these days of prolific legislation. The third is "limitation of aptitude" on the part of such bodies as compared with departments that specialize in particular subjects. Precisely here is the main hope for some sort of introduction of science into law-making. In connection with co-legislation all three of these points are of increasingly significant bearing upon the problem of adjusting representative government to the strains and stresses of an industrialized society. For in the future the nationalization of commercial and industrial relationships and of many distinctly social problems, together with the ever increasing multiplicity and intricacy of all these subjects, will produce a continual expansion of the regulative functions of Congress. Hence it is to be expected that in the period on which we are now embarking we shall see the delegation to

---

conclusions on the general issue compare the following opinion of Dicey: "The substance no less than the form of the law would, it is probable, be a good deal improved if the executive government of England could, like that of France, by means of decrees, ordinances, or proclamations having the force of law, work out the detailed application of the general principles embodied in the Acts of the legislature. In this, as in some other instances, restrictions wisely placed by our forefathers on the growth of royal power, are at the present day the cause of unnecessary restraints on the action of the executive government." He describes as "an awkward mitigation of an acknowledged evil" the modern occasional practice of delegation on the part of parliament, the practice being resorted to only where it is "obvious" that detailed statutory regulations are "either highly inexpedient or practically impossible." For in France "the form of laws, or in other words, of statutes is permanently affected by the knowledge of legislators and draftsmen that any law will be supplemented by decrees. . . . Foreign laws are, what every law ought to be, statements of general principles" (Law of the Constitution, p. 50, text, and n. 1). In a word, the continental method is approved, and should be systematized and regularized and not be the rare, exceptional, and haphazard expedient that it is in Anglo-American legislative practice. Cf. the opinion of Sir Courtenay Ilbert: "If however, the delegation of legislative powers is kept within due limits and accompanied by due safeguards, it facilitates both discussion and administration . . ." (The Mechanics of Law Making, p. 147).

the President [122] of more and broader powers of co-legislation than ever before in any period that was not a national crisis. The delegation of such powers to the Executive will in all likelihood become an accepted governmental process, not any longer being merely an exceptional method used to cope with special problems or to deal with very minor details. [123] The constitutional limitations upon such delegations which are urged in a previous chapter [124] as binding, and which should if necessary be enforced in the courts in a proper case, will keep this process from becoming a veritable transfer of legislative power from Congress to the President. Yet even within these limits the frequent and systematic use of the delegation of co-legislative power will be a practice the implications and results of which will be significant indeed.

What, then, is the implication of the practice for democracy? President Goodnow in his Politics and Administration [125] drew a sharp distinction between the formulation and the execution of policies. The principle of democracy demands that the former function be performed by the people directly or through their representatives in the popular assembly; for local representatives are over a long period more keenly and directly susceptible to public opinion than is the President. But once the policies of government have been enacted into law in conformity with the will of the people, the administration of those policies is not a question of opinion but of skill, experience, and the scientific approach. There is necessary only a popular check to prevent the per-

---

[122] This includes delegations to department heads, if not special commissions. See chap. viii.

[123] In the past delegations have been fairly closely confined to war crises, administrative matters, special problems (like governing the Philippines or building the Alaskan railroad), foreign commercial relations, and the minutiae of legislative regulations. It is only the last two classes that come within the scope of the topic of discussion; though in some cases the ordinances under the last class deal with more than mere 'details.' In handling certain problems Congress has, in ordinary times, passed what Lord Herschell termed " skeleton legislation " (Carr, Delegated Legislation, p. 16).

[124] Chap. vi.

[125] Chaps. i, iii, iv.

version and misuse of administrative authority. In advocating administrative co-legislation we merely carry to its logical conclusion, merely apply to the conditions of the present day, the idea of President Goodnow. Neither the people nor their representatives in Congress have the experience or knowledge needed to work out the details of complicated regulatory enactments; while the phenomena to be regulated are often in such a state of flux that statutory regulation becomes entirely too rigid. Why, therefore, should not Congress content itself with blocking out the basic principles of legislation, leaving the elaboration of the details in part to administrative agencies with power to issue concretizing ordinances and in part to administrative tribunals with power to individualize where necessary legislative generalizations?

Viewing the same matter from a different angle, we may consider the bearing of a system of co-legislation upon the relationship between the legislative and executive departments of government. John Stuart Mill, influenced as he was by the English Constitution, maintained that " in legislation as well as administration, the only task to which a representative assembly can possibly be competent is not that of doing the work, but of causing it to be done; of determining to whom or to what sort of people it shall be confided, and giving or withholding the national sanction to it when performed." Again he says: " Instead of the function of governing, for which it is radically unfit, the proper office of a representative assembly is to watch and control the government: to throw the light of publicity on its acts; to compel a full exposition and justification of all of them which any one considers questionable; to censure them if found condemnable, and, if the men who compose the government abuse their trust, or fulfill it in a manner which conflicts with the deliberate sense of the nation, to expel them from office, and either expressly or virtually appoint their successors. . . . In addition to this, the Parliament has an office, not inferior even to this in importance; to be at once the nation's Committee of Grievances, and its Congress of Opinions; an arena in which not only the general opinion of the nation, but that of every section of it, and as far as possible of every eminent individual whom it contains, can produce itself in full light and challenge discussion. . . ." [126]   Some of his points are inapplicable in a Presidential type of government; [127] but the essential conception of the relation of the two great political departments is fundamentally sound.   It is the business of the Executive to govern, of the legislature to control the Executive.   The former should not only conduct administration [128] under the general control of the latter, but should take the initiative in the enactment of a legislative program and guide the legislature at every turn.   It is the active force,—the assembly being the organ of opinion, the controller of policy, and the judge of efficiency.   But can we not go further?   Can the legislature find the time,[129] or has it the ability,[130] to pass upon details of legislation any more than of administration?   Must it not determine merely the general principles of the law and leave to the Executive— subject to the proper processes of legislative or popular control—the elaboration of those principles, in its sound discretion, and on the basis of scientific or fact-finding inquiry and the advice of interested parties? [131]   This would seem to be a general principle growing out of the nature of present-day representative government.   Our American practice of concrete and specific enactments by the popular body is thus a method [132] that under present economic conditions is becoming more and more intolerable.

---

[126] Representative Government, chap. v.

[127] For example, his idea of the majority party in the assembly practically choosing the prime minister; as also and especially his idea of having the assembly vote out a ministry.

[128] This involves the issuance of executive co-ordinances or even ordinances (see sec. 2 of this chapter).

[129] Carr, Delegated Legislation, pp. 19-20.

[130] Ibid., pp. 20-21.

[131] Garfield, "Recent Political Development: Progress or Change?" in American Political Science Review, February, 1924.

[132] This method has not worked so badly in the past as it is working today, for the simple reason that the problem of governing was much simpler under a régime of laissez faire.   But that régime is passing away.

VII

The final aspect of the problem of co-legislation relates to the best means of organizing, regularizing, and systematizing the practice in the American federal government. Phases of this subject like the maintenance of popular control and the protection of individual rights, and technical matters like the form, preparation, and publication of ordinances embodying co-laws, will be given more detailed treatment in the next chapter and in the Appendix. At this point we shall merely enumerate some outstanding features of organization, and outline some needed reforms in technique and some necessary political safeguards.

In the first place we must fit the practice into our existing system of presidential government.[133] There are certain aspects of popular control under responsible government which are superior to the corresponding features of the American scheme. But we cannot in this treatise discuss the purely academic question whether we should introduce responsible government into the United States. All federal ordinance making, then, is and must be technically Presidential ordinance making.[134] We have already shown that the heads of departments are responsible to him for the exercise of their discretionary powers; while many such powers which the statutes delegate to the President are exercised by him through the departments. In practice only important matters will be submitted to the Chief Executive for his approval; while the preparation of even these will be in the hands of the subordinates of the head of the department concerned.[135] The problem, therefore, is to insure that responsibility is definitely fixed. The President cannot be served with compulsory process;[136] and at times he can dodge political responsibility.

---

[133] In chap. xi the political responsibility for ordinance making under presidential and cabinet government is briefly discussed.

[134] Unless, indeed, ordinance making by commissions can be placed upon a quasi-independent basis. Cf. chap. viii.

[135] See Fairlie, "Administrative Legislation," in Michigan Law Review, January, 1920.

[136] No court can so serve him, not even the Senate sitting as

The heads of departments should be made more definitely responsible than they are by any machinery now in operation in our system.[137] Unfortunately the hierarchical type of responsibility tends to become a merely nominal responsibility.[138]

In the development of commission government the boards and commissions were in practice set apart and made independent or quasi-independent of executive control.[139] This has been done away with in part by state administrative reorganization;[140] but the federal commissions have never been closely connected with the regular administration or so closely under the control of the President as department heads. The reason seems to be the quasi-judicial character of the work of the Interstate Commerce Commission and the other boards. Whether this is wise in such cases more than in cases of ordinary ordinance making is a question for serious consideration. This is a matter which deserves study in connection with federal reorganization.

Where ordinances are issued by a governmental department, it is better to have one officer rather than a commission responsible for their issuance. There is a great deal of truth in the assertion attributed to General Goethals that administrative boards are long, narrow, and wooden. Mill emphasizes the inadequacy of the board system when he quotes Bentham as saying that " Boards are screens." According to

a high court to try impeachments, though it can serve notice of the trial and later of conviction, in case he himself has been impeached. But impeachment and conviction result in removal of the President from office, which creates a sort of personal responsibility. In practice it has never, however, come into play, and it is effective if at all only as an ultimate threat.

[137] This might be done by having them appear on the floor of the House to defend their actions; or by requiring them to lay their ordinances before Congress. In the latter case Congress might annul an ordinance within a certain period (cf. Carr, Delegated Legislation, p. 38 ff.).

[138] Whereas, in collective responsibility of all the chief officers for the action of each there is no chance to shift responsibility to one's superior or to one's subordinate.

[139] The President removes for cause the members of such commissions; but they are set apart from the regular administration, and he does not ordinarily attempt to control them in the way he controls the heads of the ten regular departments. Cf. chap. viii.

[140] See the Illinois Civil Administrative Code.

Mill, responsibility is "enfeebled" when it rests upon a board.[141] The final power of decision should be in a single officer.

Nevertheless, Mill himself declares that " it is also a maxim of experience that in the multitude of counsellors there is wisdom." Former Fuel Director Garfield has recently laid stress on the importance of what he terms "the advisory function" in government. Associated with the officer who makes the decision should be groups of advisers selected by, and thus really representative of, the interests affected by the ordinances of the said officer.[142]

Then there should be the technical experts connected with the bureau under which the particular matter comes. The technical functions involved in ordinance making consist of the processes of fact-finding,[143] scientific investigations of various sorts,[144] and the drafting of ordinances.[145] The fact-finding and scientific functions are intended to furnish the basis of judgment and the guidance of discretion. The drafting operations are important in the same way that expert bill drafting is important in the process of legislation.[146] Each of these duties should be definitely and systematically provided for and organized in each department of the government; and in the matter of forms and terminology there should be uniformity throughout the government.[147]

In matters of discretion where science can give no categorical answer and where opinions vary in fairly close correlation with interests, every safeguard should be thrown around

---

[141] Representative Government, chap. xiv.
[142] "Recent Political Development: Progress or Change?" in American Political Science Review, February, 1924.
[143] Ibid.
[144] There is an almost undeveloped field for original research as a basis for both legislation and co-legislation, especially perhaps the latter. At the least, every department that has to issue regulations should have attached to it experts trained in the scientific knowledge of that particular field.
[145] See Ilbert, The Mechanics of Law Making, pp. 86-87; Fairlie, "Administrative Legislation," in Michigan Law Review, January, 1920.
[146] Cf. Ilbert, Legislative Methods and Forms, passim.
[147] See Appendix, below.

decision so as to produce action that is based upon a weighing of the chief factors in the situation.[148]   Normally the chief factors of which account should be taken are: the relevant 'facts' so far as ascertainable; the principles of science or of political economy which are applicable; the viewpoints of the several special interests involved; the administrative aspects of the problem as viewed by government officials; and the interests of the general public, which in industrial matters correspond in large degree to the interests of consumers.[149] The function of the officer with power of decision is to take these factors as presented to him and apportion to each its proper value.   The means by which the factors are presented to him are through the permanent staff of the bureau or division and through the advice of the representatives of the interests concerned.   Then his decision must be expressed, by technically trained draftsmen in legal language which carries the proper meaning [150] and corresponds to the language in use in the statutes and antecedent ordinances on the subject.   The interests of the general public will suffer unless in suitable cases representative citizens are selected to voice them in an advisory capacity.[151]   This scheme of course applies to industrial and social [152] co-legislation especially; but it is probable that, in the years to come, these important matters [153] will be more largely handled by the federal government than they are at present.

---

[148] Discretion must be left to somebody; but its exercise becomes intolerable unless surrounded by safeguards that force men to abandon arbitrariness and to weigh the facts properly.

[149] Cf. Cole, Guild Socialism Restated, chap. v, pp. 37 ff., 67.

[150] See Appendix, below.

[151] Perhaps there is no satisfactory solution of this problem except it be through representation of consumers' interests.   But the great trouble here is that most people are primarily members of another group and only secondarily and half-consciously consumers (cf. the criticism Lowell offers of private bill legislation in Parliament: Government of England, vol. i, p. 387 ff.).

[152] The problem is different in the case of 'political' and especially 'emergency' discretion from what it is in what may be termed 'economic' discretion (see Martin v. Mott, 12 Wheat 19, for an example of political discretion).

[153] Political problems are more and more becoming economic problems.

There is no intention of depriving the President of political responsibility for the issuance of all ordinances which involve discretion and wisdom rather than science, including those that may use science as a basis but the contents of which science alone cannot furnish.   It is merely intended to give the administration a permanent machinery and facility for using both science and experience to the extent to which this is possible.   Already we have something of the sort provided in the Tariff Act of 1922, where flexible rates are provided, and made changeable by the President, with the proviso that he must first secure an investigation and report by the Tariff Commission.   It should be made clear that in all cases save where science can speak with finality the opinion of the experts should not control legally, but only morally and politically, the decision of the Chief Magistrate or the cabinet officer under him.   Furthermore, the ordinance making experts should not be independent boards but bureaus attached to the several departments of administration.   They should in general bear the same relation to the President and the department heads that the bureau of the budget now bears to the President alone under the Budget and Accounting Act, 1921.   To these scientific experts should be added other permanent employees versed in the special problems of the department, upon whose administrative experience the heads, as laymen of temporary tenure, could with a fair degree of certainty depend.

Further details will be treated in later chapters; but there are several points that require mention at this point.   With government by commission and even with executive colegislation have been associated notice and a hearing.   Mr. Taft in his book on the Presidency wrote: " The creation of many executive Commissions has given rise to qualms in the minds of some, lest we are departing from those forms of proceeding intended to protect individual right.   It may well be pointed out that the trend in all such executive tribunals is toward due judicial hearings and procedure."   It is thus in line with " the tendencies of the Anglo-Saxon to give a hearing as fair and equitable as is consistent with the effective operation of the government purpose." [154]

In all cases there must be at some stage at least a minimum of judicial review to inquire into the jurisdiction of the official who presumes to act,[155] and in most cases of particular discretionary action some sort of judicial or administrative hearing in connection with the substantive side of the decision. In the case of the issuance of uniform regulations, or ordinances, there are certain cases at least where an administrative hearing prior to issuance is neither required in present practice nor desirable in theory.[156] In other cases the statutes grant such a hearing; [157] though it is a question how far this is constitutionally necessary.

---

[154] Our Chief Magistrate and His Powers, p. 82; cf. sec. 1 of the English Rules Publication Act, 1893.

[155] The question of jurisdiction is a ' judicial ' and not a ' political ' question. It is judicial par excellence.

[156] Martin v. Mott, 12 Wheat. 19.

[157] A hearing is required of the Interstate Commerce Commission (see 24 Stat. L., 384, as amended by 34 Stat. L., 589, 36 Stat. L., 551, and 40 Stat. L., 272). But its orders may be to particular roads, although they are uniform with respect to the patrons of each such road.

CHAPTER XI

POLITICAL SAFEGUARDS AND PRIVATE REMEDIES

We want five things particularly.

(1) The delegation of legislative power should be delegation to a trustworthy authority which commands the national confidence. . . .

(2) The limits within which the delegated power is to be exercised ought to be definitely laid down. . . .

(3) In the third place, if any particular interests are to be specially affected by delegated legislation, the legislating authority should consult them before making its laws. . . .

(4) The fourth point to be insisted upon in delegated legislation is publicity. . . .

(5) The fifth and last point is that there should be machinery for amending or revoking delegated legislation as required. . . .

—CARR.[1]

The Congress is the legislative department of the government; the President is the executive department. Neither can be restrained in its action by the judicial department; though the acts of both, when performed, are, in proper cases, subject to its cognizance.

—Mississippi v. Johnson.[2]

The general rule with regard to discretionary duties and directory statutes is, that the officer who executes them is not liable for the way in which he executes them, nor may he be forced by the courts to execute them in any particular manner.

—GOODNOW.[3]

I

The term political safeguards covers several methods of holding the ordinance making officials responsible to the people for the exercise of their discretionary powers. These methods may be tabulated as follows: In the first place, there is the general check which is known as political responsibility, in its two main forms of direct and indirect responsibility. The distinction between the two as here drawn is based upon whether there is a hierarchical system with a popularly elected chief or a collegiate Executive jointly responsible to the legislature for the exercise of its ordinance making powers.

---

[1] Delegated Legislation, chap. iv.
[2] 4 Wall. 475.
[3] Principles of the Administrative Law of the United States, p. 296.

In the second place, especially in governments which embody the separation of powers in the form of having an elective Chief Executive who holds office by the calendar and not at the pleasure of the legislature, there is a special form of legislative control of all officers of the administration in the process of impeachment. A President might be impeached for misuse of ordinance making power.[4] In the third place, there is the control which the legislative department exercises over the purse and over the functions of the administration. Thus Congress can make the executive officers of the government mere clerks if it sees fit to appropriate money for minutely specified purposes and not for use by the administration in the exercise of some degree of discretion.[5] By a like token, since most of the ordinance making powers of the President are by virtue of Congressional delegations, Congress can limit or expand the discretionary power of the Executive at its pleasure according as it legislates in general or specific terms.[6] In the fourth place, there is the safeguard of publicity, which may be insured by any of several special methods. In the fifth place, there is the safeguard which comes to the special interests concerned through the method of the advisory function.[7] To several of these political checks somewhat more detailed attention may be directed.

---

[4] Impeachment really belongs among these 'political safeguards' rather than among the 'private remedies,' for the reason that it is a general check instead of a specific remedy.

[5] If, however, lump-sum appropriations are made, and if the administrator-in-chief may make, at his discreton, shifts of sums from one sub-head to another, then there is room for 'official orders' or even 'administrative ordinances' (material ordinances).

[6] Hence, if co-legislative powers are persistently abused, the power to issue them may be taken back by the authority that gave them (Congress).

[7] This has been sufficiently discussed in the last preceding chapter. It is to be noted also that the technical regularization and systematization of the process of co-legislation (as advocated in that chapter) will of itself be a safeguard, in that it will allow the public to understand the process and to realize its significance in a way that it does not now. As for the advisory function in particular, it is especially applicable in connection with the issuance of important codes of industrial rules and regulations. Where there is only sporadic ordinance making so as not to justify permanent advisory

Since the issuance of even complementary ordinances [8] is by no means a non-discretionary function, but in truth a subordinate power of legislation, we must emphasize in this connection even more than in connection with pure administration, the necessity of popular control. Such control in its general form comes either by direct or by indirect 'political responsibility.' By direct responsibility we mean that the officials who issue the ordinances concerned are either popularly elected or else appointed and removable by superior officials who are themselves popularly elected. Such is the responsibility of cabinet officers and the President in the American federal government.[9] In the case of the former, while ordinances are in practice framed under their supervision in the first instance, yet important ordinances must or should be submitted to the President for approval. He it is who bears or should bear the full burden of political responsibility for the acts of his subordinates, whether in the given instance he has approved of their action in advance or not. Unfortunately, Presidential government does not enforce this solidarity of responsibility with the same effectiveness as does the cabinet system as it works in England. In practice we

---

committees representing special interests, a provision similar to that of the English Rules Publication Act, 1893, sec. 1, is sufficient. See text below.

[8] In the case of co-legislation the problem is different from that connected with the popular control of emergency ordinance making. In the latter type of ordinances prompt and effective executive action is the prime consideration. Checks must be brought into play largely after the event. In checking executive co-legislation the aim should be to insure a scientific approach to the elaboration of already formulated general policies, to prevent the growth of bureaucratic tyranny and the stagnation of red tape, and to block irresponsibility, arbitrary action, and corruption. Improved methods of administration and standardized procedure will help; but in addition there should be the special safeguards discussed below. It cannot be said that our present means in this country secure the desired ends. Congress prescribes the methods of administration in too detailed a way; while it cannot adequately check up upon the manner in which power is exercised, because of the separation of powers (see Wilson, Congressional Government, p. 271 ff.).

[9] It is true that the heads of departments are one degree removed from the people; but we have seen that they are under the control of the President, who bears or is supposed to bear responsibility before the people for their acts.

have semi-autonomous heads of departments who are only nominally or spasmodically responsible to the Chief Magistrate.[10] This evil might be remedied in part by having them appear on the floors of the houses of Congress to answer questions and defend their acts. That has been frequently urged,[11] and would be without doubt constitutional.[12] Yet it has its own drawbacks. Chief among these are that it would tend to cause the President, in considering cabinet appointments, to give undue emphasis to the oratorical ability of the candidates; that it would make large drafts upon the time both of Congress and of the secretaries; that it would tend to cause Congress to meddle more even than it does now in matters of administrative detail; and that it would unnecessarily inject politics into administration.[13] Yet there is undoubtedly a real need for more publicity and a more effective

---

[10] As administration expands, the President tends more and more to become a political officer, interested in a program of legislation and the like, and to leave administrative matters to the cabinet members, except when they bring up to him important matters—especially those of potential political significance (see Wilson, Constitutional Government in the United States, pp. 75-81).

[11] See, for example, Leupp, " The Cabinet in Congress," in Atlantic Monthly, vol. cxx, pp. 769-778; Redfield, " Cabinet Members on the Floor of Congress," in World's Work, vol. xl, pp. 69-71; Taft, The Presidency, pp. 28-30.

[12] See S. Rept. No. 837, 46th Congress, 3rd sess., February 4, 1881.

[13] The writer is indebted, for these points of criticism of this frequently advocated change, to Mr. W. F. Willoughby, Director of the Institute for Government Research, Washington, D. C. The arguments usually advanced in favor of having Cabinet members appear in Congress to answer questions and defend their actions prove to be, when tested by these counter arguments, rather lacking in insight into the way government actually works. The fact is overlooked that, not only through formal annual reports, but also through committee hearings, heads of departments can furnish information to, and answer questions for, the persons who really determine policies—the committeemen. The case might be different if Congress could vote out an administration. As it is, the evils mentioned outweigh any advantages of the proposed change, unless it be the advantage that it would insure more publicity and more popular control of the manner in which cabinet members exercise their discretionary powers. But perhaps this end could be attained in ways of less potential danger; as, by requiring the publication of ' draft ' rules which could be subjected to criticism in Congress before they went into effect. On the evils of the present system see Story on the Constitution, sec. 869 ff.

popular control; and unless some means are found of securing these ends through the latent control of the President himself, requiring the several secretaries to appear in Congress might exert a wholesome influence upon administration in the federal government. Without some such check abuses are very apt to develop; for while statutes are given publicity by being threshed out in debate, ordinances receive no public discussion before issuance and in ordinary cases very little afterwards.

By indirect responsibility to the people of ordinance making officials is meant that they are subject to dismissal by the popular assembly, which of all organs of government is closest to the people in the long run. This is the cabinet system as distinguished from the presidential system of the United States. However, as Low has pointed out,[14] in the English government of the first decade of the twentieth century (and it has been even more so in the decade and a half since) the cabinet has in reality a responsibility to the people, who return members to parliament to support or oppose a given set of party leaders. More and more rare nowadays are votes of lack of confidence by the Commons;[15] and the cabinet can usually expect to hold office until the next regular election. Then the people will pass favorably or unfavorably upon its record while in office. In this way the English system tends to become more astronomical, and in this respect more like the American. Yet despite these transformations in the working of responsible government, it still differs very materially from the American system in respect to several major features. An ordinance making policy of the cabinet might at any time cause a vote of repudiation that would entail immediately either a resignation or a dissolution.[16]　It

---

[14] The Governance of England, passim. See especially the revised edition of 1915, pp. vii, xviii-xx, 82, 101-102.

[15] Except under conditions where a three-party system makes it possible for two of the three groups to combine at any time and repudiate the Government. But this does not affect the argument in the text that responsibility is unified.

[16] This does not mean, of course, that the cabinet resigns when one of the houses—as rarely happens—annuls ordinances which are

would not be a case of merely dismissing the guilty or the inefficient, but the whole Government would stand or fall together. This is an advantage which that system has over ours. In theory, but only in theory, the President controls all executive formulation of policy, all ordinance making. In practice the heads of departments may themselves merely accept ordinances drawn up by bureau chiefs; while the President may have only passing knowledge of the whole affair.[17] Then when the show-down comes the President or the administration as a whole can squirm out of responsibility [18] in a way that would be impossible in England. The result can be nothing less than an astonishingly slack check by the administration upon departmental wrong-doing. The further we get down in a hierarchy, the further we get from the people. In England there is a collective will of the whole cabinet. A sharp distinction is made between political and administrative officials, and the system requires full and joint responsibility of the former for everything, and that immediately and not in the distant future. In this arrangement there is a greater spur to efficiency and honesty than exists in the United States.

II

While no ordinary court can get personal jurisdiction over the President,[19] both he and his subordinates can be im-

---

required to be laid before parliament when they are issued (see Carr, Delegated Legislation, p. 39). It does mean that an ordinance making policy relative to a matter of great political significance might cause, or constitute one cause for a vote of lack of confidence on the part of the Commons.

[17] See the protest of President Madison to his Secretary of War concerning ordinances which were issued without his knowledge and of the contents of which he was apprised only through the newspapers (Writings of James Madison, vol. iii, pp. 417-419).

[18] Party politicians then claim that the President should not be held to answer for what he was not personally guilty of, and blame falls, if at all, upon individuals. They may deserve what is meted out to them; but the moral effect on the administration of government in general is almost nil. In the English system, parliament need not use the rod often, because of the wholesome effect of the knowledge that it can use it at any moment.

[19] See text below.

peached.[20] The House of Representatives has the sole power
of impeachment, and the Senate the sole power to try all
impeachments. Officers may be impeached for and convicted
of " treason, bribery, or other high crimes and misdemeanors,"
but the interpretation of that phrase rests in the last analysis
in the opinion of the United States Senate,[21] an opinion
which may be tinged by political considerations. However,
in the only case in which a President has ever been impeached,
it was strongly urged by Senators when trying the impeachment that that body must confine its consideration to the
items in the indictment sent up by the House, and must
convict only if it appeared that the acts of which the President was guilty constituted treason, bribery, or other high
crimes and misdemeanors as defined by law.[22] This precedent
has fixed the principle that Presidents and probably cabinet
officers will not be lightly convicted. Only a most flagrant
usurpation or abuse of his ordinance making powers by the
President would without other causes induce his impeachment and conviction. According to one view such abuse ought
not to have weight unless the issuance of illegal ordinances
were made a crime by law.[23] It should be added that the
penalty must be " removal from office," and at the discretion
of the Senate may be also " disqualification to hold and enjoy
any office of honor, trust, or profit, under the United

---

[20] The Constitution of the United States, art. 1, secs. 2 and 3;
art. 2, sec. 4.

[21] The Senate is, however, apt to manifest in this matter a judicial restraint. This attitude is due in part to the traditional temper
of the chamber, but also to the two-thirds majority required for
conviction (Goodnow, Principles of the Administrative Law of the
United States, p. 462).

[22] There is another viewpoint, however, according to which the
President may be convicted for misconduct which does not violate
any criminal statute. This view refuses to give a strict or technical construction to the phrase " treason, bribery, or other high
crimes and misdemeanors " (see Goodnow, Principles of the Administrative Law of the United States), pp. 460-462).

[23] It might, however, according to another view, be legitimate for
conviction to take place not, to be sure, for his policies or on purely
political or partisan grounds, but yet for gross misconduct in the
exercise of his discretionary powers, even where he violated no law.

States." [24]   After removal, the President may be indicted for violation while in office of the criminal laws.

III

The other safeguard that requires consideration in this place is the provision of publicity. There are several methods which deserve special mention. First of all, the Congress itself may, by one or both of two means, shed the light of pitiless publicity upon the manner in which the Executive has exercised discretionary powers. By concurrent resolution or resolution of one of the houses information may be requested. While these resolutions usually have a saving clause to the effect that the information is to be furnished only if supplying it is compatible with the public interest, nevertheless refusal to bare the facts connected with the exercise of executive discretion in any save special cases places the administration in a bad light. However, even if relevant documents are transmitted by the President, the inner facts of the matter can be secured only by an investigation conducted by a committee of one of the houses. Recent events have demonstrated how startling may be the revelations which such investigations disclose; but they have just as truly shown how unsatisfactory a means they are of getting at the real truth. None the less, both calls for information and committee investigations must be accounted important restraining checks upon corrupt or negligent exercise of ordinance making powers.

Then the ordinances themselves should be given adequate publicity,[25] not only for the information of those officials or private persons upon whom they are binding, but in order to give the opportunity for, and stimulus to, public discussion in the newspapers and elsewhere of the merits of their contents. Statutes are debated in Congress in the public view.

---

[24] This is clear from a careful examination of the clauses of the Constitution which relate to impeachment.

[25] Carr, Delegated Legislation, p. 36.

In ordinance making there is lacking [26] that government by discussion which Walter Bagehot [27] and Woodrow Wilson [28] so admired. Ordinance making is not ordinarily preceded by any public discussion. It is done as it were in a corner, and advertisement of its results is a minimum safeguard against arbitrary or bureaucratic co-legislation.

There are employed in England,[29] however, still other means of publicity which we might imitate with profit. The Rules Publication Act, 1893,[30] in sec. 1, provides that at least forty days before the making of statutory rules notice of the proposal to make the rules and of the place where copies of the draft rules may be obtained shall be published in the London Gazette. Representations or suggestions made in writing during those forty days by any public body interested shall be taken into consideration by the authority proposing to make the rules before such authority finally settles them. But, in case of urgency or any special reason, rules may be put into operation forthwith as provisional rules, which shall continue in force as such until rules are made in accordance with the above provisions. Some such scheme for informing the interests to be affected might well be provided in our own system. As the English statute recognizes, the method is not applicable to emergencies. On the other hand, such an antenatal safeguard, as Mr. Carr names it,[31] is peculiarly applicable to ordinances completing statutes that regulate industrial relations.

Besides requiring rules to be issued only after notice and opportunity for a hearing, parliament may require other ante-natal safeguards.[32] It may require that the rules be

---

[26] Cf. Raiga, Le pouvoir réglementaire du Président de la République.

[27] The English Constitution.

[28] See Congressional Government, pp. 78, 298 ff.; Constitutional Government in the United States, p. 105.

[29] The description of these is derived from Carr, Delegated Legislation.

[30] 56-57 Victoria, c. 66.

[31] Delegated Legislation, p. 34.

[32] These are taken from ibid., chap. iv.

laid before it in the form of drafts which shall become effective only by the tacit or the formally expressed approval of parliament. In the one case the rules go into operation at the end of a certain period unless in the meanwhile they are held up by an address being presented by either house. If such address is presented no further proceedings are to be taken on them. In the other case mentioned the rules are formally nothing but suggestions to parliament which become law by virtue of parliamentary enactment rather than departmental issuance.[33] But as a matter of fact parliament has little time to scrutinize such rules, and ordinarily approves them.[34]

Then there is in England a post-natal safeguard which " may, and often does, come upon the top of an ante-natal safeguard." [35] The rules go into effect at once, but they must be formally laid before parliament and are subject to annulment or objection in that body within a specified time, which is usually twenty-one days. Of this method Mr. Carr has said: " This provision for laying rules before the House subject to post-natal annulment is now so common that the time seems almost ripe for co-ordinating and standardizing the ante-natal and post-natal procedure and superseding section 1 of the Rules Publication Act, to the operation of which, as we have seen, there are at present certain somewhat arbitrary exceptions." [36] Why, we may ask, should not Congress, which delegates the authority to issue most Presidential or-

---

[33] These are not in strictness ordinances at all, though it would seem that in effect they are as much the product of administrative action as are other types. This is because in most cases parliament accepts them as they stand. It is interesting to note also that even where the Government frames the rules and they go into effect at the end of a named period unless one of the houses objects, it is probably true that they are no more ordinances than are those that have to be positively approved by parliamentary resolution. For the maxim that what parliament permits it commands seems to apply here. The distinction in such cases is, however, a rather artificial one. The administration is the real author just as much as if they were not laid before parliament.

[34] Lowell, Government of England, vol. i, pp. 364-365.

[35] Carr, Delegated Legislation, p. 38.

[36] Ibid., p. 40.

dinances, require that they be issued only after notice and then be laid before it for annulment? And would not this practice, if regularized, be a sufficient substitute for having the heads of departments appear on the floor to explain and justify their discretionary action?

IV

In addition to the problem of popular control there is the question of protecting the individual against executive ordinance making. This is in part a legal matter, because aside from the non-legal restraints upon executive tyranny which are imposed by popular control, it is through legal remedies that the individual finds his security against the arbitrary exercise of such rule-making discretion as may be reposed in the President. Yet the end or purpose of private remedies is political, and it is convenient to discuss them from that broad point of view.[37]

The subject is one of great practical importance as well as legal significance. We have spoken of the theoretical limits of the ordinance making powers of the President; but in practice those limits are not greater than they are made by private remedies. In the long run public opinion and the standards of public conduct may protect the citizens; but in the individual case protection is guaranteed only if it be enforceable in a court. Then, too, a limitation that cannot be enforced is merely a moral and not a legal one, even though its existence may be proclaimed from the bench or by the legal text-writers. The maxim *ubi ius, ibi remedium* really means that there is no right unless there is a remedy.

In this regard the first principle to have in mind is that the President of the United States is not amenable to com-

---

[37] For an acute analysis of the ends to be sought by the different means of controlling administration, see Goodnow, Principles of the Administrative Law of the United States, p. 367 ff. It may be added that this same problem was (in chap. vii) viewed from other angles than the one emphasized in this section. Here we consider primarily the forms of action. There we considered what questions the courts will inquire into. The two are closely related, however.

pulsory process at the hands either of any ordinary judicial tribnual or of the Senate sitting as a high court of justice in the trial of impeachments, although perhaps the Senate may serve notice upon him in case the President is himself impeached. In the trial of Aaron Burr [38] Marshall issued a *subpoena duces tecum* to President Jefferson directing him to appear and bring with him a certain letter wanted as evidence in the defense of the accused; but upon the President's refusal either to appear or to furnish the letter, the great justice declared that the court would not consider that the President had acted in contempt of court nor proceed against him as against an ordinary individual, the propriety of withholding the paper being a matter for the President himself to decide. This incident set a precedent which has never been departed from.

In the case of Mississippi v. Johnson [39] the Supreme Court of the United States refused to issue an injunction to restrain President Andrew Johnson and General Ord from executing the Reconstruction Acts, which were declared in the plea for the writ to be unconstitutional.[40]

It is the better view that under our system the President is exempt from all judicial control over his person while he is in office; the ground for this being no theory of divine right or executive sovereignty, but the practical inconvenience that would arise from having the head of the state subject to arrest or to other distraction from his official duties at the dictation of any other authority whatever.[41] From this it follows that the President could not while in office be enjoined from issuing any ordinance,[42] compelled by man-

---

[38] Beveridge, Life of John Marshall, vol. iii, chap. viii.

[39] 4 Wall. 475.

[40] See Taft, Our Chief Magistrate and His Powers, pp. 47-48.

[41] The principle, with reference to the President, is thus upon a broader basis than the exemption of officers from judicial interference in the exercise of 'discretionary' or 'political' powers. For while other officers can by mandamus be compelled to perform purely ministerial acts, the President cannot, under the rule as here stated.

[42] Cf. Mississippi v. Johnson, 4 Wall. 475. Ordinance making was not involved in that case, but the principle of the case applies a fortiori to this function.

damus to issue any ordinance [43] indicted in criminal proceedings [44] or sued in damages [45] for the issuance of any ordinance, or compelled to testify [46] in any case involving any ordinance which he has issued.

There is no absolute rule of immunity from compulsory process in the case of the heads of departments and members of administrative commissions. Thus a mandamus will lie to compel these officials to perform ministerial acts.[47] Yet from the nature of the ordinance making power it follows that with respect to it they are practically exempt. The issuance of an ordinance is a discretionary act of government, and it is fundamental that a mandamus does not lie to compel the performance of such an act.[48] There have indeed been cases in our jurisprudence where administrative officers were by mandamus ordered to exercise their discretionary power in one way or another when the statute was considered to be mandatory[49] ; but even there the court would not order its exercise in a particular way.[50] With reference to heads of departments in the federal government, however, it is probable that no court would order them to perform their powers of ordinance making at all.[51]

---

[43] Cf. Willoughby, Constitutional Law of the United States (students' edition), p. 542. No mandamus has ever been issued to the President (Goodnow, Cases on American Administrative Law, p. 627n.).

[44] Congress could not by penal statutes make him amenable to criminal proceedings.

[45] Goodnow, Principles of the Administrative Law of the United States, p. 398-399; Cooley on Torts (first edition), p. 377.

[46] See Constitutional Decisions of John Marshall, 1803-1821 (Cotton, ed.), vol. i, p. 99.

[47] Kendall v. United States, 12 Pet. 524. See also Marbury v. Madison, 1 Cr. 137.

[48] Cf. High, Extraordinary Legal Remedies, sec. 10; Goodnow, Principles of the Administrative Law of the United States, p. 433. But see ibid., pp. 296, 429, and Illinois State Board of Dental Examiners v. People, 123 Ill. 227.

[49] See Commonwealth v. County of Hampden, 2 Pickering 414.

[50] Goodnow, Principles of the Administrative Law of the United States, p. 296. The writer has based this section on this invaluable treatise of President Goodnow's.

[51] See Dunlap v. United States, 173 U. S. 65;; but cf. Commonwealth v. County of Hampden, 2 Pickering 414.

It would seem that, ordinance making being by nature discretionary or political, no court would enjoin the issuance by a principal executive officer of the government of any ordinance,[52] or convict in criminal proceedings any such officer for fraud or improper motive in exercising such power,[53] or ordinarily hold him liable in damages in connection with the exercise of ordinance making powers.[54]

Thus, in the case of Spalding v. Vilas [55] the Supreme Court laid down the principle that heads of departments are exempt from the payment of damages claimed against them for a mere excess of jurisdiction, as distinguished from those claimed in case of utter lack of jurisdiction. In Robertson v. Sichel [56] the Court held that they are also exempt from damages for acts of their subordinates where there is no personal fault on their part and where they have not acted negligently in selecting such subordinates. For entirely unauthorized ordinances and ordinances of their subordinates where they had been negligent they might under some circumstances be liable in damages.[57] The same rule might be applied in case of flagrant abuse of discretion, as when in a suit they admit on demurrer that they acted in an arbitrary manner.[58] But into their motives in ordinance making the court would not in all probability in an ordinary case inquire.

---

[52] Goodnow, Principles of the Administrative Law of the United States, pp. 432-433. However, note the use of the writ of certiorari in some jurisdictions to review the determinations of officers, ibid., pp. 433-434.

[53] That is to say, it is doubtful whether, in the absence of clear and unmistakable statutory provision to that effect, an American court would consider 'motive' in such a case. Furthermore, it is not likely that such a statute will be enacted.

[54] Goodnow, Principles of the Administrative Law of the United States, pp. 399-400; see ibid., pp. 400-401.

[55] 161 U. S. 483.

[56] 127 U. S. 507.

[57] This possibility may be negatively inferred from Spalding v. Vilas and Robertson v. Sichel, above.

[58] Cooley on Torts, p. 411, p. 480 of second ed. With this compare Bradley v. Fisher, 13 Wall. 335, and Wilson v. The Mayor, 1 Denio, N. Y., 595, 599.

V

If the President can never while in office be subjected to compulsory process, and if the heads of departments who act in his name can only in rare cases be held liable in connection with ordinance making, nevertheless the ordinances of both the Chief Magistrate and his subordinates can by several methods and in several forms of action be attacked when once issued. The distinction between the two methods of calling into question official action is summed up by the opinion in Mississippi v. Johnson [59] in the following language: " The Congress is the legislative department of the government; the President is the executive department. Neither can be restrained in its action by the judicial department; though the acts of both, when performed, are, in proper cases, subject to its cognizance." The types of cases in which executive ordinances are or might be [60] under our system of law liable to be questioned may be summarized: [61]

1. Criminal proceedings may be instituted against the officer or officers who in enforcing a given ordinance are guilty of a crime defined in the statutes of Congress. It may, however, be questioned whether it is just to punish criminally a ministerial officer for carrying out in good faith an ordinance issued by his superior.[62]

---

[59] 4 Wall. 475.

[60] While some of those types listed below may not now be used for this purpose, the aim is not to give a picture of the law as it is at the present moment, but rather as it may be without any radical changes in our judicial system. That such radical changes might be worth considering will, however, suggest itself to every person who is familiar with the French *droit administratif.*

[61] In American public law it is a recognized principle that the state itself cannot be sued without its consent. Congress has provided for suits against the United States in the Court of Claims, but only with reference to claims growing out of contractual relations. The federal government could not be sued in tort for the issuance by one of its officers of illegal ordinances or for the enforcement by its officers of the same (see Goodnow, Principles of the Administrative Law of the United States, Book 6, div. 2, chap. ii).

[62] Whether it is to be done depends entirely upon Congressional legislation. But while it may be sound public policy to hold a ministerial officer personally liable in damages for carrying out orders of his superior when there was utter lack of jurisdiction to give the

2.   Where the violation of an ordinance is by Congress made a crime or misdemeanor, the illegality or unconstitutionality of the ordinance may be offered by way of defense in case of prosecution for violation.   In such a case the court will have to pass upon the validity [63] of the ordinance.

3.   Where the interests of private persons are affected by the ordinance, its validity can be called into question in the course of a civil suit prosecuted by one private person against another.   In such a suit a right may be claimed under the ordinance, or the claim may be that the ordinance infringes upon a legal or constitutional right.   When either claim is made by plaintiff or by defendant in the suit, the courts may have to pass upon the validity of the ordinance.[64]

4.   Application may be made for a writ of mandamus to compel a ministerial officer to apply or enforce an ordinance under which a right is claimed by the appellant.[65]

5.   Application might conceivably be made to a court of

---

order, nevertheless it would seem that in case of criminal liability *respondeat superior* should be a sufficient answer, unless the ministerial officer were personally guilty, else there would be liability without fault.

[63] " The courts have . . . very generally held to the rule that their control is, ordinarily, limited to the determination of questions of jurisdiction and regularity of action upon the part of administrative officers.   They will not, as a general rule, make use of this power of control to interfere in any way with the discretion which may have been accorded to administrative officers " (Goodnow, Principles of the Administrative Law of the United States, pp. 394-396, referring specifically to the " execution of the law by judicial process ").

[64] But here again the courts do not ordinarily inquire into the wisdom of the act which results from an exercise of discretion. They may refuse to consider an ordinance involved in a case only because it is ultra vires or issued without the proper procedural methods, or because the authorizing statute is itself unconstitutional, or because it is clearly unreasonable or involves corruption or fraud.   The cases are rare where corrupt motives or fraud would enter into a decision.

[65] If a valid ordinance lays upon an officer a specific ministerial duty, then the writ could be used to compel performance of said duty.   If, however, it is a matter of compelling an officer to ' enforce ' an ordinance, it is a question whether that function would be considered ministerial or discretionary in this connection.

equity for a writ of injunction to restrain subordinates of the President from enforcing an invalid ordinance.[66]

6. Application may be made for a writ of habeas corpus on behalf of a person who is under restraint by authority of, or for the violation of, an ordinance. In such a case the court will have to inquire whether the ordinance in question is valid.[67]

7. An action in damages may be brought against the ministerial officer who enforces an ordinance which, it is claimed, violates some statutory or constitutional right. Under certain circumstances enforcement of an invalid ordinance renders the enforcing officer liable in a damage suit.[68] The value of such a suit is diminished by the fact that minor officers are not apt to have sufficient property against which judgment may be executed.

8. In proper cases other forms of action against enforcing officers, such as actions in ejectment in states where such a suit does not involve trial of title, may be used to call into question the validity of Presidential ordinances.

---

[66] In Mississippi v. Johnson the court indicated that the duty of law enforcement with reference to the Chief Executive was discretionary or political in the relation of those terms to the issuance of an injunction. Would the same principle apply here? This query is similar to that raised in note 65 above. Is a distinction to be drawn between higher enforcement officers and ministerial officers?

[67] On this point cf. Ex parte Siebold, 100 U. S. 371, where the court took jurisdiction of a petition for the writ of habeas corpus in a case where the petitioners had been convicted by a court under a statute alleged to be unconstitutional. It seems that the same principle would apply where a person was restrained by an officer under an ordinance of alleged illegality.

[68] Points seven and eight will be discussed below. The others are sufficiently clear as stated. In all cases, the remedies either arise under state law (the case being originally tried in either a state or the federal district court) or else depend upon Congressional legislation, since there is commonly said to be no federal common law. Yet the significance of the remedies as prescribed by the States or by Congress tends to follow the historical meaning thereof. It may further be added that we have not herein considered suits against ministerial officers who negligently or with malfeasance perform their duties in the enforcement of ordinances. This is a broader problem, a problem of general administrative law, which has no especial peculiarities in relation to ordinances.

VI

It is not our purpose to go into the details of this subject of private remedies, but a few cases may be cited by way of illustration. Let us consider especially cases involving damage suits against ministerial officers.

In Little v. Barreme [69] an action in damages was prosecuted on the following facts:

The *Flying Fish,* a Danish vessel, was captured December 2, 1799, by the United States frigate *Boston,* commanded by Captain Little, and was taken into Boston port and libelled as an American vessel that had violated the non-intercourse act. The fifth section of that act authorized the President to instruct the commanders of armed vessels to stop any suspected American vessel on the high seas, " and if, upon examination it should appear that such a ship or vessel is bound, or sailing to, any port or place within the territory of the French Republic or her dependencies, it is rendered lawful to seize such vessel, and send her into the United States for adjudication."

In holding Captain Little liable to damages to the owner of the vessel, Mr. Chief Justice Marshall, who delivered the opinion for the Court, said in part:

It is by no means clear that the President of the United States, whose high duty it is to " take care that the laws be faithfully executed," and who is commander in chief of the armies and navies of the United States, might not, without any special authority for that purpose, in the then existing state of things, have empowered the officers commanding the armed vessels of the United States, to seize and send into port for adjudication, American vessels which were forfeited by being engaged in this illicit commerce. But when it is observed that the general clause of the first section . . . obviously contemplates a seizure within the United States; and that the fifth section gives a special authority to seize on the high seas, and limits that authority to the seizure of vessels bound, or sailing to, a French port, the legislature seems to have prescribed that the manner in which this law shall be carried into execution was to exclude a seizure of any vessel not bound to a French port. Of

---

[69] 2 Cr. 170. But of course Congress may leave ' discretion ' to the President. With this the courts would in such a case not interfere, especially where it is of a ' political ' nature (Luther v. Borden, 7 How. 1).

consequence, however strong the circumstances might be which induced Captain Little to suspect the *Flying Fish* to be an American vessel, they could not excuse the detention of her, since he would not have been authorized to detain her had she been really American. . . .

These orders given by the executive under the construction of the act of congress made by the department to which its execution was assigned, enjoin the seizure of American vessels sailing from a French port. Is the officer who obeys them liable for damages sustained by this misconstruction of the act, or will his orders excuse him? If his instructions afford him no protection, then the law must take its course, and he must pay such damages as are legally awarded against him; if they excuse an act not otherwise excusable, it would then be necessary to inquire whether this is a case in which the probable cause which existed to induce a suspicion that the vessel was American, would excuse from damages when the vessel appeared in fact to be neutral.

I confess the first bias of my mind was very strong in favor of the opinion that though the instructions of the executive could not give a right, they might yet excuse from damages. I was much inclined to think that a distinction ought to be taken between acts of civil and those of military authorities; and between proceedings within the body of the country and those on the high seas. . . . But I have been convinced that I was mistaken, and I have receded from this first opinion. I acquiesce in that of my brethren, which is, that the instructions cannot change the nature of the transaction, or legalize an act which, without those instructions, would have been a plain trespass.

Captain Little, then, must be answerable in damages to the owner of this neutral vessel. . . .

A similar case was Tracy et al. v. Swartwout.[70] This was a suit prosecuted in the lower court to recover damages from the defendant as collector of the customs. Mr. Justice McLean, in his opinion, states the facts with sufficient fullness:

It is admitted that the law imposed no more duty on the article than fifteen per cent. ad valorem; although the collector, acting under the instructions of the secretary of the treasury, required . . . a duty of three cents per pound. . . .

It was admitted by the council of the plaintiffs, that the defendant acted throughout with entire good faith, and under instructions from the treasury department. . . .

The collector of the customs is a ministerial officer: he acts under the instructions of the secretary of the treasury, who is expressly authorized to give instructions, as to the due enforcement of the revenue laws. . . .

The secretary of the treasury is bound by the law, and although in the exercise of his discretion he may adopt necessary forms and

---

[70] 10 Pet. 80.

modes of giving effect to the law: yet, neither he nor those who act under him, can dispense with, or alter any of its provisions. It would be a most dangerous principle to establish, that the acts of a ministerial officer, when done in good faith, however injurious to private right, and unsupported by law, should afford no ground for legal redress. The facts of the case under consideration will forcibly illustrate this principle. The importers offer to comply with the law, by giving bond for the lawful rate of duties; but the collector demands a bond in a greater amount than the full value of the cargo. The bond is not given, and the property is lost, or its value greatly reduced, in the hands of the defendant. Where a ministerial officer acts in good faith for an injury done, he is not liable to exemplary damages; but he can claim no further exemption where his acts are clearly against law. . . .

Some personal inconvenience may be experienced by an officer who shall be held responsible in damages for illegal acts done under instructions of a superior; but, as the government in such cases is always bound to indemnify the officer, there can be no eventual hardship.

Gelston v. Hoyt [71] was an action for trespass growing out of the seizure of the ship *American Eagle,* property of the plaintiff in the original suit. One of the pleas set up by the original defendants (plaintiffs in error) alleged the instructions of the President of the United States issued to them as customs officials under an act of 1794. The argument was, that as the President had power under the said act to employ the naval and military forces to execute the prohibitions and enforce the penalties of the act, a fortiori he had the power to employ the civil force, to which the officials in the case belonged, for that purpose. In upholding the main objection to this plea, Mr. Justice Story, speaking for the Court, said of the plea:

The power thus entrusted to the president is of a very high and delicate nature, and manifestly intended to be exercised only when, by the ordinary process or exercise of civil authority, the purpose of the law cannot be effectuated. . . . Whenever it is exerted, all persons who act in obedience to the executive instructions, *in cases within the act,* are completely justified in taking possession of, and detaining, the offending vessel, and are not responsible in damages, for any injury which the party may suffer by reason of such proceeding. . . . It is certainly against the general theory of our institutions to create great discretionary powers by implication; and in the present instance we see nothing to justify it. (The court had said the act is in terms limited to the use of the naval

---

[71] 3 Wheat. 248 (Italics in quotation below are the author's).

and military force). The third plea is, therefore, for this additional reason, bad in its very substance, and the state court were right in giving judgment on the demurrer for the original plaintiff.

To be contrasted with these cases, however, is that of Erskine v. Hohnbach.[72] Here Hohnbach sued Erskine, a collector of internal revenue, in an action of trespass for the seizure by the said collector, and conversion to his use, of certain personal property belonging to the plaintiff. The defendant justified the acts complained of on the ground that they were done by him as collector of internal revenues, in the enforcement of an assessment chargeable against the plaintiff, duly made by the assessor of the district, and certified to him, with an order directing its collection. In holding the collector not liable on the facts, Mr. Justice Field used the following language:

Whatever may have been the conflict at one time, in the adjudged cases, as to the extent of protection afforded to *ministerial officers* acting in obedience to process, or order issued to them by tribunals or *officers invested by law with authority to pass upon and determine particular facts, and render judgment thereon*, it is well settled now, that *if the officer or tribunal possess jurisdiction* over the subject-matter upon which judgment is passed, *with power to issue an order* or process for the enforcement of such judgment, and the order or process issued thereon to the ministerial officer is *regular on its face, showing no departure from the law, or defect of jurisdiction* over the person or property affected, then, in such cases, the order or process will give full and entire protection to the ministerial officer in its regular enforcement against any prosecution which the party aggrieved thereby may institute again him, *although serious errors may have been committed by the officer or tribunal* in reaching the conclusion or judgment upon which the order or process is issued.

The last case is cited to show that the liability of the subordinate officer is not absolute and unlimited. The distinction [73] seems to be, in general terms, this: In the first three cases cited the orders of the superior officers were not justified by the statutes, and hence were ultra vires. There was an entire want of jurisdiction. On the contrary, in the last case the superior officer was invested by law with authority to

---

[72] 14 Wall. 613.   (Italics in quotation below are the author's).
[73] See Goodnow, Principles of the Administrative Law of the United States, pp. 400-402.

make the order, but merely committed a mistake in the performance of his statutory duty. In such case his order has color of authority to the extent that it will justify a ministerial officer who acts under it. Of course the courts will not go behind an ordinance to question its wisdom; but there might be a type of mistake made by an officer who had jurisdiction which would render his order invalid and yet exempt his subordinate from damages.

VII

An action in ejectment as well as an action in damages may give rise to a refusal of the courts to enforce illegal ordinances of the President.

United States v. Lee [74] was a case in which the defendant in error sued in a state court of Virginia a number of persons to recover possession of a parcel of land known as the Arlington estate. The case was removed to the Circuit Court of the United States by writ of certiorari; and from the decision of that court a writ of error was filed with the Supreme Court by the United States, *eo nomine,* and one by the Attorney General of the United States, in the name of two of the original defendants. The decision of the Court, delivered by Mr. Justice Miller, stated the question before the Court with which we are here concerned as follows: " Could any action be maintained against the defendants for the possession of the land in controversy under the circumstances of the relation of that possession to the United States, however clear the legal title to that possession might be in the plaintiff?" The plaintiff established his title to the real estate in question; but it was urged at bar that, since the United States could not be sued without its consent, no action could be maintained against any individual without that consent,

---

[74] 106 U. S. 196. President Goodnow has pointed out that this case illustrates how the courts entertain suits against officers in situations where they would not consider suits against the government itself directly. In effect, but not in theory, this Lee case is a suit against the federal government (see Goodnow, Principles of the Administrative Law of the United States, pp. 392-394).

where the judgment must depend on the right of the defendants to hold property as officers or agents of the government. This the Court denied, holding that even the fact that the property was devoted to lawful and public uses, did not justify the deprivation of the lawful owner without due process of law or just compensation. The opinion said in part:

> This right being clearly established, we are told that the court can proceed no further, because it appears that certain military officers, acting under the orders of the President, have seized this estate, and converted one part of it into a military fort and another into a cemetery.
>
> It is not pretended, as the case now stands, that the President has any lawful authority to do this, or that the legislative body could give him any such authority except upon payment of just compensation. The defense stands here solely upon the absolute immunity from judicial inquiry of everyone who *asserts* authority from the executive branch of the government, however clear it may be made that the executive possessed no such power. Not only no such power is given, but it is absolutely prohibited, both to the executive and the legislative, to deprive anyone of life, liberty, or property without due process of law, or to take private property without just compensation. . . .
>
> Shall it be said, in the face of all this, and of the acknowledged right of the judiciary to decide in proper cases, statutes which have been passed by both branches of Congress and approved by the President to be unconstitutional, that the courts cannot give a remedy when the citizen has been deprived of his property by force, his estate seized and converted to the use of the government without lawful authority, without process of law, and without compensation, because the President has ordered it and his officers are in possession?
>
> If such be the law of this country, it sanctions a tyranny which has no existence in the monarchies of Europe, nor in any other government which has a just claim to well-regulated liberty and the protection of personal rights.
>
> It cannot be, then, that when, in a suit between two citizens for the ownership of real estate, one of them has established his right to the possession, . . . the wrongful possessor can say successfully to the court, Stop here, I hold by order of the President, and the progress of justice must be stayed.

With this significant illustration of the protection by the courts of individual right against arbitrary executive orders we may fittingly close this study.

APPENDIX

TECHNICAL ANALYSIS

There is no approach to uniformity in nomenclature. Rules, Regulations, Instructions, General Orders, Circulars, Bulletins, Notices, Memoranda and other terms are given to different series of publications by different government offices, with no clear distinction as to the meaning of these terms. . . .

In the matter of publication there is a maximum of variety and confusion. Not only is there no general system, but no department has developed a system for itself. Each bureau, and often each local office, has its own methods, or more often lack of method. . : .

There is need first, within each department and in the government service as a whole, for more systematic and uniform methods in the preparation and publication of administrative regulations. There should be in each department an agency for supervising the preparation and issue of all such regulations within the department. The number of classes of publications should be reduced, and a more uniform terminology established. Finally there should be an official publication which will record all regulations and instructions issued by all branches of the government service.

—FAIRLIE.[1]

I

We have examined the ordinance making powers of the President from the standpoints of analytical jurisprudence, constitutional history, constitutional law, and political science. It remains in the appendix to suggest another point of view from which the subject may be approached, and to offer a few facts relating thereto.

The first matter of technique is the forms of executive ordinances in the federal government. From what has been said in the text of the lack of technical terminology, and of the failure to recognize the ordinance as a distinct juristic category, it need not be a cause of surprise that the ordinances of the President and the heads of departments are neither called ' ordinances ' nor assembled in any one place nor issued in any one form. It is characteristic of the Anglo-American traditional attitude on executive orders that parliament once complained because at that time the royal proclamations were being published together as if they were statutes! [2]

The chief forms of written Presidential acts are the ' Proclamations ' of the President and his ' Executive Orders.' But while these two forms contain most or all formal acts of the Chief Executive, aside from his Messages to Congress, it is by no means true that all Proclamations and Executive Orders are ordinances in the technical sense defined in Chapter II. Thus the merely hortatory document known as the annual Thanksgiving Proclamation is issued in the same collection and bears the same form and name as Proclamations of a co-legislative character. Again, the Executive Orders con-

---

[1] " Administrative Legislation," in Michigan Law Review, January, 1920.

[2] Hallam, Constitutional History of England, vol. 1, p. 323.

tain not only ordinances but at times such matters as individual exemptions from civil service rules.[3]

Executive Orders deal more exclusively with matters of an administrative or executive nature than do Proclamations. Executive legislation usually takes the form of Proclamations, especially when it is of general interest and application within the continental United States. Sometimes, however, the Proclamation of the President merely outlines an ordinance and mentions Rules and Regulations to be issued.[4] A Proclamation in both England and the United States is a form of publication or promulgation. It is not only printed, but published, and is deposited in the archives of the Department of State as a part of the public record of the government. Thus it gets its name from this purpose of proclaiming or publishing something, while its contents may be declaratory, informatory, or hortatory, as well as, upon occasion, legislative. Executive Orders are less formal, and are apt to be used either for such ordinances as those for territories like the Panama Canal, or, especially, for ordinances in the material sense of the term. Civil service rules usually or always take the form of Executive Orders. Such rules are of considerable public interest, but they do not directly affect private persons.

Both forms are used for ordinances under delegated power as well as for ordinances under constitutional authority. For certain types of both sorts of ordinances special names are employed in popular or even legal usage. However, many at least of these types appear either as Proclamations or Executive Orders. We have mentioned that 'civil service rules' are issued as Executive Orders. Amnesties are, on the other hand, issued as Proclamations.[5] The texts of treaties are also embodied in Proclamations for the sake of promulgation, though treaties themselves do not take that form. Since, however, treaties are part of the law of the land and as such on a parity with statutes, it is fitting that they be formally proclaimed to the public.[6]

The form of Presidential Proclamations has been the same since the beginning of the government.[7] It bears a striking similarity

---

[3] Another type of Executive Orders that are not ordinances, is those establishing 'administrative sites.' Even those that do embody ordinances vary greatly in importance. At one extreme we have No. 973 issued by President Roosevelt excusing veterans and sons and members of the Women's Relief Corps desiring to attend the unveiling of General Seridan's statue from duty at 1 p. m. on a given day. This is a *Verwaltungsverordnung*, yet one of relative insignificance. At the other extreme there is an Executive Order like No. 1083 issued by President Taft amending the tariff of United States Consular Fees as prescribed by a prior Executive Order, or No. 1990 issued by President Wilson for the operation and navigation of the Panama Canal.

[4] For example, see 40 Stat. L., part 2, 1716 ff.

[5] For examples of civil service rules and amnesty proclamations see Richardson, Messages and Papers of the Presidents.

[6] Treaties, like Proclamations, are printed in the back (or latterly in Part 2) of the volumes of the Statutes-at-Large.

[7] See examples of Washington's Proclamations as set forth in Richardson, Messages and Papers of the Presidents, vol. i.

to the form of proclamation used by the king of England;[8] and the reader of the Journal of William Maclay will at once suspect, and no doubt correctly, that this similarity is something more than a coincidence. Its general character may be indicated by giving a short Proclamation of President Wilson;[9] though it may be noted that in certain details the wording varies from time to time. Thus, for example, in the phrase "I have hereunto set my hand," one proclamation may use the word "hereunto" and the next "hereto."

(Revoking Proclamation of January 1, 1918, Prohibiting Aircraft Expositions)

By the President of the United States of America.

A Proclamation.

Whereas on the first day of January, 1918, a proclamation was issued forbidding the exposition of aircraft in the United States or its possessions;

And Whereas, the reasons requiring such prohibition have ceased:

Now, Therefore, I, Woodrow Wilson, President of the United States do hereby repeal and annul the said proclamation, and do remove the prohibition therein imposed upon private aeroplane exhibitions.

In Witness Whereof, I have hereunto set my hand and caused the Seal of the United States to be affixed.

Done this 16th day of December in the year of our Lord (Seal.) one thousand nine hundred and eighteen, and of the Independence of the United States of America the one hundred and forty-third.

WOODROW WILSON.

By the President:

ROBERT LANSING,

Secretary of State.

(No. 1505).

It may be added that Executive Orders are less ritualistic, less elaborate. Examples are given in preceding chapters.

Presidential Proclamations and Executive Orders are preserved in the archives of the Department of State. The former are printed in the appendices of the forty odd volumes of the United States Statutes-at-Large, from the third volume on;[10] though later volumes of the series have been printed in two parts, Part I containing the public acts of Congress, and Part II the private acts of Con-

---

[8] Anson, Law and Custom of the Constitution, vol. i, chap. iv, sec. 4.

[9] This form is taken from a loose-leaf copy of some of the war Proclamations furnished the writer by the Department of State.

[10] "The Presidents' Proclamations are believed to be all printed in the volumes of Statutes-at-Large since 1873" (Letter from the Division of Publications of the Department of State, dated 19th October, 1922).

gress, treaties, and Proclamations. The Executive Orders have been regularly printed since October 13, 1905,[11] and have been collected in bound volumes containing practically all Executive Orders since that date. There are now several large volumes, which are entitled ' United States Executive Orders.' A set is deposited in the Department of Manuscripts of the Library of Congress. There are three reasons why some Executive Orders may be omitted from these volumes. In the first place, they were not numbered for a time after they began to be published. In the second place, such Orders are sometimes given numbers which contain fractions, thus making it uncertain whether all are included, even though all those numbered with consecutive whole numbers are there. In the third place, some Executive Orders may not be sent to the Department of State at all, though all printed Executive Orders are supposedly issued therefrom.[12] For the Orders of the period before October 13, 1905, one may turn to Richardson, Messages and Papers of the Presidents, though this valuable collection does not appear to contain all of them. Richardson is also convenient for scattered Proclamations and Executive Orders of all periods.

Individual orders of administrative commissions or tribunals are usually termed ' orders.' Departmental forms of action vary. The most important form is that known as Rules and Regulations. Others which are less formal are circulars, letters, etc.[13] Rules and Regulations are the regular form for ordinances or other sorts of action of general interest and application, including acts of co-legislation, issued by the heads of the executive departments. Of course these Rules and Regulations, if discretionary, and issued under delegations to the President, involve his political and perhaps legal responsibility, and are in a sense his acts. Even if issued without his knoweldge,[14] or by virtue of authority delegated directly to department heads, his is the political responsibility, if not also the legal responsibility in case of impeachment proceedings. In form there is a difference between acts which are of departmental stamp, and those acts which the President issues personally.[15]

---

[11] See the letter from the Department of State to Mr. Worthington C. Ford,—sometime head of the Department of Manuscripts, Library of Congress,—which is printed in the first of volume i of the United States Executive Orders.

[12] " Since 1905 the Executive Orders of the President have all been issued from this Department—at least such has been the rule. But some may possibly have been issued from other Departments without this Department's knowledge. These Orders are printed in separate form " (Letter from the Division of Publications, Department of State, dated 19th October, 1922).

[13] See Fairlie, " Administrative Legislation," in Michigan Law Review, January, 1920; Checklist of United States Public Documents, 1789-1909, vol. i (Lists) : compiled under the direction of the Superintendent of Documents.

[14] See the letter of President Madison to his Secretary of War complaining because regulations were issued without his knowledge (Writings of James Madison, vol. iii, p. 417-419. Quoted at the beginning of chap. vii above).

[15] " There is no official collection of the rules which the heads of

Lieber, in his work entitled " Remarks on the Army Regulations," has the following to say: [16]

" Many systems of regulations, besides the Army and Navy regulations, have been issued, for the transaction of the business of different branches of the Government, such as the postal, patent office, Indian office, civil service, customs, internal revenue, revenue cutter service, and other treasury and consular regulations, etc. But these systems of regulations, as they are here called, form by no means the whole of that mass of regulation law which constitutes so large and important a part of our administrative law. All regulations are not collected together in systems or groups, but an enormous mass of them consists of individual regulations, the knowledge of whose existence even is ordinarily limited to the few who have to apply them to the subject to which they relate."
Some well known codes of regulations are:

1. Civil Service Rules.
2. Consular Regulations.
3. Army Regulations.
4. Navy Regulations.
5. General Orders.
6. Customs Regulations.
7. Postal Regulations.

It is desirable for the sake of exactness and clarity for ordinances to be called ordinances, and for the different types to be distinguished from each other. Furthermore, ordinances should be published separately from other executive acts. This would emphasize the distinctions, and facilitate a clear understanding of the relation of the ordinance making power to other functions of government. In fact, there is no reason why all acts of government should not be designated according to some such classification as that set forth in Part I of this treatise. Certainly the present methods of nomenclature are hopelessly confusing and meaningless. The situation might be expected to improve if only our ideas were once cleared up. For the disorder of our terminology is due to the historical and unscientific character of our concepts.

II

Besides the question of forms and terminology, there is the matter of preparation and publication. This matter is best discussed in

---

Departments issue in regulating their Departments, or where authorized by Congress to complete or supplement the statutes. . . . For regulations particularly applicable to the several Departments application should be made to each Department separately. . . . There is no list of the different forms of executive regulations, nor of the different kinds of executive acts in use in the Federal Government " (Letter from the Division of Publications, Department of State, dated 19th October, 1922. But see Checklist of United States Public Documents, 1789-1909, vol. i. (Lists) : compiled under the direction of the Superintendent of Documents).

[16] Pages 45-47.

an article on "Administrative Legislation " [17] by Professor John A. Fairlie, who was Chief of the Orders and Regulations Section in the Purchase, Storage, and Traffic Division of the General Staff in 1918-1919. He points out that " comparatively little attention " is paid to this subject, and that the drafting of executive regulations is more careless than that of legislative bills, despite the fact that it is a highly technical duty.

Of Presidential Proclamations and Executive Orders he says that " no definite agency " is charged with their preparation; drafts made in the department concerned being submitted to the President for approval and then issued through the State Department. Also, regulations issued in the name of heads of departments do not always or even often receive their personal attention; and when personally signed by them are prepared by others.

We may summarize some of the requirements of an improved methodology in the preparation and publication of ordinances which Professor Fairlie mentions as follows:

1. Each department should have an agency for the purpose of preparation manned by men trained in law and legal language and experienced in the constitutional and statutory aspects of the functions of that department. Some but not all services have an agency at the present time.[18]

2. There should be a clear and unmistakable distinction between mandatory administrative orders and mere advice or information such as is not now maintained under the existing haphazard terminology.[19]

3. There should be a uniform system of terminology and forms for all federal administrative services; and such system should be based upon differences in content. Ordinances should be differentiated from executive and other acts of government, and different

---

[17] Michigan Law Review, January, 1920.

[18] Cf. the situation in England. " Under the Minute of 1869, it is part of the duty of the Parliamentary Counsel to draw or settle all such Orders in Council as he may be instructed to draw or settle on special occasions. This is an exceptional, and not a general, duty, and the great bulk of Orders in Council are drawn outside the Office, by or under the instructions of the Departments by which they are initiated. Most of the statutory rules are drawn in the same way. But where an Order in Council or a set of statutory rules is of exceptional importance or difficulty, it is sometimes drawn in the office of the Parliamentary Counsel " (Ilbert, Legislative Methods and Forms, p. 94).

[19] See the English terminology. There are Orders in Council, which may be prerogative or statutory as regards the source of their authority. "The statutory Order in Council is the most important form of delegated legislation." (Carr, Delegated Legislation, pp. 54-55). These statutory Orders in Council come within the definition of Statutory Rules and Orders. See the Rules Publication Act, 1893, and the Treasury Regulations made thereunder, quoted in Carr, op. cit., Appendix I. But see ibid., pp. 45-47. Proclamations are forms of promulgation. Anson, Law and Custom of the Constitution, part 2, p. 47 ff., gives the forms " in which the royal will is expressed for executive purposes." See also ibid., part 1, chap. iv, sec. 4.

types of ordinances should be carefully distinguished from each other.

4. An Official Bulletin of Executive Ordinances and Orders should be issued from time to time containing, and keeping up to date, all ordinances and other executive acts of government. In this Bulletin differences of form should indicate differences of content.

5. Better arrangements should be made for the distribution of ordinances of a particular kind or type to the officials upon whom they are binding, and for making them available for the private persons to whom they apply.[20] They should to this end be issued, not only seriatim, but periodically in collected and revised form and with adequate indices and digests or summaries.[21] This should supplement the general collection of all types in the Official Bulletin.

6. Care should be taken that ordinances of one department be distributed to all other departments and services which have an official connection with the subjects covered thereby.

7. There should be uniformity in the methods of issuing amendments to Rules and Regulations and other ordinances.[22]

III

Regulations that purport to be ordinances may be held void by the courts; but at least those tribunals will not require evidence to prove their existence, but will take judicial notice of them as of other formal official acts. In Caha v. United States [23] the Supreme

---

[20] " Since 1893 statutory rules and orders have been printed on a methodical plan under the editorship of Mr. Alexander Pulling. Each one is headed with a main serial number year by year. The legal orders and the Scottish Orders also have a subsidiary serial number preceded by the letters L. and S. respectively. All are classified and labelled under their general heading of law and are usually prefaced with a brief summary stating by whom they are made, at what date, and under what Act of Parliament. As the documents are printed in uniform octavo size and thus placed on sale, it has ceased to be necessary to print them also in the different type and setting of the ' Gazette '. . . . Nevertheless, the title Statutory Rules and Orders is not synonymous with delegated legislation, for the official system of publication does not cover the whole field. . . ." (Carr, Delegated Legislation, pp. 44-45).

[21] This would of course be in addition to publication in the newspapers of ordinances of interest to the public, such publication to take place at the time of original issuance.

[22] Cf. Carr, Delegated Legislation, p. 36 ff. At p. 43, Mr. Carr cites the following clause from a set of regulations of 1920: " The provisions of the . . . Regulations, 1914, and the corresponding Regulations applicable to Scotland, Ireland and Wales, shall so far as inconsistent with these Regulations, cease to have effect." This he rightly characterizes as a ' riddle ' for the layman. Clearness is needed in making amendments, as well as uniformity.

[23] 152 U. S. 211. Cf. the Documentary Evidence Act (31-32 Victoria, chap. xxxvii, sec. 2), by virtue of which " Statutory Rules and Orders are admissible in evidence in legal proceedings " (Carr, Delegated Legislation, p. 44).

Court said, with reference to rules and regulations of the Department of the Interior in respect to contests before the Land Office, that they "were not formally offered in evidence, and it is claimed that this omission is fatal, and that a verdict should have been instructed for the defendant. But we are of opinion that there was no necessity for a formal introduction in evidence of such rules and regulations. They are matters of which courts of the United States take judicial notice. Questions of a kindred nature have been frequently presented, and it may be laid down as a general rule, deducible from the cases, that whenever, by the express language of an Act of Congress, power is entrusted to either of the principal departments of the government to prescribe rules and regulations for the transaction of business in which the public is interested, and in respect to which they have a right to participate, and by which they are to be controlled, the rules and regulations prescribed in pursuance of such authority become a mass of that body of public records of which the courts take judicial notice."

It is doubtless true that the rule applies to all ordinances, whether of departments, commissions, or the President.

IV

When does a Proclamation take effect? This was the only point of inquiry in the case of Lapeyre v. United States.[24] " The Proclamation of the President, of June 24, 1865, was not published in the newspapers until the morning of the 27th of that month; nor was it published or promulgated anywhere, or in any form, prior to said last-named day, unless its being sealed with the seal of the United States, in the Department of State, was a publication or promulgation thereof." Upon these facts the Court held the Proclamation in question operative on June 24. In so doing it declared that the same rule applied to Proclamations that applied to statutes; namely, that in the absence of statutory provision to the contrary, they go into effect from the first moment of the day of their date, any inquiry into fractions of days being inadmissible. The Court say:

" As no mode of publication is prescribed, and those suggested will answer, we do not see why applying the seal and depositing the instrument in the office of the Secretary of State may not be held to have the same effect. The President and Secretary have completed their work. It is there amidst the archives of the nation. The laws of Congress are placed there. All persons desiring it can have access, and procure authenticated copies of both. The President signs and the Secretary of State seals and attests the proclamation. The President and Congress make the laws. Both are intended to be published in the newspapers and in book form. Acts take effect before they are printed or published. Why should not the same rule apply to proclamations? We see no solid reason for making a distinction. If it be objected that the proclamation will not then be known to many of those to be affected by it, the remark applies with equal force to statutes.

---

[24] 17 Wall. 191.

"But the gravest objection to the test of publication contended for by the defendant in error remains to be considered. It would make the time of taking effect depend upon extraneous evidence, which might be conflicting, and might not be preserved. The date is an unvarying guide. If that be departed from, the subject may be one of indefinitely recurring litigation. . . . Conceding publication to be necessary, the officer upon whom rests the duty of making it should be conclusively presumed to have promptly and properly discharged that duty."

One may agree with the Court that there is no reason to make a distinction with regard to this point between statutes and ordinances. Yet is the rule correct or just with respect to the former? The argument given above by the Court sounds plausible. But the continental European idea on this matter is different from ours. We are told that " Promulgation takes place when the President (of France) signs a law, affirming that it has been regularly passed by both chambers and that it will be executed as a law of the state. . . . . The date of a law is the date of its promulgation; but it does not go into effect until it has been published in the *Journal officiel*." [25]

---

[25] Sait, Government and Politics of France, pp. 44-45; cf. Esmein, Droit constitutionnel, p. 502; Carr, Delegated Legislation, pp. 3-6.

SELECTED BIBLIOGRAPHY

(The list which follows may prove helpful to the reader who desires to pursue further some of the problems suggested by this treatise).

I. SOURCES.

Checklist of United States Public Documents, 1789-1909, vol. i, (Lists) : Compiled under the direction of the Superintendent of Documents.
Constitution of the United States.
Documentary Evidence Act. (31-2, V., c. 37, s. 2).
Dodd, Modern Constitutions. (2 vols.).
Farrand, Records of the Federal Convention. (3 vols.).
The Federalist.
Goodnow, Cases on American Administrative Law.
Journal of William Maclay.
Letter from the Division of Publications of the Department of State, 19th October, 1922. (mss.).
McBain and Rogers, The New Constitutions of Europe.
MacDonald, Documentary Source Book of American History.
MacDonald, Select Documents Illustrative of the History of the United States, 1776-1861.
Magoon, Reports on the Law of Civil Government under Military Occupation. (Government Printing Office, 1902).
McPherson, Political History of the United States of America During the Great Rebellion.
Michigan Public Acts, 1921.
Pulling, Manual of Emergency Legislation.
Revised Statutes of the United States. (With 2 supplementary vols.).
Richardson, Messages and Papers of the Presidents. (20 vols.).
Rules Publication Act, 1893. (56-7 V., c. 66).
Scott and Beaman, Index Analysis of the Federal Statutes. (2 vols.).
Statute of Proclamations. (31 H. 8, c. 8).
United States Executive Orders. (Several volumes).
United States Statutes-at-Large. (42 vols.).
United States of America v. Chemical Foundation, Inc., District Court of the United States, District of Delaware: in equity, no. 502: Brief and Reply Brief on Behalf of the United States, and Closing Arguments on Behalf of Defendant.
United States Supreme Court Reports. (263 vols.).

II. TREATISES.

Adams, Constitutional History of England.
Anson, Law and Custom of the Constitution.
Arndt, Die Notverordnungen nach dem Verfassungsrechte der modernen Staaten.
Barthélemy, Le problème de la compétence dans la démocratie.
Berdahl, War Powers of the Executive in the United States.

(University of Illinois Studies in the Social Sciences, vol. ix, nos. 1 and 2).
Black, The Relation of the Executive Power to Legislation.
Blackstone, Commentaries on the Laws of England.
Boelling, Das Recht der Prüfung von Verordnungen nach dem Staatsrechte des Reiches und Preussens (1912).
Borchard, Diplomatic Protection of Citizens Abroad.
Brown, Austinian Theory of Law.
Brunialti, Il Diritto Constituzionale. (2 vols.).
Bryce, American Commonwealth, vol. i.
Burdick, The Law of the American Constitution.
Butler, The Treaty Making Power of the United States. (2 vols.).
Cahen, La loi et le règlement.
Cardozo, The Nature of the Judicial Process.
Carr, Delegated Legislation.
Carré de Malberg, Contribution à la théorie générale de l'État. (2 vols.).
Chambrun, Le pouvoir exécutif aux États-Unis d'Amérique.
Cleveland, Presidential Problems.
Cole, Guild Socialism Restated.
Cooley, Constitutional Limitations.
Corwin, The President's Control of Foreign Relations.
Crandall, Treaties: Their Making and Enforcement. (Columbia University Studies in History, Economics, and Public Law, vol. xxi, no. 1).
Croly, Promise of American Life.
Dicey, Law of the Constitution.
Duguit, Droit constitutionnel.
Dunning, Essays on the Civil War and Reconstruction.
Esmein, Droit constitutionnel.
Fairlie, British War Administration.
Fairlie, National Administration of the United States.
Freund, Standards of American Legislation.
Girault, Principes de colonisation et de législation coloniale, 2e partie, ch. 3, Du législateur colonial.
Gneist, History of the English Constitution. (2 vols.).
Goodnow, Comparative Administrative Law. (2 vols.).
Goodnow, Politics and Administration.
Goodnow, Principles of the Administrative Law of the United States.
Gray, Nature and Sources of the Law.
Greene, The Provincial Governor.
Greenleaf on Evidence (sixteenth edition), chap. xxi.
Hall, A Treatise on International Law.
Hare, American Constitutional Law. (2 vols.).
Harrison, This Country of Ours.
Hauriou, Précis de droit administratif et de droit public.
Holland, Elements of Jurisprudence.
Ilbert, Legislative Methods and Forms.
Ilbert, The Mechanics of Law Making.
Ito, Commentaries on the Constitution of the Empire of Japan.
James, Principles of Prussian Administration.
Jellinek, Gesetz und Verordnung.

Jèze, Principes généraux du droit administratif.
Laband, Deutsches Reichsstaatsrecht (Das Öffentliche Recht der
    Gegenwart, Band 1).
Laband, Staatsrecht des deutschen Reiches.
Lapp, Federal Rules and Regulations.
Lieber, Remarks on the Army Regulations and Executive Regu-
    lations in General.
Low, Governance of England.
Lowell, Government of England. (2 vols.).
Lowell, Governments and Parties in Continental Europe. (2
    vols.).
Mathews, Principles of American State Administration.
Maitland, Constitutional History of England.
Merriam, American Political Theories.
Meyer-Anschütz, Lehrbuch des deutschen Staatsrechtes.
Mill, Representative Government.
Moreau, Le règlement administratif. (Paris, 1902).
Nakano, Ordinance Power of the Japanese Emperor. (The
    Johns Hopkins Press, 1923).
Posada, Derecho Administrativo. (2 vols.).
Pound, Introduction to the Philosophy of Law.
Procter, Principles of Public Personnel Administration.
Raiga, Le pouvoir réglementaire du Président de la République.
    (1900).
Richardson, Constitutional Doctrines of Justice Oliver Wendell
    Holmes. (The Johns Hopkins Press, 1924).
Rosin, Polizeiverordnungsrecht in Preussen.
Sait, Government and Politics of France.
Salandra, La Giustizia Amministrativa.
Schmidt, Das Verordnungsrecht des Bundesrates des deutschen
    Reiches. (1913).
Stein, Handbuch der Verwaltungslehre.
Stourm, The Budget (tr.).
Stubbs, Constitutional History of England. (3 vols.).
Taft, Our Chief Magistrate and His Powers.
Thach, The Creation of the Presidency, 1775-1789. (The Johns
    Hopkins Press, 1922).
Thayer, Preliminary Treatise on the Law of Evidence.
Thomas, History of Military Government in the Newly Acquired
    Territory of the United States. (Columbia University
    Studies in History, Economics, and Public Law, vol. xx,
    no. 2).
Whiting, Military Government of Hostile Territory in Time of
    War.
Whiting, War Powers of the President, and the Legislative
    Powers of Congress in Relation to Rebellion, Treason and
    Slavery.
Wigmore, Problems of Law.
Willoughby, W. F., Government Organization in War Time and
    After.
Willoughby, W. W., Constitutional Law of the United States.
    (2 vols.).
Willoughby, W. W., Fundamental Concepts of Public Law.
    (Macmillan, 1924).

Willoughby, W. W., Nature of the State.
Willoughby, W. W., Prussian Political Philosophy.
Wilson, Congressional Government.
Wilson, Constitutional Government in the United States.
Winthrop, Abridgment of Military Law.
Wright, The Control of American Foreign Relations.
Wyman, Administrative Law.

III. ARTICLES.

Albertsworth, " Judicial Review of Administrative Action by
    the Federal Supreme Court," in Harvard Law Review, vol.
    xxxv, p. 127.
Ballantine, " Constitutional Limitations on the War Power," in
    California Law Review, vol. vi, p. 134.
Ballantine, " Unconstitutional Claims of Military Authority," in
    Yale Law Journal, vol. xxiv, p. 189.
Barnett, " Executive Control of the Legislature," in American
    Law Review, vol. xli, pp. 215 and 384.
Barnett, " Executive, Legislature, and Judiciary in Pardon," in
    American Law Review, vol. clix, p. 684.
Berle, " The Expansion of American Administrative Law," in
    Harvard Law Review, vol. xxx, p. 430.
Berthélemy, " Le pouvoir réglementaire du Président de la Ré-
    publique," dans la Revue politique et parlementaire, janvier
    et février, 1898, pp. 1 et 322.
Biklé, " Power of the Interstate Commerce Commission to Pre-
    scribe Minimum Rates," in Harvard Law Review, vol. xxxvi,
    p. 5.
Blachly, " Who Should Organize State Administration ? " in
    Southwestern Political and Social Science Quarterly, Sep-
    tember, 1923.
Bogart, " Economic Organization for War," in American Poli-
    tical Science Review, vol. xiv, p. 587.
Brinton, " Some Powers and Problems of the Federal Adminis-
    trative," in Pennsylvania Law Review, vol. lxi, p. 135.
Brown, " The Separation of Powers in British Jurisdictions," in
    Yale Law Journal, vol. xxxi, p. 24.
Bryce, " Conditions and Methods of Legislation," in University
    and Historical Addresses, p. 75.
Carbaugh, " Martial Law," in Illinois Law Review, vol. vii, p.
    479.
Carpenter, " Military Government of Southern Territory, 1861-
    1865," in Annual Report, American Historical Association,
    1900, vol. i, p. 465.
Carroll, " Freedom of Speech and of the Press during the Civil
    War," in Virginia Law Review, vol. ix, p. 516.
Cheadle, " The Delegation of Legislative Functions," in Yale
    Law Journal, vol. xxvii, p. 892.
Cheadle, " Judicial Review of Administrative Determinations,"
    in Southwestern Political and Social Science Quarterly,
    June, 1922.
Clarke, " The Rule of DORA," in Journal of Comparative Legis-
    lation and International Law, April, 1919.

Cohn, "To What Extent Have Rules and Regulations of the Federal Departments the Force of Law," in American Law Review, vol. xli, p. 343.

Cook, "The Legal Legislative and Economic Battle Over Railroad Rates," in Harvard Law Review, vol. xxxv, p. 30.

Coker, "Dogmas of Administrative Reform," in American Political Science Review, vol. xvi, p. 399.

Curtis, "Judicial Review of Commission," in Harvard Law Review, vol. xxxiv, p. 862.

Dicey, "A Comparison Between Cabinet Government and Presidential Government," in Nineteenth Century, January, 1919.

Dobie, "Judicial Review of Administrative Action in Virginia," in Virginia Law Review, vol. viii, pp. 477 and 557.

Duguit, "Des règlements faits en vertu d'une compétence donne au gouvernement par le législateur," dans la Revue du droit public et de la science politique, tome xli, no. 3, p. 313.

Duguit, "The French Administrative Courts," in Political Science Quarterly, vol. xxix, p. 385.

Dunning, "The War Power of the President," in New Republic, vol. xi, p. 76.

Ehrlich, "Montesquieu and Sociological Jurisprudence," in Harvard Law Review, vol. xxix, p. 582.

Esmein, "De la délégation du pouvoir législatif," dans la Revue politique et parlementaire, août, 1894, p. 209.

Fairlie, "Administrative Legislation," in Michigan Law Review, vol. xviii, p. 181.

Fairlie, "The Administrative Powers of the President," in Michigan Law Review, vol. ii, p. 190.

Fairlie, "American War Measures," in Journal of Comparative Legislation and International Law, vol. xviii, p. 90.

Fairlie, "Separation of Powers," in Michigan Law Review, vol. xxi, p. 393.

Fenwick, "Democracy and Efficient Government," in American Political Science Review, vol. xiv, p. 565.

Fisher, "The Suspension of Habeas Corpus during the War of the Rebellion," in Political Science Quarterly, vol. iii, p. 454.

Fletcher, "Civilian and the War Power," in Minnesota Law Review, vol. ii, p. 110.

Ford, "The Growth of Dictatorship," in Atlantic Monthly, vol. cxxi, p. 632.

Ford, "The War and the Constitution," in Atlantic Monthly, vol. cxx, p. 485.

Foster, "The Delegation of Legislative Power to Administrative Officers," in Illinois Law Review, vol. vii, p. 397.

Frankfurter, book review, in Harvard Law Review, vol. xxxvi, p. 1046.

Frankfurter, "Constitutional Opinions of Justice Holmes," in Harvard Law Review, vol. xxix, p. 683.

Freund, "American Administrative Law," in Political Science Quarterly, vol. ix, p. 403.

Freund, "Principles of Legislation," in American Political Science Review, vol. x, p. 1.

Freund, "Substitution of Rule for Discretion in Public Law," in American Political Science Review, vol. ix, p. 666.

Garfield, "Recent Political Development: Progress or Change?" in American Political Science Review, February, 1924.

Garner, "French Administrative Law," in Yale Law Journal, vol. xxxiii, p. 597.

Garner, "Judicial Control of Administrative and Legislative Acts in France," in American Political Science Review, vol. ix, p. 637.

Garner, "Le pouvoir exécutif en temps de guerre aux États-Unis," dans la Revue du droit public et de la science politique, tome xxxv, p. 5.

Gaus, "The New Problem in Administration," in Minnesota Law Review, vol. viii, p. 217.

Giraud, "Étude sur la notion du pouvoir discrétionnaire," dans la Revue generale d'administration, mai-juin, 1924, p. 193, et juillet-août, 1924, p. 298.

Goodnow, "The Administrative Law of the United States," in Political Science Quarterly, vol. xix, p. 112.

Goodnow, "The Executive and the Courts," in Political Science Quarterly, vol. i, p. 533.

Goodnow, "The Growth of Executive Discretion," in Proceedings, American Political Science Association, vol. ii, p. 43.

Goodnow, "Private Rights and Administrative Discretion," in Century Law Journal, vol. lxxxiii, p. 165.

Green, "The Separation of Governmental Powers," in Yale Law Journal, vol. xxix, p. 369.

Guggenheimer, "The Development of the Executive Departments," in Jameson, Essays in the Constitutional History of the United States in the Formative Period, 1775-1789.

Haney, "Price-Fixing in the United States During the War," in Political Science Quarterly, vol. xxxiv, pp. 104, 262, and 434.

Hankin, "Validity and Constitutionality of the Federal Trade Commission Act," in Illinois Law Review, vol. xix, p. 17.

Hart, "Emergency Ordinance: A Note on Executive Power," in Columbia Law Review, vol. xxiii, p. 528.

Hart, "Ordinance Making Powers of the President," in North American Review, vol. ccviii, p. 59.

Harvard Law Review, Notes, vol. xv, p. 852.

Harvard Law Review, Notes, vol. xix, p. 69.

Harvard Law Review, Notes, vol. xix, p. 288.

Harvard Law Review, Notes, vol. xxi, p. 205.

Harvard Law Review, Notes, vol. xxix, p. 208.

Harvard Law Review, Notes, vol. xxx, p. 386.

Harvard Law Review, Notes, vol. xxxv, p. 450.

Harvard Law Review, Notes, vol. xxxv, p. 952.

Harvard Law Review, Notes, vol. xxvi, p. 1020.

Harvard Law Review, Notes, vol. xxxvii, p. 1118.

Harvard Law Review, Recent Cases, vol. xxxii, p. 87.

Hitchcock, "The War Industries Board: Its Development, Organization, and Functions," in Journal of Political Economy, vol. xxvi, p. 545.

Hughes, "War Powers under the Constitution," in Central Law Journal, vol. lxxxv, p. 206.

Isaacs, "Review of Administrative Findings," in Yale Law Journal, vol. xxx, p. 781.

Jèze, "Le règlement administratif," dans la Revue générale d'administration, mai, 1902, p. 11.

Leake, "The Conflict Over Coördination," in American Political Science Review, vol. xii, p. 365.

Leupp, "The Cabinet in Congress," in Atlantic Monthly, vol. cxx, p. 769.

Martin, "The Line of Demarcation Between Legislative, Executive, and Judicial Functions, with Special Reference to the Acts of an Administrative Board or Commission," in American Law Review, vol. xlvii, p. 715.

Masters, "Suspension of the Writ of Habeas Corpus," in Illinois Law Review, vol. vii, p. 15.

Mathews, "State Administrative Reorganization," in American Political Science Review, vol. xvi, p. 396.

Moore, "Treaties and Executive Agreements," in Political Science Quarterly, vol. xx, p. 385.

Parker, "Executive Judgments and Executive Legislation," in Harvard Law Review, vol. xx, p. 116.

Patterson, "Ministerial and Discretionary Official Acts," in Michigan Law Review, vol. xx, p. 848.

Paxton, "The American War Government, 1917-1918," in American Historical Review, vol. xxvi, p. 54.

Penfield, "The Recognition of a New State—Is it an Executive Function?" in American Law Review, vol. xxxii, p. 390.

Pierson, "The Committee on the Conduct of the Civil War," in American Historical Review, vol. xxiii, p. 550.

Pillsbury, "Administrative Tribunals," in Harvard Law Review, vol. xxxvi, pp. 405, 583.

Pound, "Executive Justice," in American Law Register, vol. iv, p. 137.

Pound, "Juristic Science and the Law," in Harvard Law Review, vol. xxxi, p. 1047.

Pound, "Law in Action and Law in Books," in American Law Review, vol. xliv, p. 12.

Pound, "The Revival of Personal Government," Proceedings of the New Hampshire Bar Association, 1917, p. 13.

Powell, "The President's Veto of the Budget Bill," in National Municipal Review, vol. ix, p. 538.

Powell, "The Conclusiveness of Administrative Determinations in the Federal Government," in American Political Science Review, vol. i, p. 583.

Powell, "Judicial Review of Administrative Action in Immigration Proceedings," in Harvard Law Review, vol. xxii, p. 360.

Powell, "The Separation of Powers," in Political Science Quarterly, vol. xxvii, p. 215, and vol. xxviii, p. 34.

Rogers, "Presidential Dictatorship in the United States," in Quarterly Review, vol. ccxxxi, p. 127.

Shepard, "The German Doctrine of the Budget," in American Political Science Review, vol. iv, p. 52.

Signorel "Le pouvoir exécutif en temps de guerre: Étude de législation comparée," dans la Revue générale d'administration, tome xliii, partie 2, p. 129, and partie 3, p. 5.

Smith, "War Legislation," in Central Law Journal, vol. lxxxvi, p. 116.

Turner, "Democracy in Administration," in American Political Science Review, vol. xvii, p. 216.

Walsh, "War Powers of the President" in Case and Comment, vol. xxiv, p. 279.

Walton, "The French Administrative Courts and the Modern French Law as to the Responsibility of the State for the Faults of Its Officials: Comparison with the Common Law," in Illinois Law Review, vol. xiii, p. 211.

White, "The Growth and Future of State Boards and Commissions," in Political Science Quarterly, vol. xviii, p. 631.

Whitfield, "Legislative Power That May Not Be Delegated," in Yale Law Journal, vol. xx, p. 87.

Whitney, "Another Philippine Constitutional Question—Delegation of Legislative Power to the President," in Columbia Law Review, vol. i, p. 33.

Willoughby, "The Juristic Conception of the State," in American Political Science Review, vol. xii, p. 192.

Willoughby, "The Study of the Law," Virginia Law Review, vol. vi, p. 461.

Wilson, "The Study of Administration," in Political Science Quarterly, vol. ii, p. 197.

Wood, "Military Government of Cuba," in Annals of the American Academy of Political and Social Science, vol. xxi, p. 153.

Woolsey, "The Beginnings of War," in Proceedings, American Political Science Association, vol. i, p. 54.

Wyman, "Jurisdictional Limitations Upon Commission Action," in Harvard Law Review, vol. xxvii, p. 545.

INDEX

Adams, John, delegations to, 79-84.
Administration, defined, 31, 33, 37.
Administrative control, 192, 193, 194-196, 226.
Administrative determinations, defined, 31, 37.
Administrative reform, 272-273.
Administrative regulations, relative advantages of, 275-279; relative disadvantages of, 279-281.
Administrative tribunals, 271-275.
Advisory function, 278, 281, 288, 289, 293.
Affolter, F. X., quoted, 24.
Alaskan railroad, act relating to, 1914, 97.
Alien Act, 1798, 82.
Alien Enemy Act, 1798, 83.
Amendment of ordinances, 321.
Amnesties, 316.
Amnesty, power of, 216-217; proclamations of, 211.
Analytical jurisprudence, 25 ff., 39.
Annals of Congress, quoted, 205.
Ante-natal safeguards, 300-301.
Appeal, correlative right of, 192.
Archives, Department of State, 316, 317.
Argumentum ab inconveniente, 143, 155.
Army and navy, power of Congress relative to, 240.
Army Regulations, statutory authorization of, 97, 319.
Arthur, Chester A., executive order of, 66.
Attorneys General, opinions of the, cited, 184, 189, 192.
Ausführungsverordnungen, defined, 58.

Bagehot, Walter, cited, 300.
Bill of indemnity, 61-62, 95, 101, 141, 254.

Blackstone, quoted, 134, 203.
Blanket delegations, 102-103.
Blockade, proclamations of, quoted, 213-214.
Brown, Jethro, cited, 37.
Bryce, James, quoted, 110, 270.
Budget and Accounting Act, 1921, 107-108, 273, 290.
Budgetary laws, control of administration through, 293.
Bulletin, Official, needed, 321.

Cabinet in Congress, whether wise to have, 295-296, 302.
Canal Zone, government of, in statutory lapse, 236-237.
Carr, Cecil T., quoted, 281-282, 292, 300, 301, 321.
Carré de Malberg, quoted, 251-252.
Civil Service Act, 1883, 272.
Civil Service Rules, authorization of, quoted, 109, 316, 319.
Civil Suits, 307.
Classification, not inconsistent with uniformity, 259.
Cleveland, Grover, civil service rules of, cited, 65; railroad mail rules of, cited, 66; quoted, 224.
Codes of regulations, 319.
Coke, Sir E., quoted, 47, 110, 206.
Co-law, defined, 37.
Co-legislation, 21, 33-35, 56 ff., 71, 131, 216, 265-291; political aspects of, 265-291; growth of, 265-275; reasons for its slow development in the United States, 265-268; common in continental Europe, 267; as means of adjustment of representative government to new conditions, 274-275; justifications of, 281-282; implications of, for democracy, 283-284; bearing of, upon relation of Executive to legislation, 284-285; problem of responsibility for, 286-287; its organization,

333